October 9th 2007

Happy Birthday, my special
friend, Sara,
I think you will find
this to be a really sweet
book.
It was written by a
precious lady whom I had
the pleasure of knowing
Love, Linda

A Farmer's Daughter . . .

Amazed
By Grace

A Farmer's Daughter . . .

Amazed by Grace

Ann Curtis

Open Ear Publishers, LLC
Batesville, Arkansas

A Farmer's Daughter . . . Amazed By Grace

Published in Batesville, Arkansas, by Open Ear Publishers, LLC

Scripture quotations unless otherwise noted are from the King James Version.

Scripture quotations credited to the Living Bible are taken from The Living Bible®, copyright © 1971. Used by permission of Tyndale House Publishers, Inc., Wheaton, Illinois 60189. All rights reserved.

Scripture quotations noted NIV are from the *Holy Bible, New International Version*®, copyright © 1973, 1978, 1984 by the International Bible Society. Used by permission.

ISBN: 978-0-9788080-1-3   Printed in the United States

To My Dearest Earthly Treasures

My Husband
Jay

Our Two Daughters
Brenda O'Neal—Husband, John
Deborah Alfano—Husband, Len

Our Five Grandchildren
John O'Neal, Jr.—Wife, Laine
Timothy O'Neal
Shannon Terry—Husband, Jason
Shawn O'Neal—Wife, Amanda
David Curtis Cowan—Wife, Kimme

Our Nine Great-Grandchildren
Samantha LeeAnn Terry
Daniel Jay Terry
Charly Faith Terry (in heaven)
Ethan Terry
Joshua Curtis Cowan
Elizabeth Cowan
Aaron O'Neal
Arlen Addison
Abigail O'Neal

ACKNOWLEDGMENTS

MEDICAL MINISTERING ANGELS

Dr. Kelsey

Nurse Sally Stovall

Dr. Paul Wills—my hearing ears

Dr. Ed Whiteside—a trainee who continues to share the Gospel—
even took it to Africa

Dr. Bob Delay—preserving my *smile* (by saving my eleven front
teeth thirty-five years ago after my dentists the previous twenty
years used only one treatment—*pull*)

TO THE SCORES OF YOU WHO WERE MINISTERING ANGELS TO JAY AND ME

Your names are not included because of space, but they were written
on my heart, and our Lord's list will have your name and reward in
heaven.

> *For God is not unrighteous to forget your work and
> labor of love, which ye have shown toward his name,
> in that ye have ministered to the saints, and do minis-
> ter.* (Heb. 6:10)

Steve Gaddis summed up my life desire, as well as his, in his tribute to
me: "My commitment is to follow your example and always lead
people to the cross . . . till my last breath."

CONTENTS

Part IV: Ministry and Going Home

FOREWORD

It is my high honor and special joy to write the foreword to this book because it unveils the life of one of the truly remarkable servants of Jesus Christ of our times—Mrs. Ann Curtis. There are many remarkable ingredients in the life of Mrs. Curtis, but her distinction lies in one dominating, God-given motivation:

She was exceedingly grateful that she was saved,
and she was extraordinarily glad to share with
the whole world how they could be saved too.

Mrs. Curtis worked diligently and untiringly at my side in First Baptist Church, Fort Smith, Arkansas, for almost twenty years (1967–1986). All of her *labors of love* focused on winning the lost, and she was without equal in this noble and God-given assignment.

The Great Commission of our Risen Savior—*to make disciples of all the nations*—was burned into her heart by the Holy Spirit from the day she was born again. She literally looked upon the Great Commission as her personal *Orders from Headquarters*, and she carried out those orders without ceasing, in season and out of season, and with contagious enthusiasm. Only in eternity will we know the number of souls she has won, but it will be an amazing multitude. Most persons desire to be wise in the eyes of men, but Mrs. Curtis sought wisdom in the eyes of God and found it. God himself declares *He (or she) who winneth souls is wise* (Prov. 11:30). Based on this divine and infallible criterion, if there ever was a wise person on this earth, it was Ann Curtis.

Some autobiographies are dull and prosaic, the mere recounting of events in one's past. But Mrs. Curtis' story throbs with life and excitement. She accomplishes this by quoting herself and the persons in her life *verbatim,* thus permitting them to speak for themselves, and when you hear them speak, it seems like they are in the room with you. Of the like I have never found in any book on this earth.

Mrs. Curtis calls herself *The Farmer's Daughter* which speaks of her pride in her humble beginnings and her immense gratitude for the values instilled in her home. However, while she was the *Farmer's Daughter*, she carried herself as if born into royalty and as though she had just stepped out of Harvard. Excellence was stamped upon everything she did with a capital *E*—from her wardrobe to witnessing, and all for the glory of Jesus Christ.

There are numerous other wonderful facts that I could share about Mrs. Curtis, but I hesitate in saying more because I want you to read for yourself in her own words and the own words of others her inimitable story. You will find it absolutely thrilling beyond my ability to express. I have some nine to ten thousand volumes in my library, consisting of great biographies, but I have never read one so personal, so passionate, so powerful, so Christ-honoring, so precious as the one you are about to read. Why? Because it describes on paper the exceeding great joy of one life totally surrendered to the greatest task this side of heaven—the winning of lost persons from sin to salvation, and ultimately to a home in heaven. And she did it all because of her overflowing love for Jesus Christ and the souls He died to save. So I urge you to get your copy without delay, if you have not already done so, and I predict you will enjoy it so much that you will pass it on to your dearest friend.

In closing I would summarize the life of Ann Curtis, not in my feeble prose, but in the infallible word of the prophet Daniel:

Those who are wise will shine like the brightness of the heavens, and those who lead many to righteousness, like the stars forever and ever. (Dan. 12:3).

Soli Dei Gloria

Dr. Bill Bennett

A NOTE TO READERS

This book could just as well be entitled *The Evangelist.* We evangelicals normally think of an evangelist as the itinerate preacher who holds revivals and moves from town to town seeking to encourage and assist churches in reaching the lost. The image was broken for me by observing the life of Ann Curtis. This book is no doubt the story of an evangelist.

This dear lady was the most faithful witness for Jesus Christ that I have ever known. She was *gifted*, I believe by the Holy Spirit, to do this work. She was motivated by this same Holy Spirit. She was tireless, enthusiastic, and hopeful for all souls. Truly her life was a life well lived. Her life and testimony is one and the same with the Apostle Paul, *For I am not ashamed of the gospel of Christ* (Rom. 1:16).

Mrs. Curtis never really retired. She worked along side Dr. Bill Bennett for nineteen years and with my ministry in Fort Smith for nearly fifteen years. She was in her mid-80's when her health would not allow her to press on. She was always looking for *one more*. I know that you will enjoy this story, but most of all I pray that you will be inspired. I encourage you to take the journey through these pages and experience a life that was an incredible mixture of humility, boldness, and confidence in the Savior and His Gospel.

Dr. Dale Thompson
Pastor, First Baptist Church
Fort Smith, Arkansas

PREFACE

Often I am asked, "How do you remember what you said in those early years?"

Actually, I don't—not word for word, not even act by act.

As I read my account of Part I, I asked myself, "Could I stand in a court of law and raise my right hand and say, 'This is the truth, the whole truth, and nothing but the truth.'?"

No, I could not. It is embellished at times. I told myself it was to make it readable, but then one of my daughters asked after reading it, "Were you really that good, Mother?" I knew I had shielded myself because the real me was not *that good* as she perceived in reading my account.

In essentials if not in detail, the life story is true, and whatever else it is, you can count on it being a *true love story* between a man and a woman. Finally, the story reveals a love that transcends all earthly passion.

You may not like me at times, but you will love Jay, and I pray you know and love our heavenly Father. If you don't know Him, our story will tell you how we became His children and pilgrims in this world on our journey to heaven.

(There is no embellishment in the account of His moving in my life as a child or through the later years.)

Ann Curtis

Ann

Introducing a Farmer's Daughter

Mama said I made my entry to planet earth upside down and feet first. She may not have thought about it the day I was born, but even my birth reflected the trend of the female gender that year.

Most young women were not fighting for their rights; they were just doing the unthinkable. They bobbed their hair, rolled their stockings, and flipped their shortened skirts revealing at first ankles and then their legs. Some scorned the secret snuff boxes of their mothers but boldly puffed cigarettes and openly used lipstick and rouge. A few dared to vote.

Model T Fords supplied wheels for young men to whisk giddy flappers away from their front porch swings and the eyes of their puritanical parents. Jazz bands blared as the young and restless generation following World War I kicked up its heels and danced the Charleston with gusto.

The glitter of false prosperity prevailed in 1922, and a light-hearted spirit replaced the gloom of the war years. Girls were starved for romance and soldiers were home again, but they were not the same hometown boys they were before their European exposure.

Right in the middle of all that national hullabaloo Aaron and Annie Thompson stopped working on their dairy farm long enough on March 2 to welcome me as their third child.

Daddy didn't leave the farm during the war years, and he remained relatively unaffected by the social changes that followed it. Mama was sheltered under his protection, but she succumbed to some of its influence. She surprised Daddy and shocked her parents the day she cut her long hair. Her bobbed hairdo called for stylish shortened skirts and up hers went—so far that her mother gasped, "Annie, people can see your knees!"

Mama didn't stray much further into the vices of the Roaring Twenties. Her venture stopped abruptly when an unmarried cousin disgraced the family that year by being the only woman to vote in their precinct.

There I was, born during a social revolution and in a generation intoxicated with prosperity—either looking forward to it as Daddy and Mama were, or like many others, already tasting it. I remained a contented farmer's daughter until the crash. No, not the stock market—the crash of my childhood. I almost skipped adolescence as I plunged headlong, or maybe it was feet first, into an adult world when I was ten years old.

The family economy was progressing steadily when I arrived and continued at a comfortable rate for seven years. Then, almost overnight the whole nation plunged from joyful prosperity to abject poverty when the stock market crashed in 1929.

Daddy set aside his dream of becoming a successful dairyman. He used nearly every acre of his pasture land to produce food for his family to survive. And survive we did— with plenty to eat, but no money.

Daddy planned, labored, sweated, and cussed as he literally forced our livelihood out of his land. His greatest fear was that a day might come when he could not pay his taxes. Farmers were having their land taken when they couldn't pay their mortgages, and Daddy feared the same if he couldn't pay his taxes. So far, he had managed to meet the deadline by selling a cow or a pig, but then a year came when he couldn't find a buyer.

One night he sat brooding over the matter and reading his newspaper, one of the few luxury items he managed to keep in his budget. Suddenly he jumped up, and with clinched fists fighting the air he thundered, "It won't be a pitch fork I'll use to meet them if they come to take my land—it will be my shotgun!"

For the first time my child's mind grasped a little of the impact of Daddy's words, and I knew we were living in hard times.

Prayer was not a part of our household, but I remembered how Aunt Fletcher asked God to help when she didn't know what to do. I looked up—or maybe I looked down. Whichever, I remember I asked an unknown God to pay my Daddy's taxes. My fear vanished instantly, but Daddy's didn't until he had a tax receipt marked *paid* in his pocket.

Later, I heard Daddy tell Uncle Glenville, "Remember how I tried to sell that scrub cow and no one had the money to buy it? Well, I sold it today. Now I can pay the taxes and buy extra seed for spring planting." I relaxed, knowing that it would be another year before taxes would be due; when that time came again, I would know what to do.

I was protected from most of the grueling misery of the ten poverty years that history records as the Great Depression. Daddy's farm, ten miles west of Little Rock, was surrounded by aunts, uncles, and cousins living on tracts of land his grandparents first owned. These blood-related neighbors added social interchange and acceptance to the serenity of my already secure family unit. The youngest child of Mama and Daddy, little sister to Marie and Kenneth, and the apple of Grandpa's eye (Mama's daddy who lived with us)—I scarcely knew it was hard times, as everyone kept saying it was, except when taxes were due. I was not only the baby of my family, but I was also the youngest child of any of the relatives whose land joined ours. I learned early where kittens, puppies, and calves came from, but the question of where I began didn't enter my mind. I was the only baby I knew and that satisfied me.

The words *I love you* were not voiced and hugs were unknown in our household, but I didn't miss them. When Mama looked at me in her own special way and said, "Ann, you are cute," I felt loved all over.

I chided her the last time she said it to me, the year she was ninety-three, "Mama, who ever heard of describing a sixty-six year old woman as cute?" But I knew she was expressing her love and approval of me as her grown-up baby daughter.

Daddy was seldom complimentary in words, but I felt his approval when he included me in grown-up activities. He was an avid fisherman and hunter. I sat enthralled, listening to him and my brother Kenneth rehearse deer, coon, squirrel, or quail hunts. Daddy sensed my longing one night as he rounded up his coon dogs, shotgun, lantern, and other hunting gear. He turned and said, "Anna Mae, do you want to go with us?"

I jumped up and was ready to go by the time they went out the door into the dark cold night. The first hour was sheer bliss, following Daddy and his lantern through the deep woods with the limbs swatting my body as the hunters pushed a path for us to walk through. Just as I thought I couldn't walk another step, they stopped and built a fire. We sat around the brush fire warming our hands and listening to the dogs bark as they chased a scent. I understood then what Daddy meant when he called it music to his ears.

Finally, the triumphant sound of the head coon dog barking "He's treed!" rang through the night. The hunters almost ran as they pursued the sound coming from up and around the mountain. My short legs were making two or three steps to their one as we climbed the mountain and my chest was almost exploding for air when Daddy reached back, caught my hand, and half pulled me the last lap of the hunt.

I thought coon hunting was heady stuff, but when Daddy asked me to be his partner at the card table, I knew I had made first team.

The family and any friend who stopped in to visit gathered around the pot-bellied wood heater in the living room on the long, cold winter nights. Pans full of popped corn and roasted peanuts provided ample snack food for everyone. Daddy played cards and Mama sewed or hooked rugs until bedtime.

Aaron Thompson was known as a man of integrity throughout the community, and his honesty was clearly revealed around the card table. No player, man or child, dared to play except with all cards on the table. Daddy was as avid a poker player as he was a sportsman, and he played to win. My heart leaped with pride the first time he asked me to be his partner as I knew he must value me as a team winner.

Marie was my long-legged, slim, and graceful big sister who could flip cartwheels on a foot log across the creek. I was afraid of walking on the log for fear of falling in. Her five years' seniority gave me a glimpse of teenage life before I entered it. Carefree and, I thought, generous to a fault, Marie shared her limited possessions not just with me, but also with our visiting cousins.

Anything we could not produce on the farm was a luxury during the depression years, and facial soap was a luxury. Mama made lye soap after hog killing time each winter, and we used it for all our cleaning purposes throughout the year.

I learned soon after I was school age not to wash my face with lye soap. A lady from the city (ten miles and a day's journey away) visited Mama, and as she was leaving, she tipped my chin up with her finger, observed my face closely, and said, "Child, you have a beautiful complexion. See that you take care of it. Stay out of the sun. Wash it gently every day, and don't ever use that lye soap I just used to wash my hands." She made a terrible face at just the thought of it. I remembered her expression afterward when I smelled lye soap.

Marie had a new bar of toilet soap and she shared it with me. I treasured it as if it was pure gold, and I hesitated each time I put it back with her belongings.

Soon afterward, I found the soap left in Marie's wash pan and beginning to dissolve in the pool of water. Suddenly, I realized she was taking a bath with that precious soap and not keeping it just for her face. Carefully, I rescued the treasured bar and hid it leaving the soapy water in the pan.

My heart said, *Don't do it. The soap belongs to Marie. She shared it with you, and now you are hiding it from her.*

My mind reasoned, *She won't take care of it. If she keeps using it for bathing, there won't be any left for her or for me. Besides, if I hadn't found it, the soap would have dissolved in the water where she left it. Anyway, she won't ever know. She will think it melted when she finds that soapy water.*

I used the bar sparingly as I washed my *complexion* each day and carefully dried the bar before hiding it away. It lasted for months, and by that time Mama was able to purchase another bar.

During those months I usually felt at ease with Marie, but not with Daddy—especially at the card table. His honest appraisal, as he looked across the table at me, caused me to lower my eyes under his steady gaze. I was afraid he would see the truth, only now it was deception.

Kenneth was my big brother, my idol. I followed after him like a puppy dog follows its owner. He basked in my girlish adoration and in turn treated me like a little princess. When he crossed the highway from school after lunch time, I waited until he was seated at the grocery counter before I ran across the highway and jumped up beside him. I never asked, but whatever he ordered for himself he ordered for me: two five cent cokes or two five cent candy bars—enough for both of us for two dimes.

In a similar fashion, but with a different motive, Grandpa followed me like I did Kenneth, adoring me in his own special way and trying to give me anything his dear heart could imagine. Mama explained that her daddy had a sunstroke soon after her mother died, and it left him not quite himself.

And there was Grandma Nancy, Daddy's mother, the matriarch of the family clan. She lived on the old home place about a half mile from us. Once redheaded, now white haired, slim and straight as a ramrod, she had little time to coddle her youngest granddaughter. Past sixty and too old to work, she spent hours engrossed in her books. She guarded her small library as a miser does his gold. The great value she placed on her books served to whet my appetite to get the opportunity to read at least one of them.

Nestled in this isolated family community—ten miles from the city with no telephone, radio, or car—I remained the baby of the family almost as innocent as the day I somersaulted onto planet earth. Anything beyond our family compound was outer space to my unsophisticated mind.

My blissful status changed overnight on May 10, 1932. The previous night I stayed with Aunt Fletcher, my *other mother*.

Uncle Glenville's place was across from Daddy's back pasture, and I had a path worn smooth from running to and fro to their house. They didn't have any daughters and only one son. Aunt Fletcher called me her daughter, the one she never had.

Before we left her house that morning, Aunt Fletcher took two tin buckets—once filled with sorghum molasses that Daddy made each fall—and said as she picked them up, "Strawberries are beginning to ripen in your mother's garden. Let's go pick some."

As we approached my house, we saw people huddled together talking in little groups outside the back door and others arriving at the front porch. Aunt Fletcher turned abruptly to me and put a bucket in each of my hands saying, "Ann, can you go pick the berries, and let me go help your mother?"

"Oh, yes. Let me," I answered. "I can eat some too while I'm picking them."

I hurried across the road to the garden and found the strawberry patch glistening with red berries. Without taking time to eat any, I joyfully began filling the gallon buckets thinking, *Mama must be having a bunch of company for dinner today. I wonder if Daddy caught a big mess of fish after I left yesterday. That must be why so many people are coming. Mama always says fish must be cooked soon as it's caught. If it's kept overnight in Grandma's spring house (our refrigerator), it begins to smell fishy. If she is having a fish fry, I hope she makes strawberry shortcake too.*

My clean blond hair that Aunt Fletcher and I had shampooed the night before felt good when a cool breeze tossed it about my face as I skipped happily from the garden to the house. Balancing a bucket of luscious red strawberries in each hand, I raced up the back steps with my bare feet and stopped dead still in the open door.

A baby—a beautiful baby boy—lay lifeless on the kitchen table. The room was filled with people and the doctor was explaining to them what happened. Every eye was on the baby as Dr. Lamb said, "He's a perfect baby in every way except his heart didn't work properly . . . that's why he was so blue when he first came . . . . It's leakage of the heart . . . there is no more I can do for him. . . ."

If the proverbial stork had dropped that baby right down out of the sky, I wouldn't have been any more surprised. I stood without uttering a sound, almost as lifeless as the dead baby.

The only one who noticed me standing in the doorway was Grandma Nancy. She moved over and stood between me and the table and said with the kindest voice I ever heard her use, "Child, why don't you come home with me."

She took my hand and gently led me down the back steps. She had that *no questions asked* expression so we walked silently down the road, and she went directly to her bookshelf as we entered the house. Cautiously, she handed me one of her treasured books and immediately instructed me, "Ann, take care of this book. When you return it in good condition, you can have another one."

As I reached up to take the book, I caught her off guard. I glimpsed an expression that reminded me of what I heard Daddy tell Mama one day, "Now, Annie, Mama doesn't mean to sound as hard as she does. She really has a soft spot when you know where to find it."

I had no idea where to look for her soft spot, but in that instant I thought, *She really does have one—I just saw it.*

Slowly, I walked back homeward holding the book tightly, but with no immediate interest in it. As I walked up the hill from Grandma's house, the road curved at the top showing Daddy and Mama's place. I stopped at the sight of it and turned around to run—to run away—but even with the thought came the answer, *There is no place to run but home.*

As I drew closer, I saw Daddy at his workbench. He was using his hand plane smoothing over pine planks. I recognized those planks as ones he had stored carefully away sometime ago telling Mama, "I will make you some nice cabinets to replace the shelves in the kitchen as soon as I find the time and we have the extra money for the finishing material."

I asked one of my cousins who was standing with a group at the well, "What is Daddy making?"

Doyle didn't answer immediately. Then he said, "He is making a casket, a box to bury the baby in."

I walked up hesitantly to Daddy's side, and without turning he said as if to himself, "When I finish, it will be smooth and soft as silk." The curled shavings were falling on the ground as he carefully planed each piece.

I watched him measure and saw the planks and then begin fitting the pieces together. I didn't tell him, but what he was making didn't look big enough for a doll. I hadn't played with dolls so I didn't know how big it ought to be, but I still thought it was too little. Silently, I turned away and went inside.

Aunt Fletcher, Aunt Dill, and, I think, Aunt Paralee were busy in the living room laying out material to use to line the baby's casket. After a lot of planning and discussion, I heard one say, "Let's use this fine batiste material Annie saved from sugar sacks and cover it with the white satin material from the wedding dress to line the sides."

Another said, "And we can make a pillow to lay him on with the same material. Let's stuff it with goose feathers. There is no softer stuffing than goose down. Let's cover it with the white satin and use Mama's tatted lace to edge the seams."

It was strange for the thought to enter my mind at such a time, but when I heard them mention goose down, I thought, *That must be what Grandma Nannie's mean geese are good for—to make soft pillows for tiny babies who can't live.*

Her geese literally chased me off her place when I visited unexpectedly and she wasn't outside to rescue me. Daddy often said Grandma didn't need a watchdog as long as she kept her geese. I was more afraid of them than I was of Daddy's bull. He said the bull would kill me dead if I ever got in the pasture with it. At least the bull didn't run loose, ready to catch me, like the geese did.

Aunt Fletcher interrupted my reverie by saying, "Now, we need to dress the baby. We can't do any more about lining the casket until Aaron finishes making it."

"Let's ask Annie what she wants him to be buried in," one aunt spoke up.

They all agreed, and after a moment's silence another tearfully spoke, "But who wants to ask Annie that?"

I thought, *Let Aunt Fletcher ask Mama. I heard her ask God to help Mama today when she was praying this morning.* I didn't voice it as none of them ever mentioned prayer.

Just as I thought it, Aunt Fletcher got up without saying a word and walked slowly in the closed bedroom to talk to Mama. Later, she came back carrying an open box of baby clothes. As she held them up for us to see, I suddenly remembered seeing Mama make some of them—especially the crocheted booties. I had thought at the time it was just some more of her *doodads* that Daddy teased her about making every time she had a spare moment. The family sewing, mending, canning, washing clothes on a rub board, and working from early to late each day left her precious few spare moments.

If craft fairs had been in vogue, Mama would have been a great supporter. She delighted in making knickknacks out of knickknacks. But we were not looking at doodads. These were baby clothes for a real live baby that everyone was expecting but me.

I watched spellbound as all the aunts, I think Aunt India and Aunt Bessie may have come by then, gathered around to dress the baby in the burial clothes that Mama selected. Aunt Fletcher said, "Annie wants to see her baby again when we get him dressed. Call Aaron and ask him to come go in with us."

When Daddy came in, I ran outside and stayed until they came out of Mama's room. When I came back in the living room, Daddy was telling his sisters and Aunt Fletcher that it would be the next day before they could line the baby's casket. "It's almost four o'clock and milking time, so I won't be able to finish it today. Can you have everything ready and line it early in the morning?" he asked.

As he left the room, he said almost under his breath, "Now I need to see that someone has the grave ready for one o'clock tomorrow." Uncle Glenville and Kenneth went that afternoon and dug a grave in the family graveyard for little Aaron W. Thompson to be buried in the next day.

Daddy worked all night, stopping now and then to drink coffee with friends and family who came to sit up with the body. He finished the casket and made a bigger box to put it in. It was four o'clock and milking time the next morning before he was satisfied that he had done all he could do to make it suitable for his son's burial. It was a beautiful baby casket and it was not too little. It was just the right size for my baby brother.

Early that morning the lining was carefully stitched and tacked in place and the baby cradled inside on the soft goose-down pillow. I didn't touch him. I looked and looked and kept looking, thinking I had never seen or heard of anything as beautiful.

When Daddy began closing the satin-covered lid, I ran outside to be by myself. I grabbed Grandma Nancy's treasured book on the way out and hurried to my hideaway, the toilet. When it was first built, Mama decorated the wall with an oval framed mirror that had a crack right down the middle. We never called it an outhouse.

I looked at myself that morning, and for the first time I knew I would never be the baby again, and I didn't want to be. I made a vow to myself, looking me straight in the eye in the cracked mirror, *I don't ever want to be the only one "who doesn't know" again.*

Grandpa died not much more than a year later, but Daddy didn't make his casket. Uncle John, who was my mother's brother, and Aunt Mary hired a funeral company in Little Rock to come bury Grandpa. A black box-shaped car came out to take him to the cemetery where Mama said he was being buried beside her mother.

Uncle John was the city jailer in Little Rock and one of the few people we knew whose income wasn't altered by the Depression. We rode with him in his new car and followed the black funeral hearse that carried Grandpa across the country to be buried by his beloved wife.

With tears slipping out of Mama's eyes and down her cheeks, she repeated over and over again some of the many ways her daddy was never quite himself after her mother's death. Then, crying visibly, she sobbed, "Oh, how I wish I had been more patient with Dad all these years he lived with us. Why wasn't I as good to him as I wanted to be?"

I cuddled close to Mama's side saying fiercely, "Mama, you were good to Grandpa and to me too. Even when we got in your way while you were working so hard, you were good to us, Mama . . . " and we cried together.

I stood and watched another one of my family buried in a freshly dug grave. My body shook uncontrollably as men shoveled the reddish dirt back in the grave and covered the coffin of my beloved grandpa. I vowed again, as I did at my baby brother's grave, *I won't stay in that ground if anyone ever puts me in it!*

It took me ten years to shed my babyhood, and I almost skipped adolescence. Soon after I was eleven, I was no longer a child. My cycle of approaching womanhood had begun.

I was thrust out of my childhood in one short year, but I remained encircled in the security of home as I launched out to make my mark in the world—a mark that Daddy said we all make, whether we want to or not.

First School Buses - 1926 Vintage
Ann's uncle, Glenville Thompson, is at far left.

PART I

Early Childhood to Marriage

Ann's search for heaven begins,
but no one shows the way.

1

Elementary Years

I must have been one of the happiest little girls in the whole wide world on my first day of school. Off and on during the previous summer months, I overheard Mama and Daddy discuss whether I should start in September or wait until the following year. Daddy always emphasized that I was only five years old and I wouldn't be six until March. Mama's plea was that she thought I was ready for school. Enrollment time was fast approaching and Mama turned the tide by saying, "Aaron, don't hold her back. She wants to learn and she already knows how to read. I hear her picking out words on everything she sees written."

Mama said it right: I did pick out words. But I knew I couldn't actually read. I almost spoke up to say, "No, I can't read—except just words. I can't read your newspaper, Daddy, no matter how hard I try." It made me feel good for them to think I could read, so I remained silent.

The next day Mama's sewing machine began whirling merrily as her feet moved steadily on the treadle. I watched spellbound as she turned strips of material into skirts and blouses.

My concept of school was seeing books on top of books and reading them all day long. I thought even heaven couldn't offer better than that, but having new skirts and blouses to wear wasn't hard for me to add to my heavenly dream.

Then came the crowning item—school shoes. Mama seldom went shopping. Instead, she made a list and Daddy did it for her. But before school started each year, Mama took her butter-egg-chicken money that she had saved all year and went to Little Rock. This time she took me with her and she bought my school shoes. That day I knew it was a settled fact that I was going to start to school.

Finally, my big day was arriving. Now it was *tomorrow* instead of *when school starts*. Mama scrubbed me the night before until I was clean as a whistle. It was not the usual washbasin bath I took every day. Instead, this was a number two wash tub filled with warm water and sweet smelling soap bubbling all around me. Mama had no idea as she was lavishly soaping me that in just another year or two the very soap we bathed with would be a luxury item. Next, she shampooed my hair and rinsed it until, as she said, it "squeaked."

Later, I lay in bed too excited to sleep. Marie and Kenneth and I shared the same bedroom, but I didn't feel cramped for space or privacy. Marie and I slept in a big double bed on one side of the room and Kenneth in one on the opposite side. My mind was racing with questions about the coming day, but their sleepy answers didn't tell me much. Then I realized they weren't hearing me at all. *How can they sleep when they know they are going to get to go to school tomorrow?* I thought.

But even I went to sleep for the next thing I knew Mama was tapping my shoulder saying, "It's time for breakfast, Ann. Hurry, you are going to school today, and you don't want to miss the bus."

The possibility of missing the bus made me sit upright immediately. I bounded out of the bed and was in my chair at the breakfast table in time to see Mama take a big pan of biscuits out of the oven. A platter of fried eggs was ready in the warming closet over the cook stove. A mold of fresh churned butter was on the table in front of me. I knew it was fresh because I churned it the day before, a monotonous task that I talked my way out of completing most of the time. Sitting in one place, moving the pestle up and down in the cedar churn gave me no glimpse of what was happening to the milk inside. It caused me to ask, long before it was ready, "Mama, have I churned it long enough?"

After the third or fourth time I stopped her to ask, she would answer, "No, it isn't ready, but I guess I can finish it for you."

I waited impatiently, watching Mama carefully stirring white gravy in an iron skillet. Daddy often said that his mother, Grandma Nancy, made smooth white gravy without a single lump in it, and Mama seemed to try her best to do as well. Finally, I said, "Mama, your gravy tastes good even if it does have lumps in it. Hurry, I don't want to miss the school bus!"

But Daddy and Kenneth weren't back from the dairy barn, and Mama didn't serve any meal until Daddy was seated at the table. Marie wasn't in her chair either. She always came in late and helped Grandpa get seated after Daddy and Kenneth came inside.

While I waited for everyone to be seated at meal time, I often looked at the roses in a painting hanging over the dining area windows. Everything seemed bigger, better, and more beautiful on that special day. The roses looked fresher and I tried to imagine how they must smell, but the smell of strong coffee boiling in the granite coffee pot blotted out the aroma of roses in my imagination. Then Daddy came in the back door and Mama began pouring the coffee. I knew it was time to eat.

Soon, all six of us were seated around a bountiful breakfast. We didn't bow our heads and thank God for our food before we ate. The only time I heard thanks given audibly in our house was when Aunt Fletcher ate a meal with us, or when Brother Jack Taylor, the circuit riding Methodist preacher, was our guest. When Daddy picked up his fork, it was our signal to begin eating.

Mama sat down at the table with us, but when we began eating, she quietly got up and moved back to the cabinet area and prepared three lunches for Kenneth, Marie, and me to take to school. I wondered why Mama didn't get as hungry as we did; for even in my excitement on that memorable day, I ate a hearty breakfast. The thought of going to school made me feel older and wiser than my years warranted, and I drank an extra cup of the coffee (half coffee, half cream) when Daddy had his cup refilled.

Marie never ate as much as I did, and she was dressed and combing her hair when I rushed in the bedroom after breakfast. Half scolding, she said, "You better get ready if you're going to school with Kenneth and me."

The night before Mama had pressed my new skirt and blouse carefully and hung them on a chair by my bed. My shoes were on the floor beneath the chair with the toes peeking out at me from under the edge of the skirt. Everything was ready and now it was time to get dressed.

Mama called from the kitchen, "Marie, help Ann with her skirt and blouse. See that she buttons them in order."

I called out loud and clear, "I can do it. I know how to button them." And in a quieter tone, "I tried it over and over last night and I could do it every time."

Marie turned from the mirror and asked, "When did you do that? Did you get up and try your clothes on after I went to sleep last night?" Before I had to answer, she lost interest as she took one last look at her dark wavy hair in the mirror and glided in her own graceful way out the doorway.

I was glad I didn't have to admit that it was all playlike, and I was pretending I was buttoning my blouse and skirt as I lay in bed the night before.

Finally, it was not pretense. My hands and arms slid easily through the blouse sleeves. I buttoned the bottom button, and all the other buttons went in their right places just as they had in my imagination the night before. Then I stepped in the skirt and pulled it up to my waist, tucking my blouse inside just as Mama did when she tried them on me. I buttoned the waistband and thought, *I did it.*

Now came the best of all—my new school shoes. First, I slipped on the short socks Mama bought the day we went shopping. These were not the brown ribbed cotton stockings Daddy always bought when he did the shopping. Instead, these were socks that didn't require garters to hold them up. I hadn't tried them on even in my imagination, and I thrilled at the feel and looks of them on my feet as I stepped in my treasured shoes.

Getting ready posed no problem until I came to the shoe laces. Tying a bow didn't work even in my imagination the night before, and it certainly didn't now. The bow kept slipping through each time I tried to loop it. Grandpa did it so easily when he put his shoes on. I heard Marie calling from the living room, "Are you ready yet, Ann?"

What if I don't ever learn how to tie my shoes? I thought.

I turned toward the tilted mirror over the dresser and twirled round and round as I had seen Marie do when she finished dressing. I smiled at my reflection standing there ready for school, my shining clean blonde hair in a Buster Brown cut and my skirt and blouse fitting just right. Then the mirror tilted downward enough to add my feet to the scene. The gaping shoes and dangling shoe strings changed the whole picture I was seeing, and I ran frantically to find Mama.

Mama was sitting at the kitchen table eating her delayed breakfast. Sheepishly, I stood in the doorway and asked, "Mama am I ready?"

Her expression when she saw my flopping shoe strings caused me to hurry across the room to get her to tie them. Mama put both her arms around me and pulled me close to her body as she stooped over me to tie my shoe laces—it was as close to a hug as Mama ever gave me. Then, as though she knew I didn't want anyone else to know that I couldn't tie my shoes, she almost whispered, "Once you do it, Ann, it will come easy as pie."

Hope leaped up in my heart when I heard her words, and I looked up gratefully trying to find a way to express it. Laughing, Mama said, "Ann, you're cute," and she gave my backside a playful push to send me on my way.

It sent me back to the mirror to see what she meant by "cute." As I looked in the tilted mirror and saw my feet, I thought: *My shoes really are cute with the strings tied in a bow and I am going to learn how to tie them. Just as Mama said it will be "easy as pie" once I do it.*

"Come on, Ann, it's time to go," Marie called from the front porch.

Mama hurried in and shooed me out the door. She handed Kenneth my lunch, saying, "Take care of Ann and check on her at lunchtime to see if she needs anything."

Down the front steps we went and we were finally on our way to the bus stop. West Twelfth Street (later named Kanis Road) was paved all the way from Little Rock to within one half mile of Daddy's place. It was at the end of the pavement that we met the school bus.

Somehow, *hurry* was a word in my vocabulary that I did not seem to understand, and even Kenneth was telling me to "hurry up" now as we went down the gravel road. I was trying to walk in the smooth places as Mama said the gravel would wear out my shoes. *It would be a lot easier to skip barefoot than to hurry in my new shoes. But I guess I'm too old to skip, and I sure don't want to pull off my new shoes,* I thought.

The big school bus rumbled around the corner almost as soon as we got there and stopped right at our feet. I looked up so excited I could hardly breathe as Kenneth had me step up first. My stepping on board the big jet planes of the present age has never produced the exhilaration I felt as I climbed on board that school bus.

A long bench went the full length on both sides of the bus with a double bench down the middle aisle. The open windows had roll-up canvas curtains (or roll-down, according to the weather). The benches and windows comprised the comforts of the bus, but Cinderella's carriage couldn't compete with the pomp and grandeur I sensed as I traveled that ten miles to my first day in school.

The glory diminished, but never completely departed, as I rode that same route every following school year until my graduation day. I learned early in life that what is waiting at the end of one's journey determines the grandeur of the trip.

Joe T. Robinson, a new consolidated school (grades one through twelve) located on Highway 10 just out of Little Rock, was waiting for me that day.

Kenneth took me directly to the first grade room. As he opened the door, I couldn't believe my eyes. Instead of books on top of books as I had pictured in my imagination, I saw a room full of boys and girls all about my size, or not much bigger. Aunt Fletcher was at the front of the room, and I ran excitedly toward her. With an expression and tone I had never known her to use, she said, "Good morning. Please come in and sit down," as she pointed to a desk on the front row.

I sat down wondering if she didn't recognize me all grown up and dressed for school. I turned around looking at all the boys and girls sitting behind me and got caught up in such excitement I guess I didn't hear the teacher's instructions. In the midst of my exuberance, she suddenly stood by my side, took both of my hands and tapped them firmly with a ruler. She repeated her instructions—this time directly to me.

Whatever else Aunt Fletcher taught me my first year in school, it all began in that instant. I immediately learned that being *the daughter she never had* didn't give me the privileges in her classroom that it did in her kitchen at home.

I jumped down from the school bus at the end of my first school day humming under my breath a tune Mama sang on good days, "Oh, Happy Day, Happy Day!"

As my feet hit the ground I thought, *Now I can pull my shoes and socks off and skip all the way home.* My bare feet felt so good that I sat a moment wiggling my toes in the cool dirt, and I began to feel drowsy.

Marie and Kenneth didn't bother to tell me to hurry as they trudged up the hill. Suddenly I realized, and the thought jarred me wide awake, *I went to school today but I still can't read. What if Daddy asks me to read his newspaper tonight?* Then I told myself, *Maybe he won't ask until tomorrow.* Carrying my shoes, I started slowly on my way home.

Mama was waiting in the kitchen with homemade yeast rolls, butter, and muscadine jelly on the table. She stopped working and sat down with us. I told her everything that happened to me at school—well, almost everything. She interrupted me saying, "Ann, run see if your granddaddy is out front. I haven't been able to get much work done today without you here to play with him. He asked, seems like a hundred times or more, 'Where's Ann?' I no sooner told him you were in school than he asked it again. It seems like he can't remember anything. Go and let him see that you are home again. Maybe he will settle down."

I found him sitting on the front door steps with his head in his hands. When he heard my voice, his head came up and with outstretched arms he pulled me down beside him asking, "Where have you been?"

"I've been to school, Grandpa; let me show you." I stood up in front of him and began repeating everything I could remember that Aunt Fletcher told us. I pretended I was the teacher and Grandpa was one of the pupils. When he didn't heed my instructions, I tapped his hands firmly with my new pencil and repeated them directly to him. He was accustomed to our playing pretending games so playing school was just part of having me home again for Grandpa.

Teaching Grandpa after my school day became a pattern that we both looked forward to each day. Mama said he sat on the front steps waiting all afternoon. Even though he seemed to be waiting for me, he still asked intermittently, "Where is Ann?"

Later, I began using Daddy's newspaper for Grandpa to read during our *school time*. He couldn't see well, and as he slowly read the words, I sat down beside him to help him as Aunt Fletcher sometimes did during her reading class. I followed the words along with him and I soon learned the *connecting words*. Then I began actually reading Daddy's newspaper, not just picking out words.

Meanwhile, reading at school was easy as pie, but I still couldn't tie my shoe laces. Mama tied them each morning and when one got untied at school, I learned to ease my foot out when Aunt Fletcher came down the aisle. Almost without stopping, she would bend over and tie them without looking right or left.

Toward the end of the school year, Aunt Fletcher had me read to one group in the class while she was helping another group. During one of these sessions, Miss Latin, a tall olive-skinned, long-nosed lady from the State Department of Education came in for her regular inspection of the classroom teaching. She sat down with my reading group and afterward she asked Aunt Fletcher, "How do you account for this child's reading ability?"

Aunt Fletcher paused a moment before she answered, "I'm not sure. I think she came to school expecting to read the first day—and somehow, she almost did it."

EAGLE TO TURKEY

I soared like an eagle during my first grade in school, but my wings must have been clipped in my second and third grades. I can't remember my teachers' names, or even their faces.

I do remember three things occurring during those two years. One was the A's on my report card. I carried it proudly home to show Mama and Daddy. Somehow, I wished I could make better than an A, and maybe they would be happy again. Both were overwhelmed with making ends meet during those depression years, and I seldom saw the happy excitement on their faces that I once had seen.

I remember Miss Latin. She continued to periodically visit the classrooms, and I began to dread seeing her face when she came to our room. She not only inspected the class procedure, but she inspected me. Her possessive interest in me and in my progress in school caused my childish imagination to run wild. I wondered, *What if she comes one day and takes me away to be her pupil—and I won't ever see Mama and Daddy again.*

Then one morning Miss Latin's picture appeared in Daddy's newspaper. It was her obituary. That was one section in the newspaper that I avoided reading, but seeing her picture caught my attention. I read the account of her death and the enumeration of the good works she was known for doing. Relieved, I thought, *Now I won't have to see her again.*

I was ashamed to share my reaction to her death, and I didn't mention it to anyone until I told Aunt Fletcher several years later. She was appalled that she had not recognized my fear of Miss Latin. "Oh, Ann," she said, "I had no idea you were thinking such thoughts about her trying to help you. She was interested in your scholastic ability, and she wanted you to have every opportunity to develop it. Had she lived, she would have sponsored you in any educational field you were qualified to enter."

Looking back, I could see how Miss Latin kept me involved in extracurricular projects that challenged me to go beyond my regular reading, writing, and arithmetic assignments. She encouraged me to enter a writing contest during my third grade. It was open to any student from first through eighth grade. Each could pick his own subject and would be graded according to his age and grade. The winner would get a five dollar prize.

I wrote on Robert E. Lee and I won the prize—a subscription to *Child Life* magazine and a congratulation card containing a fifty cent piece.

Remembering, I was ashamed again—this time of my ungrateful feelings toward a lady who had been my benefactor.

It was three years later before another mentor emerged in my life. During those years I continued to make A's in subjects that were too easy to challenge me. Instead, growing up was challenging me to my utmost. The unexpected birth and death of a baby brother and later the burial of my beloved grandpa sent me groping for answers to questions I didn't know how to ask. It was then that Grandma Nancy's library opened the door to a world that fascinated and challenged me to find answers to *Life* instead of to humdrum school subjects.

I had vowed to myself the day my unexpected baby brother was buried, *I don't ever want to be "the only one who doesn't know" again.* I became a secret detective in my own household. I spied on the activities of Marie and Kenneth and our teenage cousins. I eavesdropped when Mama and Daddy and other adults were talking, determined that nothing was going to happen again unexpectedly in our household that everyone knew about except me.

When the teenagers didn't want to include me in their escapades, I threatened to tell Mama what they were doing. Telling on another was known as *snitching*, a crime no self-respecting family member could tolerate in his or her life. Threatening to tell was tantamount to snitching, and even though I didn't commit the crime, the threat separated me from my siblings more than our age gap had ever done.

Fortunately, their activities were relatively harmless until the day I discovered they were smoking cigarettes. I spied on their secret meeting place and caught them puffing cigarettes, joking and laughing merrily together. I was scared to smoke even if they let me, but I determined not to be left out of anything so I insisted that they include me. At first Kenneth was adamant in refusing to give me a cigarette, but this time I said, "If you don't, I'll tell Daddy what you are doing." He reluctantly relented.

Terrified, I smoked my first cigarette. My head went round and round. My stomach churned. I began coughing so violently I almost upchucked—but I smoked. "I did it!" I exclaimed, but not with the good feeling I had felt in previous accomplishments.

We met secretly and smoked every day for the rest of the summer. The first three days were terrible, but by the end of the week nicotine had hooked me, and I looked forward to our smoking time each day.

Kenneth never treated me like a little princess again. I was his peer. He remained my adored big brother, but I felt cheated—almost as if I had sold my birthright.

I no longer soared like an eagle. Instead, I walked with the turkeys.

ANSWER TO IGNORANCE

Even in the summertime the wood-burning cook stove stayed hot from sunup to sunset as Mama cooked breakfast, dinner, and supper. She canned garden produce on it and heated the flat irons she used on starched dresses, aprons, shirts, and the crocheted scarves that graced every tabletop in the house.

Although no wood was added to the stove after supper was cooked, the heated house remained almost unbearably hot even after the fire died down. We migrated from the supper table in the middle of the kitchen to the front porch each night. It was our family room as well as our bedroom during the summer months. If there was any breeze stirring, it blew across the open porch, cooling us as we lay sleeping on folding cots or on pallets (sleeping bags in the modern vernacular) that Mama spread on the floor.

Daddy led his family to the front porch after supper each night. He pulled his wooden rocking chair up by the open window where a kerosene lamp burning in the living room provided barely enough light for him to read the newspaper—not even the Depression could take that from him.

Summer dragged relentlessly on that year. I thought rain, cool weather, and school days would never come again. Hot winds swept across the dry fields on the dairy farm, swirling dust clouds often thick as fog and stifling our breathing. Elderly people in their fifties and sixties began dying throughout the area from the extended drought and heat wave. Barnyard language, hitherto reserved for the barn, blazed out in unexpected places. The breakdown of household appliances, which Daddy previously took in stride, provoked outbursts of profanity. I heard his exasperation as he replaced a broken axe handle for my brother Kenneth to chop the firewood, or as he stopped to fix the frazzled rope caught in the well pulley. It may well have been the summer that spawned the plot for the book *Grapes of Wrath* that was published a few years later.

One night, as Daddy sat reading his beloved newspaper, suddenly he looked up and said, "Listen to this." He read aloud a news account of a man being killed when he was decapitated in a local accident.

Rather than acknowledge my ignorance, I ran inside, searched, and found the family dictionary. Quickly, I looked up the word *decapitated* and rushed back, excitedly explaining, "It cut his head off, Daddy. That's what that word said—it cut off his head!"

Daddy didn't laugh, but I sensed by his amused expression I was the only one on the porch who needed the explanation. I was embarrassed, but I was still tingling with the excitement that engulfed me as I tasted the power of finding an answer to my ignorance. I clutched the dictionary close to my breast and claimed it for my very own book. It became my Bible—a book I had not read.

FAMILY LIFE

The entire nation plunged from joyful prosperity to abject poverty almost overnight, and the Roaring Twenties came to an abrupt halt when the stock market crashed in 1929.

Its full impact began hitting our household in 1932. I was ten years old, just jolted out of my warm nest of childhood by the unexpected arrival and death of a baby brother, and a year later the burial of my beloved playmate, Grandpa.

Even as the economic collapse affected the nation, changing it from an aggressive, joy-riding society to a despondent and almost defeated people, our family life changed dramatically.

SUPPLIES
Kerosene
Flour
Matches
Meal
~~Sugar~~
Salt
Coffee
Soda
Baking Powder

Mama's shopping money for school supplies was already spent each year as she used her butter-eggs-chicken money to help Daddy buy bare necessities.

Just before she gave her list to Daddy, she marked out *sugar* saying she could substitute sorghum molasses. Daddy and Mama literally forged a living for us from their sixty acres of land. They harvested potatoes, peas, beans, corn, turnips, cabbage, strawberries, popcorn, peanuts, watermelons, and sorghum cane. Apples, peaches, and pears came from Grandma Nancy's orchard. Milk and eggs were plentiful; hogs supplied ham and salt meat; fishing provided recreation and food; and Mama continued setting a bountiful table throughout the grueling years.

There was no money for extras. Daddy struggled to have cash to pay the taxes on his land and to buy seed to plant each year. He refused to charge a single dollar, and even the thought of someday having to mortgage his land for living money (as many were doing) threw him into a rage. Instead, Daddy planned, worked, sweated, cursed, and battled his way through the ten years that later were named The Great Depression. His dream of becoming a prosperous dairy farmer was delayed by the necessity of supplying food for his family.

Mama's body went through physical changes during those depression years that caused her indescribable agony. Sick headaches, accompanied by severe hemorrhaging, altered her happy, carefree personality. But she continued staying on her feet, working from 4 a.m. until 9 p.m. each day. Her voice changed to a loud, shrill tone as she struggled through each miserable day. Then, all of a sudden the physical change finished its vicious cycle, and Mama was well—a subdued version, but my Mama again.

School shoes, coffee, and a daily newspaper were considered essential items, and Daddy budgeted them along with taxes, seed, and bare necessities. He used a stubby pencil on a pocket-sized note pad and sat under a kerosene lamp pondering the list night after night. I never saw him count his money. It wasn't necessary. He knew exactly to a penny how much he had at all times. The bottom line was there to show him.

Since the only clothing budgeted was for shoes, Mama had to provide the rest. She made our school clothes out of anything available, but after a year or two she had used up every scrap of material in the house.

Dr. Lamb's wife bought butter and eggs from Mama and she must have sensed her plight in dressing three children with no cash available. In earlier years she had admired Mama's hooked rugs, so she emptied her closets of unused clothing and brought it to Mama, saying, "I know you like to hook rugs. See if you can use some of these garments in your rugs."

Dr. Lamb was a well-known physician in Little Rock. His family clothing was of the finest fabric available. Mama carefully ripped the seams and used the material to make our school clothes, saving the strips for her hooked rugs. Daddy was a proud man. He was seemingly unaware that Mrs. Lamb continued bringing *hooked rug* supplies each summer and Mama was turning them into school clothing for his children.

The lack of things money can buy was no insurmountable hurdle for me. I was enchanted, intrigued, and challenged by a whole new world opening up to me through the books I was reading. Grandma Nancy's library was open to me one book at a time, and they covered a whole range of thought: *Ben Hur, Little Women, Uncle Tom's Cabin, Les Miserables*—Hawthorne, Dickens, Longfellow. Along with her books I now had access to the school library. My mind was whirling with new information.

If the Roaring Twenties no longer roared, I didn't miss it. School was still a great adventure, beckoning me on to higher ground each year.

GOOD NEWS IN A GRAVE YARD

Churchgoing was not a regular part of my childhood and growing up years. Daddy felt no need for church attendance. His philosophy was, "If a man lives as good a life as he knows how, that ought to be good enough for God or anybody."

Mama knew better, but she said she would wait until Daddy changed his mind and then we could all go together.

Before I was school age, Mama encouraged me to go to church and not wait for her and Daddy. She shampooed my blond hair one Saturday night, woke me up early on Sunday morning, and brushed my hair until she said she could see glints of gold shining through. She dressed me in the prettiest dress I owned—white organdy, encircled in white ruffles across the shoulders, down the side seams, and along the front and back of the hem. Mama ironed those ruffles with a flat iron, and they stood out crisp and beautiful.

I skipped off down the gravel road to church, eagerly expecting to have a good time, as I only wore that dress to special events. Everyone was quiet, no laughter or even smiles as I entered the church doors. Immediately, I felt out of place without my daddy and mama and sitting among families who read the Bible and talked aloud to a God that I couldn't see. *If this were real, Daddy would be here,* I thought.

In later years I rationalized, *Daddy lives as good a life, or better, than the men going to church, and if he doesn't need it, why should I?*

I knew too that his daddy had had the same philosophy: Be honest, work hard, pay your debts, and don't harm anyone.

Daddy's mother, my grandmother Nancy, came from a different culture. The land we all lived on in that section was bequeathed to us by her ancestors. The small Methodist church built on land donated by her family was a visible testimony of churchgoing families. A plot of land behind the church that began as the family graveyard was now a community cemetery.

The church was one that never had a pastor. Methodists sent a circuit riding preacher three or four times a year to preach, and often he stayed overnight at our house. Brother Jack Taylor was a godly man; even Daddy said he was. He gave me a New Testament and he wrote Matthew 6:33 on the flyleaf. I cherished that verse when I was old enough to read it: *Seek ye first the kingdom of God . . .* , and I pasted the flyleaf in my scrapbook. I thought "kingdom of God" surely meant *heaven*, and I wanted to go to heaven whatever and wherever it was.

Funerals were held in the graveyard alongside the open grave. Daddy was asked to be a pallbearer for nearly all the funerals in the community. We went as a family to show our respect. The graveyard became my church— it was there I heard the Bible read and people pray.

I was ten years old the first time I watched a coffin lowered in the ground and men shoveled dirt in to cover it. I decided right then I didn't want to stay in a grave when I died.

Daddy's creed didn't fit me. I couldn't "live as good as I knew how" as he said he did, and God seemed to have a higher standard than Daddy. I discovered it was impossible for me to live a good enough life to deserve it, but the desire to go to heaven when I died continued to haunt me.

A TURNING POINT

I saw it in my mind's eye, heard it in my inner ear, and felt its power surge throughout my eleven year old body. I may have even voiced it. If I did, only one person heard the message, and she didn't respond audibly.

The year was 1933, right in the middle of the Great Depression when everyone was poor—but if I was poor, I didn't know it. I was a country farmer's daughter on a rare shopping trip, and if that wasn't excitement enough, quite unexpectedly I came face to face with three black people in downtown Little Rock, Arkansas.

Daddy's farm was ten miles west of Little Rock, but that didn't make it a suburban community. Electricity, running water, gas, and telephone lines all stopped at the city limits. Isolated from the outside world, I could have been living in the remotest mountain village in Arkansas.

Western Pulaski County must have been one of the most segregated areas in the nation as black people were unknown to me except for what I heard. The warning I heard to blacks was, "Don't let the sun go down and find you here," used with an insulting term. It came over the grapevine in a community that had no telephone lines.

Black people wisely took that warning seriously, and they didn't travel West Twelfth Street Pike outside the city limits even during the sunup time, at least not after one did. The grapevine reported, "He woke up dead the next morning."

Daddy wore many hats besides being a dairyman. Folks looked to him as the community veterinarian and as their barber. A nook behind his barber chair on our front porch provided a hiding place for a small girl to listen undetected on dark nights as men lingered on our front steps after getting Daddy to cut their hair. They cussed and discussed the hard times of the Depression days along with other subjects that children and ladies were not supposed to hear. Daddy was not an active part of the shenanigans about which some talked and snickered, but neither did he confront them with their obvious cruelty and blatant disregard for what little law existed then to protect a black person.

Segregation lawfully kept the races apart, and no one, white or black, was championing a black person's rights in that section of Pulaski County. He had none. To speak up for a black person would label you with a derogatory name ending with *lover*, and the penalty for that was deadlier than being black itself. I listened and pondered in my heart all that I heard.

But segregation didn't enter my mind the day Mama said I could go with her to buy my school shoes. Daddy cranked up his Model T Ford that he usually drove only on the back country roads. The motor sputtered, but finally started, and away we chugged on our way to the big city. We stopped at the streetcar tracks on the edge of town and Daddy showed us where to stand to wait for a trolley car to come and take us downtown.

Mama had five one-dollar bills, and as Daddy counted out some change to go with it, he said, "Now, Annie, don't spend all of this. Be sure you keep enough to pay your way back. Meet me right here. If you get lost, I'll never know where to find you."

The thought of getting lost prompted me to speak right up, "She won't spend it all, Daddy. When I get my shoes, we won't spend another cent."

Riding a streetcar was a rare adventure for Mama as well as for me, and we were both nervous as we stepped on board the clanging, shaking vehicle when it stopped alongside us. The conductor tipped his special cap and kindly put us at ease, showing us where to drop our six-cent fare and smiling as I fumbled with the pennies that Daddy had given me. Pointing to a seat up front he said, "Sit up here, Goldilocks, and I'll show you the city."

Before I could answer and tell him, "I'm not here to look— I'm here to buy my school shoes," the streetcar stopped and right before me were three black girls. One may have been the mother, or she could have been the sister of the two younger girls. Except for their skin and hair I was amazed that they looked like me or anyone else I knew. I thought, *Well, what difference does color make?* I soon found out.

Mama and I may have been nervous when we waited for the streetcar, but these girls stood motionless with fear when the conductor opened the door for them to enter. "What are you waiting for?" he called out. They cautiously stepped inside and the older one dropped in the correct fare for all three. She stood blankly watching the coins jangle down to the bottom while the younger girls hid behind her trying to wrap themselves in her skirt.

The conductor barked, "See that sign. Get to the back. Can't you read?" As if petrified, she stood speechless. Standing up he yelled even louder, "Can't you hear, either? Get off, or get to the back!"

For a moment she turned as if to run, then grasping the hands of the younger ones who were clutching her skirt, she lifted her head, and with downcast eyes slowly moved toward the back of the streetcar.

I instinctively scooted over to make room beside me. As she passed by, I looked up in her frightened eyes and thought, *I wish you could sit by me.*

Immediately, an inner voice moved throughout my body, and I saw and heard:

> *Someday you will be free to sit*
> *anywhere I can . . . . You just wait*
> *and see.*

Hope sprang up in her face as if she too heard the message. Her lips moved but no sound came. Our eyes made contact and that silent conversation marked a turning point in my life.

It was a brief encounter, but it convinced me there was an unseen and mostly unheard *Power* surrounding me. Not understanding what happened, I kept it secret and pondered it in my heart.

I waited and watched for another glimpse, another message. A fleeting few came over the years, but I was nearly thirty-four years old before I finally met the Author.

2

Junior High Years

The long, hot summer of 1934, my first year in junior high school, extended on through the month of September and into October. We continued to sleep on the front porch until the first frost finally cooled the sweltering days and nights that had seemed to have no ending.

School started in mid-September. I woke up early that first day moist with perspiration. A soapless wash pan bath and the sprinkling of Arm and Hammer soda (the Depression substitute for bath powder and for toothpaste) did little to freshen my body or my spirit.

Mama called us to breakfast, a table set with ham and eggs, hot biscuits and gravy, fresh churned butter, muscadine jelly, and hot coffee. In her special way Mama tried to make our first day of the school year a celebration. Without money to buy our school supplies, she did what she could do—she prepared a bountiful breakfast. Good farm food was never a shortage in our household throughout the Depression years, and Mama enjoyed cooking for us even in a steaming hot kitchen.

On that day I didn't eat as much as Marie, who was known for eating like a bird. Mama looked disappointed, and I hurried out of the hot kitchen to go get dressed for school.

Dressing was almost methodical until I slipped on my new blue suede shoes. Standing before the tilting mirror, I smiled at my reflection. I remembered looking in that same mirror and seeing my untied shoes on my first day in school six years earlier. That seemed a long time ago, and somehow I didn't feel as grown up, or as important as I did on that unforgettable day.

Later, a spark of excitement ignited when I stepped up on the school bus. I thought, *Maybe junior high will have the answers to my questions.*

My excitement, along with my anticipation, grew as the bus bumped along on the dusty road carrying me closer to my beloved Joe T. Robinson School. I stretched out my legs full length trying to make them look long and slim. They never did look as long as Marie's, no matter how long I stretched them, so I contented myself by admiring my blue suede shoes.

Then leaning back, I soon became mesmerized in thinking about my future. By then my life goal was etched indelibly on my mind.

A civic minded daddy and a mama who voiced her opinion at home (but never cast a vote at the polls) exposed me to social issues that burned in my young mind and soul. Gross injustice to black people prevailed in that segregated county. Daddy was not an active part of the shenanigans that local men laughed and talked about while resting on our front steps, but he did not confront them either.

On my eleventh birthday I resolved in my secret heart to make good grades, go to college, and then go to law school. I planned to be a lawyer, but not to remain one. I wanted to be a judge to sit on the bench and exact justice to all races. Sandra Day O'Connor may never have dreamed that she would sit on the Supreme Court, but I dreamed that I would. Segregation was the law of the land, and I purposed to work for a change of the law and then one day be a judge who would rule by the law and not by the color of one's skin.

I was engrossed in planning my lofty future, and before I expected it, the long bus ride came to an end. I moved forward in the seat anxiously waiting for the bus to come to a complete halt as it turned slowly in the school driveway and circled around to the parking lot.

The Home Economics cottage, built of native stone, stood majestically in view when I jumped down from the bus. It sat apart from the main building and I hurried to be one of the first to register in Miss Martindale's homemaking class.

I wasn't particularly interested in learning to cook and sew, but a glimpse in a friend's textbook the year before convinced me I needed that class. I marveled at pictures of table settings which showed fine china, crystal, silver, and the instructions to use it properly—even to the folding of the napkins. I sensed I would need social as well as academic skills to succeed in the prestigious field I planned to enter, and I wanted to be prepared.

Miss Martindale, secretly called the *Old Maid* by the pupils, had a reputation of ruling the Home Ec cottage with an iron hand. She prided herself on making a *lady* out of every pupil she accepted in her class. A lady was what I wanted to be, so I rushed in jubilantly to fill out a registration card.

Her startled expression when I came rushing in could have said more than I was aware of at the time. The stale tobacco odor that any nonsmoker can detect, my blue suede shoes, and my confident manner may have made her think a Roaring Twenties flapper had invaded her domain.

She didn't welcome me with the warmth teachers usually have for all their pupils on the first day of the school year. Instead, without smiling she asked if I had a textbook, and immediately instructed me that no pupil remained in her class without one.

She handed me a registration card and a list of fees:

Textbook	$1.25
Pattern, material, thread	$3.75
Total	$5.00

My jubilance faded as I read the list. I hadn't owned a text-book for three years, not since Mama's butter-egg-chicken money had to be added to Daddy's budget book. It helped buy the bare necessities, or as they said, "It made ends meet."

Mama's sick headaches seemed to get worse when she didn't have money to buy us things she knew we needed. The beginning of school each year—once a happy time—was especially hard for her. I tried to find a way to ease it, and I said, "Mama, you don't have to buy books for me. I can listen in class and Coy will let me borrow her books to study on the bus. I can still make A's. I'll show you." And I had for three years. Coy and my teacher each year were the only ones who knew I didn't have any books. I studied Coy's books on the bus, and if I needed them, my teacher let me take her books overnight.

My first day in junior high school didn't give me the answers I had hoped to find. Instead, I went home unsure of what to expect. Later, I lay in bed reliving the day and trying to imagine how the next day surely would be a better one.

I thought, or it could have been I dreamed:

> *Maybe Miss Martindale will let me use her text-*
> *book. If I don't cook or sew, I won't need to pay*
> *the fees. I'll listen carefully in class. Someday*
> *when I have the money to get what the fees re-*
> *quire, I'll already know how to cook and sew. I'll*
> *learn everything that book says and everything*
> *Miss Martindale teaches the other girls. She'll see*
> *that I can.*

If it was a dream, I had a rude awakening in class the next day. Miss Martindale looked out over her small group of *young ladies* and asked that we hold up our textbooks. I sat way down in my desk chair hoping I wouldn't be seen. She said, "Ann, you are dismissed to go to the study hall. If you have your textbook by the end of the week, you may come back to my class."

I looked around the room thinking someone would offer to share her book with me, but every girl's head was turned downward. I didn't know Miss Martindale meant for me to leave immediately until she said, "Now."

Feeling wet and unfamiliar tears rolling down my cheeks and dripping on my blouse, I stood up and looked hopefully into Miss Martindale's face. Her unmoving eyes told me there was no need to plead. Slowly, I walked out of her classroom.

Outside I stood still for a moment. I was unaccustomed to shedding tears, and I scarcely knew what to do with them. Wiping my eyes with both hands, I hoped I was removing all traces of them as I deliberately tried to regain my composure. Then I hurried across the school yard wondering what I would say when I reported to the study hall teacher.

Across the way in front of me I saw a sign at the back of the school yard: *Smoking Area*. A group of seniors who had the early lunch hour were going in that direction. I fell in step with them and soon found myself smoking with the seniors.

Physically I was as mature as any of the girls, and by then I was a veteran smoker. Everyone was hurrying to smoke and get back on schedule, and there was no time for idle talk. I fit in with the group, and no questions were asked.

GENIE IN MY POCKET

Later, at the end of my second day in junior high school, I went home *sick*. The ten-mile bus ride that, magically, was never long in earlier days seemed endless. Finally, I staggered through the back doorway at home and slid down in a chair at the kitchen table gasping, "Mama, have I caught your sick head-ache? My head hurts and I'm sick all over."

Mama was standing over the wood-burning cook stove steril-izing Ball fruit jars that she used for canning fruits and vegeta-bles. The steaming hot kitchen flushed her face beet red. She looked at me and almost screamed, "This hot weather—oh, Lord, we're all going to die if it doesn't rain and cool things off!" When she said we were all going to die, I almost fainted, or maybe I did. Next thing I knew, I was lying down on the front porch and Mama was fanning me. She seldom stopped working from early morning until late evening, but she stopped everything that day to sit beside me on the daybed. The wet cloth she put on my forehead and her constant fanning soon began to cool me.

I was feeling better until I read the words *Drummond's Fu-neral Parlor* in bold print on the oval-shaped hand fan. It stirred my imagination to wonder fearfully, *Is this hot weather going to kill junior high girls like everyone says it is doing to old folks in their fifties and sixties?*

If I was dying, dirt would be shoveled in to cover me like it was on my baby brother and Grandpa. With that thought, my body shook uncontrollably.

The back screen door slammed shut as Daddy came through the house looking for Mama. She called out, "Aaron, I'm out here. This weather is killing us. Ann is having an awful chill. I can't help milk tonight."

Daddy came hurrying out on the porch and stopped long enough to feel my forehead and to say, "You're going to be all right—yes, you are." The gentle touch of his work-hardened hand, and the healing message he spoke surged throughout my body. *I'm not dying after all,* I thought.

Sure enough by suppertime I was feeling well enough to be up again. Mama must not have received the healing message I did as she still seemed fearful I was going to die and kept me lying down. She made potato soup, her antidote for any major illness, and spooned it slowly into my mouth. Doctors may not have yet learned of potato soup's healing value, but they do acknowledge the power in tender loving care. Mama dispensed plenty of that, unaware it was exactly what I needed to heal my hurting spirit after the turmoil of my second day in junior high school.

The next morning I jumped out of bed ready to eat breakfast and dress for my third day of the school year. No answer to my textbook problem had come to my imagination or to my dreams during the night. But when I dressed and looked in the tilted mirror, I thought, *I'm not sick.* I stopped to think what else was good about it and I added, *And I still have my blue suede shoes.* That brought a smile to my reflection and sent me tripping, my grownup version of skipping, on my way to catch the bus to take me to my beloved school.

A breeze blowing through the open bus window felt cool and I leaned back resting, trying not to think of my truancy of the day before. I reminded myself that no one knew what I had done except the smoking seniors, and they weren't apt to tell. With that thought I dozed off to sleep and was startled awake when the bus came to a stop on the school ground.

Hurrying to my homeroom, I was barely seated when the teacher handed me an open note: *Report to the principal's office.* I asked, "Now?"

She nodded, "Now."

That summons marked the ultimate of trouble in a pupil's life. It meant your teacher couldn't handle your problem, and when the principal had to solve it, you were in real trouble.

Mr. Hoggard was a young man who had replaced Mr. Hall as principal the year before. He made changes that caused some of the older teachers to raise their eyebrows in protest, but the younger ones thought he was super.

The only reprimand I had received in my six years' schooling was on my first day of school. Aunt Fletcher tapped my hands with a ruler and taught me immediately to respect a teacher's authority. I thought as I approached the principal's office, *I wish Mr. Hall was still principal.* I remembered how he patted me on the shoulder when he saw me in the hall and often told me I was a good student.

Mr. Hoggard never had done that, and after this incident he wasn't apt to ever do it. His office door was open, and I entered holding out the summons in my hand. He looked up and turned from his conversation with a parent long enough to take it and say, "Sit down (pointing to his desk) and I will get to you as soon as I can." He continued talking to a woman at the counter who was upset and objecting loudly to her daughter's grades from the year before.

I sat in his chair at his desk and waited all morning growing more apprehensive by the minute as he talked to a steady stream of people—pupils, parents, and teachers. Communication was face-to-face or through a written message, not by telephone or any of the modern means of today. People brought their problems directly to him, and he handled some that day in ways even my young mind thought was unusual.

It was noon before he left the open counter and finally turned to me. Pulling up a chair and sitting down in front of me —I was seated at his desk— he said, "Ann, I received a note this morning saying you have been smoking on the school grounds. Is that true?"

All I could say was, "Yes, sir." Then I almost whispered, "was it Miss Martindale?"

He ignored my question, but a brief twinkle in his eye told me it was. Then he asked, "Were you in the designated area?"

Again, I answered, "Yes, sir."

Leaning forward and looking me straight in the eyes, he said, "Ann, you have too good a record here to mess it up now. You owe it to yourself and to Joe T. Robinson School to keep up your good record. If you will continue making straight A's in all your subjects and in citizenship throughout this seventh grade, I will see that you pass to the ninth grade at the end of the school year. Will you do it?"

Numbly, and not understanding how that could help the problem I was facing, I nodded, "Yes, sir."

I stood to leave, but he said, "Sit down. I want to talk to you. There is a government program called National Youth Administration that will pay certain qualified youth in an on-the-job training program. I am entitled to train one person in my office. It pays six dollars a month.

"You will be assigned various duties as the needs arise. Among other things you will hear discussions, even as you have this morning, which must be kept in complete confidence. It will mean coming here as soon as you arrive each morning. You will have no study hall time and a limited lunch hour. Even some of your class time may be required. I will train you in all phases of school and office administration. By the time you graduate, and I hope with honor, you will be known throughout the school as my office assistant. Can you do this and still make straight A's?"

Tingling with excitement, and with no voice to answer him, I breathed, "Yes, sir!"

Feeling a little like I did when mama rescued me by tying my shoes on my first day in school, I struggled to find words to express my gratitude. When none came, he smiled as he stood and motioned for me to leave saying, "If you still want in that Home Economics class, take this note to Miss Martindale."

How did he know I wanted in that class? flashed through my mind as I left his office with the note in my hand. *I didn't tell him.* I didn't bother to try to fathom the answer as my next thought jolted me out of my dazed reaction to the rapid turn of events. *I have a job. I'm going to get a paycheck. Money, money, money—I'm going to have money—six dollars a month!*

Mama will smile again. Daddy will lend me five dollars until I get paid, and I can take Home Ec. I'll have a dollar besides that. I can buy notebook paper, a writing pen, a bar of toilet soap, and . . . . My thoughts raced on as I rushed jubilantly toward the Home Ec cottage.

Then, stopping abruptly before I entered the door I thought, *I don't need this class. Lawyers and judges don't cook and sew.*

They hire it done. I can buy that textbook and teach myself how to set a table properly.

With that decision I turned and retraced my steps to the main building. On my way I opened the note in my hand that I was taking to Miss Martindale. There were three words—*J. Kendall Hoggard.*

Folding it carefully, I slipped it in my pocket feeling a power that the proverbial Aladdin must have felt when he rubbed his magic lamp and the genie appeared to do his bidding.

A glory and a grandeur that surpassed that of my first day in school surrounded me. My clipped wings, branding me forever one of the turkeys, took flight and I soared upward once again to mingle with the eagles.

COCKY BANTAM ROOSTER

Mr. Hoggard was dubbed a *cocky bantam rooster* by some adults in the community. He was small in stature, quick in speaking his opinions, and he managed to make his voice heard in any group. He had the zeal and fervor of a crusader. Looking back, I wonder if he detected some of that in me when he dealt with my encounter with Miss Martindale.

Whatever, he was true to his word. The next three years he remained as principal of Joe T. Robinson School, and he tried to train me in every phase of school administration.

Beginning with Aunt Fletcher in the first grade, then Miss Latin, later Mr. Hall, and now Mr. Hoggard—all seemed to take it for granted I would one day enter the educational field.

As yet, I hadn't shared my secret ambition, actually my obsession, with anyone. It burned in my soul and affected every choice I made in preparing for my future. I quietly studied to excel academically and to be ready to enter college. My goal to be a lawyer, then a judge, and to one day see black people receive the same treatment as I did, goaded me on to be prepared.

Segregation was the law of the land, and I vowed in my secret heart to one day be a part of changing that law. That was not a subject people in Pulaski County thought about, or if they did, they didn't voice it. Well, I didn't voice it either, but I thought about it, and I expected one day to see it changed. In retrospect that does sound like a cocky bantam rooster, doesn't it? But I didn't qualify in gender to being a rooster—so surely it didn't fit me. Well, maybe Daddy had a name for that, *a crowing hen.*

MUTT AND JEFF

Whatever people thought of J. Kendall Hoggard and his new way of handling the various situations that cropped up on any given school day, I found him to be a man of his word. At the end of my seventh grade he checked my record and promoted me to the ninth grade. Miss Martindale and Mr. Bundy had difficulty adjusting to many of the changes under his administration, and they openly voiced their objection to this action. He seemed to thrive on opposition, and he marched blithely on making his own decisions about each situation he encountered.

My promotion to ninth grade put me in a different world. Grades one through twelve were all on the same campus at Joe T. Robinson, but there were three distinct divisions: elementary, junior high, and then the zenith, high school. Ninth grade was still junior high, but I began enjoying the privilege of the senior high activities. My body matured early, and for the first time since childhood I felt at ease with my peers.

Life took on a new meaning socially, as well as academically. Senior high boys began to look at me when they came in the principal's office, and soon they were asking me to all their activities.

Life was wonderful. When I signed *Ann Thompson* on the back of my paycheck each month, I felt richer with that six dollars than I would today signing a $6,000 check. I boarded the school bus each morning thinking I had the world by the tail, and Mama smiled with me when I came back home surging with the excitement of each new day.

Soon after registration day a new teacher was added to the faculty. He and Mr. Hoggard were friends, the same age, almost the same stature, except Guy Jones was even shorter, probably no more than five feet tall. He identified himself as *Mutt* Jones, but I never knew who the *Jeff* was as his counterpart.

He strutted more than any bantam rooster Daddy had. What Mr. Hoggard couldn't think of to change the status quo, Mutt Jones could. There were no dull moments at good old Joe T. that year.

He was the coach, taught civics, government, and a new subject added to the curriculum—debating. Civics was a ninth grade subject, and I was automatically enrolled in it, but debating was a high school subject. The moment I heard he was teaching it, I knew it was for me. I walked in his class and confidently expected to register.

He looked me up and down (unlike Mr. Hoggard, he was single and he did like to look at girls) and said, "Ann, you're in my civics class. Aren't you in the ninth grade?"

"Yes, sir, but I need to take debating," I replied, seeing no problem that couldn't be surmounted.

"Why?" he asked, looking at me in a different manner this time.

"I need it to do what I'm going to do," was my direct, but evasive reply.

Without asking what I was going to do he winked and said, "You may be right. I believe you do need it. I bet I can make a real debater out of you. If the office okays it, I'll let you in this class, and I'll make the best debater in the country out of you."

I thought of my *genie* that I hadn't used, and I hurried to the office to see if it was still operable. If Mr. Hoggard's name could get me in Miss Martindale's class, surely it could get me in Mr. Jones'.

Without hesitation Mr. Hoggard said, "You can audit the debating class—no credit and no trips with the debating team until you're in tenth grade."

My thoughts raced ahead as fast as my feet, and I hurried back to register. *I'm going to learn how to stand on my feet before a group of people and present my case. That is what a lawyer does, and now I'm on my way.*

3

Joe T. Robinson Senior High

Mr. Jones, a pint-sized version of a modern-day Newt Gingrich, was soon recognized throughout the campus as Mutt Jones. One could trace his tracks as well as hear his voice all over the place, a natural-born politician from head to toe, all five feet of him. He stayed at Joe T. Robinson one year before going into politics full time.

My other mentors—Aunt Fletcher in first grade, Miss Latin in elementary, Mr. Hoggard in junior high—all tried to groom me for the educational field. Mr. Jones only recognized one field of service—politics.

He would jump on his soap box at the flip of an eyelash and say his piece. It began with "Let's make the world a better place," and then he gave his solution to whatever he thought the problem was. I listened intently, fully expecting him to tell us how to make the world a better place for black people; I would have an advocate in whom I could confide my secret reason for wanting to study law. But if he saw a problem that needed a solution in that area, he didn't reveal it.

Segregation lawfully kept the races apart, and no one, white or black, in that section of Pulaski County was championing a black person's rights—he had none. It was a silent subject that even a feisty, pint-sized Newt Gingrich personality like Mutt Jones didn't have the courage to tackle, or maybe he was just biding his time until he could politically change the law.

His one-year tenure changed Joe T. Robinson from a rural consolidated school to a progressive, almost-urban high school. Little Rock was a metropolitan city, the capital of Arkansas with all its government functions, and it lay untapped at our doorsteps until he took us there. His civics and government classes sat in on legislative sessions at the state capitol, attended trials in the county courthouse, met the mayor in city government, made field trips to industrial plants, and enjoyed every opportunity he could think of to expose us to the outer world.

"A school newspaper is a must," Mr. Jones declared soon after he arrived on campus. He immediately organized a Journalism Club. Again, it was for senior high students and again, my genie got me in it. The officers were all boys in the twelfth grade, and the editor was my school boyfriend that year. At the end of the final semester new officers were elected for the coming year. Since all of them were graduating and could not be reelected, I was nominated and elected editor.

I began my first year in high school as editor of the school paper, but I didn't wait until the coming year to proclaim it. I immediately published a bulletin announcing it.

Mr. Jones took the Journalism Club officers, the ones newly-elected along with the former ones, on a field trip to the *Arkansas Gazette* and the *Arkansas Democrat* newspaper offices in Little Rock. He introduced us right and left as future reporters and editors of tomorrow. He was either already known everywhere he went, or he was remembered after he left.

It is obvious by the content of *Campus Chatter* that we were not sponsored by a Journalism teacher:

```
                    BULLETIN

    The Journalism Club presents this bulletin
to the school as a foreword to the permanent
paper, "The Campus Chatter."

    The staff which was chosen for this paper
is as follows:

    Editor in Chief      Ann Thompson
    Business Manager     Billy Bradley
    Circulating Manager  Perry White
    Sports Editor        Kenneth Thompson

    This paper will relate the activities,
happenings, and spirit of the school. We feel
that it will be a success if the student body
will cooperate with the Journalism Club.

    The Campus Chatter will be published semi-
monthly and will sell for five cents a copy.

                    LIBRARY

    With the assistance of the P. T. A. the
school has been able to buy new books and re-
pair some of the old ones which were badly
soiled and torn. About 15 books that have
been discarded are now patched and glued to-
gether and are being used again. There is
still $36 left to spend for the library, but
we want to spend it carefully and with
```

consideration, so that the books will last and be of educational value.

Rules have been made for the library and are posted upon the wall near it. We urge that each of you read them and obey accordingly.

Mr. Hoggard has done his part toward making a good library since he has been principal. Now that it is improving rapidly he needs the cooperation of the students to keep it in good condition.

* * * * * *

We wonder why H. K.'s hair has such a glossy sheen since the Xmas Holidays. Now, now, Katy, where did you get the grease?

If some people don't believe that Sadie can write sweet love letters just ask some of the kids that ride the White City Bus.

It's a shame the creeks were up—eh—Popsie?????

An ideal couple: Shirley and Jean

The teacher who said that Robinson students "don't function above the neck" certainly hasn't observed some of our girls chewing gum.

Just who was the little girl who had so many boys on their knees Friday night—and what was the motive?

Even in its informal style, I sensed a power in the printed and published word that, had I not already made a vow to myself to study law, would have caused me to choose the newspaper to make my mark in a changing world. My goal was to make it a world where black people could have the same chance to succeed as I had.

FIRST DATE—MOVIE—KISS

Remember your first car date? Sure you do. How could you forget? Men may have different memories, but women surely recall the sheer ecstasy of daydreaming about what a grownup date would be like and, of course, planning what they would wear.

I felt like a millionaire, fourteen years old, in the tenth grade, and earning a six-dollar paycheck each month. Can you believe that? Perhaps you could only believe it if you lived during the Great Depression years. I had money to spend, a job that kept me right in the middle of all the activities of my beloved Joe T. Robinson School, and along with all that—boys.

I looked for the best-looking senior boy who would notice me, and soon one was escorting me to classes and to all the school activities. If heaven promised more than that, I didn't know it. But then came weekends, and I lived in a different world. High school boys didn't have cars, and none of us had a telephone. I lived on a dairy farm ten miles away from the school and was isolated from my school friends from Friday afternoon until Monday morning each week.

Suddenly a door opened, and I stepped out into a whole new world. Little Rock boys in their late teens and early twenties began cruising out West Twelfth Street, known as Kanis Road today. Soon they were dating the young country girls.

Randall, a tall, blonde, good-looking fellow, cruised out one night and stopped in at a neighborhood party at his cousin's house. Sue told us about her city cousin. She said he was out of high school; he planned to further his education and one day be the director of a big-city zoo. He didn't have much time for girls or parties, and she was as surprised as we were when he breezed in the doorway.

No school boy stuff about Randall. He walked up close beside me right after we met, and looking at me in a way I hadn't been looked at before, said, "Ann, let me take you to see the big lights. There's a Fred Astaire movie on Saturday night (he glided across the floor in front of me imitating a dance step). Don't you love to see him dance?"

He kept talking and I didn't have to answer his question. I had read about Fred Astaire in Daddy's newspaper and at least knew he was a dancer, but I hadn't seen him. How could I? I never had been to a movie.

Randall took it for granted I was willing to go and said, "I'll come get you about seven o'clock Saturday night. Tell your mother there will be at least one other couple with us. You know how mothers want to know that about car dates."

No, I didn't know mothers were like that, but I was relieved I wouldn't be alone in a car with this fascinating young man that I didn't quite know how to talk to. He kept looking in my eyes with a message I couldn't decipher. I liked it, but I didn't know how to respond as I didn't know what it said.

"Tell her Sue and John will be with us. He is head over heels in love with her, can't you tell it? He wants to marry her. I keep telling him he has a lot of living to do before he needs to make that leap, but he won't listen," continued Randall.

His words made me feel better, as I knew I didn't have time in my life plans for love—head over heels, whatever that meant— and obviously he didn't either. Both of us had bigger plans for our lives than love and marriage.

My goal was to make the world a better place for all people to live in, whatever their race or color. It was more than a goal; I made a secret vow to myself to devote my life to that cause. Secret, because I didn't dare tell anyone as I knew what happened to those who showed sympathy for black people. No black people lived around me so I didn't know any to love, but to think it was enough to wear the label.

Thoughts travel faster than words and all of this flashed through my mind as I wondered what our movie date in "the big lights," as Randall called it, would be like.

Walking home from the party I mused, *I hope Mama hasn't gone to bed. I can't wait to tell her about Randall and the movie we're going to see Saturday night.*

She was sitting in her bedtime chair crocheting when I hurried in. My words tumbled out on top of each other as I told her about Randall coming to the party and how he liked me, and Sue didn't think he had time for girls, but he had time for me. "He does, Mama, and he asked me to go to see a Fred Astaire movie Saturday night and . . ."

Looking up from her crocheting, but without missing a stitch Mama calmly said, "Ann, you're way too young to go on a car date. Maybe in two more years you can."

There was nothing calm about my response. "Mama! Two years— that is forever!" I exclaimed. I wasn't exaggerating. Two years was a lifetime in my young mind.

My inner voice said, *What can I do? I can't tell him "No" when he comes. He will ask some other girl. He won't wait two years.*

Then words of Mutt Jones, my debating teacher, echoed in my ears, "Stay calm, Ann. Present your case." I did.

"Mama, Sue's mother is letting her go, and she and John will be in the car with us. I may not be as old as Sue, but I'm as responsible. I heard you tell Aunt Fletcher that I am more dependable than any sixteen-year-old girl you know. She agreed, didn't she? Mr. Hoggard thinks I am, or he wouldn't let me work in the school office. Daddy treats me like I am a grown woman."

I rested my case with my plea, "Mama, let me go."

Suddenly Mama's face glowed with an inner light as she said, "I remember asking my mother those very words, 'Let me go,' but instead of going in a car it was a closed-in buggy."

"Did she let you go?"

"Yes, she did," Mama answered and we laughed together.

I won my first case hands down.

Randall's words, "Let me take you to the city and show you the lights," rang in my ears all week as I looked forward to Saturday night. I couldn't wait to see Little Rock at night. I marveled at the lighting at school and in the city stores when I made my few shopping trips during the day, but soon I would see the lights at night.

Electricity didn't come out as far as Dad's place. We used kerosene lamps in the house and lanterns to light the milk barn. My Saturday night date would be my first step out into adult city life, and I was tingling with excitement. I was a fourteen-year-old girl with a body that had functioned as a woman three years and with a mind filled with reading my grandmother's classical literature; yet, I was still a farmer's daughter who knew little of the outside world.

Saturday finally came and you can bet I did more than tingle; I dressed for the occasion. My day was planned right down to the minute. I did that the night before as I lay in bed. I could see in my mind's eye just how I wanted to look from the top of my head right down—especially down to my shoes. I began early by shampooing my hair and trying out a new hairdo that Grace, the school beauty, introduced to Joe T. Robinson School. She called it a *page boy*. Rumor floated around among envious girls that Grace rolled the ends of her hair on large cans every night to get the beautiful effect.

I searched the house, the smokehouse, and even the milk house trying to find six cans. I found three, but that wasn't enough. Although Mama was skeptical about the outcome, she joined in the search and helped me find one more—but four wasn't enough either. Mama said, "If you have to do this to your hair, go see if Fletcher can find you some cans. But I think you're silly for trying such a thing."

Why hadn't I thought of Aunt Fletcher? She could solve almost any problem. Away I went, running along the path that led to her house. She joyfully joined in my search and soon I had three more cans. As I hurried away, she delayed me saying, "Ann, remember to be a good girl tonight. You will, won't you?"

Why wouldn't I be? my mind puzzled as I hurried back home.

I skipped across the pasture this time, not taking the long path around—something Daddy said "never do" as the bull might be out of his usual enclosure. I couldn't wait to get back and roll my shoulder-length hair, and this was too good a day for anything bad to happen. Besides, the bull never got out.

I ran up the back door steps clutching my three cans and called out, "Mama, can you come help me roll my hair?" It was easy to do with her help, and when we finished, Mama laughed and said, "Ann, you dangle like you're wearing cowbells." We giggled like two school girls at the sight of cans jiggling around my neck.

By midafternoon I wanted to start dressing, but I had set five o'clock to begin, so I waited. My clothes were hanging on a chair by my bed. New shoes were peeking out from under the skirt, and I contented myself by looking at them and imagining how I would look when I finally dressed for my night on the town. *This is another first*, I thought. It reminded me of my first day in school, even in the way my clothes were ready for me.

Right on the minute, at five o'clock, I began bathing. This was no everyday pan bath. Instead, I filled a number two wash-tub with warm water that I had heated on the kitchen stove. I dropped a new bar of sweet-smelling toilet soap in the water and lavishly soaped myself all over, a luxury I didn't take for granted. I remembered sponge bathing in a wash pan with no soap, but that was before I earned a big paycheck each month.

My joy overflowed as I stepped out of my bath and began to dress. Mama always made my skirts and blouses, but this was a special outfit—a navy, red, and gold plaid skirt, gold blouse, and red jacket. I stood before the mirror and tilted it to see my full reflection. I thought, *I'm ready this time. No untied shoes flopping on my feet like they did on my first day of school.* The back screen door slammed as Mama was coming in from the milk barn. I called out, "Mama, come see me before you go back to milk. The outfit does fit to a T, just like you said you wanted it to look while you were making it."

All Mama saw when she came in the door were dangling cans flopping around my neck. "How can I see what you look like until you get your hair out of those cans?"

"Take them out, Mama. You're going to be surprised if it looks like Grace's hairdo."

I brushed the ends of my hair under, and lo and behold, it looked like it was supposed to look, a first class page boy style. Even Mama said it did, and she had never seen one. We looked in the tilted mirror, and it was hard to tell which one of us was getting ready for her first date. We surveyed the reflection from the top of my shiny clean hairdo to the swing of my plaid skirt, punctuated with the gold blouse, topped with a red jacket, and down to my shoes, a burnished copper. That's what the shoe clerk said they were.

Mama may have been reliving the excitement of her first date with Daddy in a covered buggy. Whatever, her cheeks were flushed and her eyes glinted with unshed tears as she looked me up and down approvingly. "Ann, it looks better than I expected when I was making it. You did pick the right colors after all."

"What time is it, Mama?" and before she could answer, I heard a knock on the front door. "Mama, he's early," I whispered. If one's heart can come up in one's throat, mine did. But right along with it, an inner voice said, *Calm down, Ann. Don't act like a country bumpkin who has never seen the light. Just step out like you're used to going to the city escorted by a tall handsome fellow.* I glided through the house to the front door to greet my first grownup date.

Randall's tall, handsome body filled the doorway when I opened it. We looked at each other with mutual pleasure. I supposed what I saw in his eyes reflected approval. Whatever it meant, I tingled under his penetrating gaze.

He dressed for the occasion even as I did. His grey double-breasted suit made him look more like a lawyer than a future zoo director. I detected a faint, pleasing fragrance like pine needles about him, and my mind raced ahead. *I must buy a rose fragrance when my next paycheck comes.* And with that thought came another, *I'm glad I bought my first deodorant and I don't have to rely on Arm & Hammer soda to keep me dry and odor-free tonight.* All of this in a moment's time and one-sided at that as I had no idea what was racing through his mind as we stood smiling at each other.

Mama interrupted our silent conversation by coming in long enough to meet Randall. He assured her he would take good care of me, and out the open door we went. I didn't realize I was walking so fast until he took my arm and said, "We have most of the night, Ann. There's no need to hurry."

Talking and laughter filled his car as we approached it. Randall opened the door saying, "We sit in the front. Our back-seat passengers are Sue and John—you know them, and Colene, she goes to your school. The other is my friend, Jay Curtis. Guys, if you can't see Ann, I want you to take a look at her. She's all dressed up and we are going out on the town."

Sue caught a glimpse of my hairdo and she almost squealed, "Ann, how did you get your hair to look like that?"

But before I had to answer, Jay leaned over the seat saying, "You may not remember me, but I've been watching you grow up. I've visited your cousins at your Uncle Charlie's farm the last two summers. With thirteen kids in their family you probably didn't notice an extra guy in the bunch."

We all laughed at the thought of thirteen kids growing up in one family, and it gave me time to signal Sue to hush about my hair. I settled comfortably in the front seat near the door, waiting for Randall to whisk us off to the city. He teased me saying, "You don't need that much room, do you?" and reaching over, he took my hand and eased me closer to him. He kept his right arm back of my shoulder and drove with his left hand. I felt protected, as I remembered he told Mama he would take good care of me.

We drove five miles on a narrow winding road before we saw a dim light in the first house along the way. Halfway through that "Dark Hollow," as it was called, was *the Dip*. I had heard scary tales of how city guys speeded over the Dip, lost control of their cars, and landed in the treetops. Randall said, "Hold your seats," and he pushed the gas pedal down. Over, under, and up we went, and if he hadn't been holding me securely, I would have hit the top or even out the windshield. I was breathless and even more so when Randall said, "If you think this is exciting, wait till I take you on the Ferris wheel at Fair Park."

I was glad we were going to the movies instead, and when we entered the city, I could hardly restrain my excitement. I was afraid to speak for fear Randall would realize I'd never seen the bright lights of a big city, or for that matter, a small one. Apparently he didn't attribute my excitement to the lights as he said, "You really are having a good time with me, aren't you?"

All six of us bounded out of the car simultaneously when Randall parked the car across the street from the theater. He led the group, holding my arm and guiding us to the box office. I tried to linger, wanting to see everything on the way, but he quickly took me inside. He seated me, went back to get some popcorn, and just as he slipped down beside me, the show began. Then came two hours of sheer ecstasy as I sat beside a handsome fellow in a downtown theater and watched Fred Astaire dance. I could not believe my eyes and ears.

Randall whispered in my ear, "I can skate almost like he dances. I'll show you next time we go out. Do you like to skate?" He had a way of asking questions and then talking on and I didn't have to answer. No, I didn't know how to skate, not even on the frozen ponds around the dairy farm.

"Can we go to the Shack before we go home?" Colene asked on the way to the car after the show. "Let's go, can we?"

I had no idea what the Shack was. Randall answered, "Sure we can. No date is special without going to the Shack," and away he sped. The sign said *Shack* when he stopped. Beyond it stood the state capitol building —a tall, gleaming white monument to the majesty of our state government. Then I remembered Mutt Jones saying the Shack served the best barbecue sandwiches in town.

I hadn't eaten many hamburgers, and this was my first barbecue, but eating was something I knew how to enjoy, and the barbecue was delicious. Colene asked Jay to get her another one. Randall offered to get me one, but I didn't dare show my appetite as I remembered reading that well-bred girls eat delicately.

Later, on our way home I realized how the Dark Hollow got its name. Coming away from the bright lights of the city and driving into total darkness was almost frightening to me, and I never had been afraid of the dark. Randall liked it. He marveled, "Doesn't this look good after all the glare of the city lights?"

As we drove in the driveway at my place it still looked like total darkness, but when Randall steered the car in close, I could see the flicker of a kerosene lamp through the kitchen window. He swung out of the car, took my arm almost swinging us into a Fred Astaire dance step, and glided our way up the steps to my front door. I reached for the door knob and he swirled me up and around, whispering in my ear, "We'll go again next Saturday night."

I turned the doorknob and he pulled me up and kissed me full on the mouth. As he let me down, the door came open, and I slid in the opening, shutting it quickly behind me, and leaned breathless against the closed door.

What a night! I had my first grownup date, first movie, first sight of the bright lights, and my first grownup kiss. At least, I hadn't been kissed like that before. *Is that what Aunt Fletcher meant when she cautioned me to be a good girl tonight?*

I secretly liked it, but she didn't have to worry about me. Lawyers and judges don't spend their time kissing. *I'll take care of that. Next time, I'll ask Mama to leave a lamp burning in the living room window to shine out on the front porch.*

With that resolved I hurried to bed to wrap myself in delightful memories.

FAIR PARK

Saturday night finally came, and I was bathed, groomed, dressed, and excited when Randall knocked on my door. I didn't tell Mama why when I asked her to leave a lamp burning in the living room window when she went to bed. I thought, *Surely he won't kiss me good night with a light shining on us.*

Stepping jauntily in the doorway when I answered his knock, Randall stopped, and looking me up and down, took a deep breath, and slowly exhaled. He did a little two-step, took my hand, and literally glided us down the steps and to his car.

His friends, Jay and Colene, were in the back seat and he seated me in the front, close to him this time. His lips barely touched my cheek as he leaned across to make me comfortable.

"We're going to the Fair Park. You know, where the zoo and skating rink are. Wait till I take you on the Ferris wheel, Ann. Your heart will come up in your throat," he explained as he sat down under the wheel after taking another long searching look at me. He made me feel like a precious jewel when he looked at me with such intensity.

I wasn't sure I wanted to feel my heart come up in my throat, but it must be fun for him to be so excited about it.

Later, I was dazzled by all the glittering lights and nervous about being strapped in the seat of the Ferris wheel, but with Randall strapped in with me surely it would be safe.

We began to move, and Randall held me tightly as we neared the top. Just as we went over the top, he jubilantly kissed me full on my mouth. I covered my face with my hands to ward off more, but I was trembling with excitement.

Week after week we continued to date, a movie on Saturday night and to the zoo and park on Sunday afternoon.

Somehow, I didn't feel threatened by his unexpected kisses. They seemed like brief expressions of unbounded joy and occurred in places we moved out of in a moment. In both the long rides through the Dark Hollow and in other moments, I discovered traits of a gentleman under the veneer of his self-confident manners. He was a city gentleman, unlike any I knew—but exciting; I liked him.

Our Sunday afternoons at the zoo became my favorite time. We strolled along the well-kept gardens, as Randall called them, and he proudly introduced me to monkeys, lions, bears, giraffes, the elephants, and even to the snakes and birds. I had met snakes before and some of the birds, but not the proud and beautiful peacocks or the swans floating gracefully in the park.

Grandma Nancy's mean geese were as close to a swan as I had seen.

There were so many different animals that it took Sunday after Sunday for him to show me all of them. "One day I'll direct a zoo housing every animal that came off Noah's Ark," he mused as we walked hand in hand, surveying his animal world.

"*Noah's Ark?*" I thought, but didn't voice it. I identified that with the Bible, a book I hadn't read. My thoughts raced on, *I need to read that book. Maybe it is more than a preacher's book. Aunt Fletcher reads it every day and homeroom teachers read a little of it in our opening classes.*

Then, just as Randall said, "A penny for your thoughts, Ann," it raced through my mind, *Lawyers and judges read the Bible, too. They must. Don't they use it to swear people to tell the truth and nothing but the truth?*

Before I could settle that issue in my mind, Randall brought my thoughts back to him and to his goal in life that he was sharing with me. I caught a glimpse of a man who had his eyes and heart set on being a big-city zoo director, and I sensed he would let nothing get in his way of being one.

Looking in his eyes as he spoke so earnestly about his future plans, I thought, *He has a calling in life, even as I have. Maybe, just maybe, one day I'll know him well enough to share mine with him.*

I envied his freedom in talking so openly about his plans, but none of his were controversial as mine were. It is a stifling feeling to have a pent-up obsession and to have no one—not a single person—you could share it with.

"What's troubling you, Ann? Is it what I've just said?" Randall asked. Before I had to answer, he swung into a Fred Astaire dance step, and said, "Let's go skating."

I *was* troubled then, as skates had never been on my feet. "I'm not sure I know how," I said.

He answered, "That's no problem; you can watch me. Remember, I told you I can skate like Fred Astaire dances. Well, you just come and see."

Off we went, and if he didn't equal Fred Astaire, I didn't know it. I watched him floating as if on air clouds around the rink.

STOOD UP—STAND IN

Three months of Randall showing me around town was equal to a college crash course. I graduated from being a country bumpkin to a girl who thought she knew the ways of the city and especially the ways of at least one city man.

Then came the crash. It happened as unexpectedly as one of his kisses. I opened the door when I heard the knock on Friday night—our night to go to the movies—expecting to see Randall. Instead, his friend Jay was standing there. Before I could speak, he said, "Randall couldn't come and he asked me to take you out tonight."

Just like that—no explanation—as though all he had to do was send another to take his place. Well, what does one do when she is *stood up*? I wanted to hide my face and run to the bedroom, and I suppose, cry. What else can a girl do?

Then Guy Jones' debating class rescued me in the nick of time. His words popped in my mind as clear as a bell, *Learn to think on your feet, Ann. When your opponent trips you up, respond with your head, and not your feelings.*

I looked at Jay, and in a split second I evaluated the situation. I'm all dressed up and no place to go. Jay isn't tall and blonde, but he sure is dark and handsome. Why not go with him tonight? With that decision I smilingly accepted his outreached hand, and we slipped out the door and down the steps with Jay humming a catchy tune.

LANDING IN THE TOMATOES

A double date again, but this time we sat in the back seat. As Jay opened the back door, I wanted to tell him that I liked riding in the front with my date driving the car, but I squelched the thought with another one. *Just for tonight. Randall will be back next time.* And I smiled at Jay and said, "This is fun."

On our way home after seeing a Ginger Rogers movie, Jay sang in my ear, "You Are the Girl I Want to Marry." I thought it was a new song, but I learned later he liked to make up his own songs and sing to me as we rode through the Dark Hollow. It didn't matter to me as I had no plans for marriage in my life. There would be no time or way to fit a husband in what I planned to do.

Even as Randall knew how to show a country bumpkin the ways of the city, Jay knew how to make that same farmer's daughter feel like a beautiful princess. I had looked in the mirror enough to know my face, and I knew it wasn't half as beautiful as he said it was in his songs that he made up and sang to me. But I didn't use any debating tactics to reverse the issue. Why not settle out of court and come out on top?

If Jay had set out to become a millionaire with an equal strategy and perseverance as he used to try to capture my heart, he would be listed with the Rockefellers today. On Wednesday night after his first surprise appearance he knocked on my door again. This time he said, "Come, see what I have," and before I could question him, he had my hand drawing me down the steps.

"Look at her— isn't she a beauty? I got her for you—well, for us. Come on, get in. It's mine. We can ride in front now. (*How did he know I wanted that?*) I'll teach you how to drive it. Let's take a ride. We won't go far—come on."

"Let me tell Mama," I said, and I ran inside to assure her I would just go to the forks of the road, less than a mile from our house. It was my first time to be alone in a car with a boy. Double dating was a strict rule for car dates, but this was a test drive, not a date.

Jay put his car in reverse and down the driveway we went, but instead of slowing down to turn on the road, we sailed across the road and stopped right in the middle of Daddy's garden. We smashed through the gate—a double one built wide enough to take a wagon and team through—and plowed through the strawberry patch before landing in the tomato plants.

Jay was nervous. I was scared. What would Daddy say? We soon found out. Just as Jay stepped out of the car, we saw Daddy coming across the road.

"What's going on here?" he called out.

Jay walked up to meet him and answered, "I guess I got excited. This is my first car and I wanted to show it off to Ann. I must have stepped on the gas pedal instead of the brakes when I got to the road. I'll fix the gate. If I can't, I know someone who can, and we will come fix it tomorrow."

Daddy liked an honest answer. I could tell he appreciated Jay taking responsibility for what he had done when he said, "Well, let's fix it right now before Uncle Charlie's cows get in and eat my garden up." Daddy went after his tool box. Jay held the boards and Daddy fixed the gate. He built it in the first place, so he had no problem putting it back together. They stood back and looked approvingly when it was finished, and Daddy said, "It's good as new now. Come on up to the house, and let's finish eating the pie I was eating when you started this commotion."

Jay gingerly backed the car out of the garden. Daddy closed the gate behind us, and we went back to the house without taking a trial run of his new car. Later, when we walked in the kitchen to eat pie, Daddy looked up smiling and said, "Young man, you better hold on to that car and not let it get away again. I let a horse get away with me once when I was about your age, but it didn't happen the second time."

Jay didn't know it, but he hit first base with me when he won Daddy's approval that night; however, first base is a long way from a home run. We said good night on the front porch. Jay held both my hands, leaned forward, his lips barely brushing my cheek as he whispered in my ear, "We'll take that ride Saturday night." Before I could ask, "What about Randall?" he jumped in his car and away he went.

HELL HATH NO FURY LIKE A WOMAN SCORNED

Maybe I wasn't scorned, but after two weeks and no word from Randall, I realized I truly was jilted. But for what—I didn't know. Was it another girl, or was it something I did, or didn't do that changed his mind? What does a girl do when she doesn't know the answer?

I copied Daddy's method. When farming plans failed for him, he pulled out his pocket note pad, and with a stubby pencil he listed the cause, the effect, and often he found the answer. I didn't know any other method to use in my dilemma, so I made a checklist.

—Did I look good enough to please him?
  *His eyes, his words, his actions indicated he
  thought I did.*

—Did he like me?
  *I thought he did. I liked him, but he seemed to
  restrain his feelings for me.*

—Was I too young for him?
  *My age didn't stop him in the beginning. Why
  should it now?*

—Did I actually graduate from being a country
  bumpkin to a girl who knew the ways of the city,
  and especially of one city boy?
  No, I didn't. That must be the answer.

—Why didn't he tell me?
  *I don't know; maybe he was too embarrassed
  to say so.*

Now I was embarrassed. I decided to let the issue rest for the time being. In the same instant I resolved to one day find out specifically what I did that made Randall walk out of my life as abruptly as he had first appeared.

In the meantime I hadn't lost anything except a big slice of my pride. My heart was still intact, not shattered, as I had read about in broken romances. Maybe that was it—I was having fun with him, and there was room in my life for fun, but not for romance. I couldn't imagine a romantic lawyer or judge, even in my wildest imagination.

This was the last question on my list:

> —What do I do now?
> *Close the case for lack of evidence.*

Even as I slowly penned the answer to the last question, I thought, *But I'll show him. I'll always be a farmer's daughter, but no one will think I'm a country bumpkin when I wear a judge's robe.*

My wounded pride was healed as I pictured myself in such a lofty role, and I tore my list into shreds. Fire was popping in the big wood-burning heater, and I wadded the torn shreds into a ball and threw it into the fire. As the flames consumed it, I thought, *That takes care of him.*

Randall's exit made way for Jay's entrance. They were boyhood friends, and it almost smacked of being a conspiracy— but what sense did that make?

Jay jubilantly filled the gap and boldly staked his claim. Beginning the night he knocked unexpectedly on my door saying, "Randall couldn't come tonight, and he asked me to come instead," Jay claimed me as the girl he wanted to marry. I thought he was playing a game as he jauntily sang about it each time he took me out. It was fun playing the game even though I knew marriage was not for me. But why not take a time for romance before I settled down to the serious business of my life goal? I wondered what he would think when he knew my plans. What kind of songs would he sing to me then?

I told myself, *Don't worry about it. There's nothing wrong in being a beautiful princess until you get out of high school, even if it is in his imagination.*

Jay had a deep singing voice that would thrill any girl's heart, but he swore no one had heard him use it until he met me. I asked, "Why don't you sing for others? If I had a voice like yours, I would sing every chance I had."

"It's just for you," he crooned in reply and added more lines to make the words flow into another love song. Composer, singer, lover, all in one man—*I liked him.* He made sure I did by being so lovable there was no way to resist him.

Imagine being romanced by some of his delightful ways:

- Stopping to pick a daisy and presenting it to me with the elegance of a rose
- Seeing a rose blooming along a stranger's fence, stopping the car, and innocently clipping one for me
- Picking an armful of jonquils blooming profusely in the springtime, and singing a new song as he joyfully put them in my lap
- Teaching me to drive his car, and remembering how we landed in Daddy's garden the first time he drove it
- Saving his lunch money to take me on an airplane ride over Little Rock
- Treating me to two movies a week, one to a deluxe theater downtown and another to a neighborhood movie
- Taking me swimming in the summertime
- Roasting wieners and marshmallows in the winter

- Hunting rabbits in the snow (but not shooting them)
- Buying me two barbecue sandwiches at the Shack without asking me if I wanted more than one.

The list reveals a few of the ways Jay stayed on the front burner of my dating life without being my steady boyfriend. He was steady, but not exclusive, and that didn't seem to bother him a bit.

He showed me everything he knew about Little Rock except the zoo and Fair Park. But after nearly a year he drove us through the park one Saturday night and pulled in alongside the skating rink. Randall was gliding in his Fred Astaire style, almost a solo skater around the rink. I recognized him immediately. He was still his tall, blond, handsome, debonair self and I thought, *Jay, why have you done this?*

Randall saw us even as we saw him and called out, "Come on, Jay. Bring Ann, and let's skate."

Jay jumped out saying, "Man, you know I don't skate, but why don't you teach Ann?" And without asking, Jay opened my door saying, "Come on, Ann. Let's try it. I bet he can have you skating in a few rounds." Before I knew what was happening, I was seated inside, and Jay was lacing skates on my feet.

Randall took my hands saying, "Remember, I told you I could skate like Fred Astaire dances? Well, I can teach you how in two or three easy lessons. And without waiting for an answer he put his arms around me, drew me up to my feet, and began swirling me around the rink until I felt like we were dancing instead of skating.

All the way round and round the rink we went before he glided me breathlessly back to a viewer's bench. As we sat down together, our eyes met, and not knowing what to say, we laughed —apparently at each other.

Jay smiled as he stooped down to remove my skates saying, "I told you he could teach you," and to Randall, "we'll be back again, maybe next week."

As Randall glided off, I answered almost angrily, "No, we won't. Once is enough. This isn't for me."

Jay looked pleased. I must have looked puzzled so I thought, *This is like a big jigsaw puzzle—all put together but one piece is missing.*

"Wait till you see me play ball," Jay said as he walked me to my door after our skating excursion. Then half-joking and half-serious he continued, "You know how Randall brags about skating like Fred Astaire dances. Well, I tell him I can pitch ball like Dizzy Dean—even his name was Jay until they nicknamed him Dizzy.

"You and Randall have been friends a long time, haven't you?" I asked.

"Since we were kids, lived next door to each other, went to school together, played backyard ball . . . "

I interrupted, "Even dated together for awhile, didn't you?"

Jay didn't answer that, just kept on talking about a baseball game for the next Saturday. A movie sounded like a lot more fun to me, but I could tell he wanted to show me he could pitch like Dizzy Dean so I agreed to go.

It didn't take long for me to realize this was not a one-time affair. They played every Saturday and Sunday afternoon. Before the game ended I was hot, tired, itching all over from insect bites, and I wanted to go home.

Even in my discomfort I soon saw that pitching was more than a hobby to Jay. He was their star player and suddenly it struck me that this would go on all summer. I thought, *I can't spend my weekends sitting on a hard bench watching ball games. Once is enough.*

The game finally ended. Jay was jubilant as his team practically carried him off the field, screaming their victory. His expression changed abruptly when he saw mine.

"Ann, what do you think? Didn't you like it?" Jay asked as he hurried me away from his friends and out to his car.

He was sweaty, dirty, and smelly. I was itchy, irritated, and maybe smelly too as we sat facing each other in the hot car. His display of pitching ball like a champion failed to impress my feminine instinct. My eyes must have revealed it, and as he read the message, defeat settled on his face. My heart went out to him, and I reassured him, "Jay, you go ahead and play ball, but I want to do something else."

"What will you do?" he asked and before I answered, he said, "If I play ball every weekend, someone else will start taking you out."

I interrupted, "Jay, we're not going steady."

"No, but I want your weekends." he said. "Those school boys can date you during the week, but I want Saturday and Sunday."

We sat silently looking at each other. I saw no way of compromise. Jay's hopeless expression reminded me of Daddy's the year he didn't have the money to pay his taxes. I remembered asking God to give him the money, and He did. But I couldn't bother God with a ball game. Besides, I didn't know much about God. What if He thought I ought to go to the games with Jay? I better leave Him out of this, so I just sat there.

Jay pitched the ball in the glove from one hand to the other as though he was weighing balances. Finally, struggling physically as well as emotionally, he said slowly, "Baseball will have to wait."

He threw the ball and glove over his shoulder, and as they landed in the back seat, I caught a glimpse of his expression. It showed the same determination Randall's had when he declared he would one day be a big-city zoo director. Nothing would stand in his way.

It was then I knew Jay hadn't been playing games with me when he made up those songs and sang in my ear. He meant it when he sang, "You Are the Girl I Am Going to Marry."

I thought, *All three of us—Randall, Jay, and I—know what we want in life. Randall wants to be a big-city zoo director, Jay to marry me, and I to make our world free to all people without respect to color; each one of us is determined to reach his goal, whatever the price.*

Then came a sobering thought, *But at least one of us will miss it.*

Defiantly, I told myself, *Well, it won't be me. I know where I am going, and I intend to get there.*

TENTH GRADE—LIFE IS MAGNIFICENT

Fourteen years old and going on fifteen, I welcomed again the first day of another school year. I felt more grown up and had more answers than I do today.

Finally, I was a bona fide senior high school student in the tenth grade. I dressed carefully and inspected my appearance from head to foot in the same tilted mirror that years before revealed my untied shoes. This time I smiled as I waved back at my reflection. I called out a happy "Bye, Mama" as I raced out and down the gravel road to catch the school bus.

With sheer joy I stepped on board the bus to see windows and padded seats had replaced the rolled-up curtains and the built-in benches. This bus seemed almost luxurious compared to my earliest ones. As I thought, *Life is g-o-o-o-d,* a nagging shadow began clouding my thoughts. *What if Mr. Hoggard isn't principal again? Mr. Jones won't be back, but I can live without him, even without debating. But if Mr. Hoggard leaves, I won't have a job, and I can't live without that six-dollar paycheck each month.*

Oh, yes, you can, my subconscious answered, but I shrugged off the thought of trying to figure out how by telling myself to wait and see if I had to. It was too good a day to ruin it with thoughts of disaster.

Mr. Hoggard was in his office giving instructions right and left when I arrived. He acknowledged my appearance by handing me a card showing my work schedule for the day. As I reached out to take it he said, "Ann, I'm glad you're here. I need you."

I wanted to answer, "You don't know how much I need you," but no words came.

As I looked at my schedule I realized again that he was a man of his word. My study hall time was taken as well as most of my lunch period. A possible new assignment was added: *Be prepared to fill in at times when an elementary teacher is absent unexpectedly.* He penciled in at the bottom, *Register in required subjects only—no clubs except Journalism.*

I could be editor of the school paper. I would continue making six dollars a month. I thought, *Life is more than good— it is magnificent!*

ELEVENTH GRADE—NEW MANAGEMENT

The first day of each school year was like a taste of heaven, and this one began on a high note as my previous ones had. I boarded the faithful school bus with a spring in my step and joyful expectancy in my heart. I was on my way to a good job as well as to classroom teaching that challenged me to reach for the stars. I planned to reach until I scaled the utmost height, the Supreme Court of the United States of America. No one suspected that but me, but the secrecy made it even more exciting.

I could close my eyes and see black people free to sit up front on streetcars in downtown Little Rock, drink from the same water fountain as I did, use the same restroom, drive Ford cars like Uncle John, and wear pretty clothes like Mama made me. Free, even as I was, to dream and touch the highest star of their dreams.

The principal's office was the highest star at Joe T. Robinson, and I was an active part in it. I jumped off the bus, bouncing with enthusiasm as I hurried to the office to see Mr. Hoggard and get my work schedule before class time. He always had it ready, and after a brief greeting, would hand it to me. I was almost inside his office before I saw it was not Mr. Hoggard at the desk. Instead, a woman I had never seen was sitting in his chair.

Startled, I didn't utter a sound, but she quietly said, "I'm Mrs. Stewart, the new principal's wife. I will be teaching here. What grade are you in?"

My heart sank as I heard of a new principal, but I mustered a smile and said, "I am Ann Thompson in the eleventh grade. I hope you will be my teacher."

A flash of recognition registered in her eyes as she heard my name. She obviously assessed my appearance before she replied, "Just remember, Ann. There won't be any teacher's pet around here."

I was silent, not knowing how to respond. She turned to papers on the desk and I felt dismissed, so I hurried out the door. As I slowly walked down the long hall toward my home room, hot tears welled up in my eyes, but this time they didn't overflow.

What did she mean? Did she think I was someone's pet? Now I won't have a job—no money. What can I do?

Well, you can go to school, I told myself as I walked in my home room and found an empty desk.

Just as I settled down in the seat and looked around greeting my fellow students, Mrs. Stewart walked into the room. She was my home room teacher. I remembered telling her that I hoped she would be my teacher. I didn't know why I said it then, and I I thought that was what she meant. What kind of a pet does she think I am? But before I could imagine any more, she got right down to business.

It wasn't long before I realized she was a born teacher—all five feet, six inches, slim as a model. She stood before us addressing us as intelligent adults and obviously expecting us to respond as such. I forgot about the pet peeve momentarily as I basked in the academic atmosphere she created.

I discovered she was teaching three of my five subjects. *Maybe I shouldn't have hoped so soon to have her for a teacher,* I thought. *What if she is another Miss Martindale and requires pupils to have textbooks to stay in her class. With no job and no paycheck, what can I do?*

At the end of the day, I found out. Mrs. Stewart said, "Ann, stay in after class. I want to talk to you."

When the last pupil filed out of the room, thinking I already knew what she was going to say, I stood and looked her full in the eyes, needing to make my appeal: "I must stay in these classes. May I tell you why?" For the first time I was willing to share with another person my secret ambition. It was my only hope, and somehow, I thought she might understand.

But before I could say a word she calmly said (as she placed three books between bookends on her desk), "Ann, these are my textbooks. Feel free to take them home any time you choose."

Without waiting for my response she continued, "Mr. Stewart will see you in his office first thing in the morning."

Out the door she went, a real live genie, but not one I could put in my pocket as I had with Mr. Hoggard's name. I sensed I had met the force behind Mr. Stewart, our new principal, even before I met him.

4

Graduation—What Now?

Mrs. Stewart kept my nose to the grindstone all the way through the eleventh grade and then again my senior year. If I made a perfect score on a test, it seemed she made certain it was impossible for me to do it again. She was a brilliant woman, and I longed to one day know as much as she did.

Mr. Stewart, our new principal, had a quiet, unassuming manner in direct contrast to his wife's aggressive personality. I continued to be the principal's assistant and receive a six-dollar monthly paycheck, but I missed the excitement of trying to march to the beat that his predecessor, Mr. Hoggard, challenged me to follow. Mr. Stewart didn't do much for me to assist, but what he lacked in leadership, his wife gladly supplied.

With less work to do in my job I had more time to study and her assignments made sure that I did. This new arrangement in my school life worked well for me in the eleventh grade, but my senior year found me pulled up and down like a yo-yo in her hands. As a teacher who once warned me that Joe T. Robinson

School would have no pets, she began showing subtle preferences to help a male student.

Blake had a brilliant and analytical mind akin to hers, and she challenged him to graduate with the top honor. If he disciplined himself to study, I knew he could surpass me academically, and it struck fear in my heart.

My goal since junior high was to graduate in first place and earn a scholarship to help pay my college tuition. Blake outranked me by one to two points in math and science without seeming to study. I sensed he could do the same in his other subjects if he applied himself. Mrs. Stewart knew that too, and one would have thought he was her son in the ways she favored him.

Despite his aptitude and the perks Mrs. Stewart offered him, Blake casually drifted through the twelfth grade and graduated, with little effort on his part, as salutatorian.

I won the prize. I was valedictorian.

The day it was final my joy overflowed, and I danced up and down telling anyone who would listen, "I'm the valedictorian of the 1939 graduating class." Their nonchalant response to my excitement puzzled me, as they seemed to think it was false humility. They thought it was a done deal from the beginning. Only Mrs. Stewart and I knew how close the race could have been, and who could have been the victor had he tried.

FULL DRESS

The excitement a bride or a future Miss America feels as she prepares for her big event swept through me when my graduation day finally had a date. I marked the days on my calendar and thrilled at the notes I scribbled in on the coming days to remind me to be ready. My speech—every valedictorian makes a speech—what would I say? And, of course, what would I wear? There were numerous details, but these were more than details.

The 1939 class would be the last to graduate in full dress at Joe T. Robinson. The junior class already had their robes ordered for the coming year. They looked academically correct in the catalog, but my feminine instinct rejoiced that my graduation would be more like a celebration. Mrs. Stewart said it sounded like a party instead of an academic affair, and she immediately set about changing the procedure for the following year.

"A party" failed to capture the picture in my mind. I thought of it as a beautiful, but solemn event. In my imagination as one who didn't plan to get married, graduation must have equaled the excitement a wedding would arouse in most young girls' minds.

I would have time for the academic look in the future when I would be wearing a judge's robe. For this occasion I had a young girl's heart, and I looked forward to my first store-bought wardrobe. If it sounded and looked like a party to Mrs. Stewart, well, so be it.

Do you remember Aunt Mary and Uncle John? They were the ones whose income was not altered by the Depression. They paid for Grandpa's funeral and later showed their appreciation to Mama for taking care of Grandpa by outfitting all three of her children in lavish style for each one's graduation.

Imagine a sixteen-year-old country girl who had been dressed well by her mother, but not once had gone in a store and purchased a ready-made dress. Now picture this same girl going to a big department store in downtown Little Rock and selecting any dress she wanted from what they had to offer.

Carefully taking my cue for city shopping from Aunt Mary, I followed her into Gus Blass Department Store. A handsome older black man in full uniform tipped his cap at us as we stepped on the elevator. I didn't have a cap to tip back, so I said, "Good morning." We smiled at each other and I wanted to ask him if he had a daughter getting ready to graduate, but the door opened and we were on the second floor. I caught my breath audibly as it stopped, and almost lost it as we stepped out. I caught a glimpse of models in full dress looking so lifelike that I almost spoke to one.

I turned to say "Thank you" to the elevator man, but the door was shut and he was gone. Not wanting to embarrass Aunt Mary, I covered my mouth as I gasped and pretended to cough, hoping I didn't look like a country bumpkin. She seemed unaware that all this was new and breathtaking to me and kept moving on through the store. A saleslady hurried over to greet her, called her by name, and asked, "Who is this lovely young lady you have with you?"

Her words made me feel lovely, and I discarded the country bumpkin image from my mind. I wanted to go from rack to rack and look at all the dresses, but Aunt Mary whispered as she sat down in a rose upholstered chair and pointed to one facing it, "We'll sit here, Ann, and let her bring them to us."

But how will she know what I want? I thought. I soon found out. Aunt Mary said, "This young lady is getting ready to graduate with top honors, and we want a dress suitable for the occasion. It must be long, white, formal, and yet youthful. Show us the best you have."

The saleslady turned her head to one side, and it seemed for a full minute she looked me over from head to foot. Then she snapped her fingers, apparently indicating she had the situation in hand as she said, "I'll find the very dress you want. Sit here and let me show you."

Aunt Mary asked after viewing several dresses, "Ann, is there one you like?"

I could only say, "They are all beautiful."

"Ann, it must be more than that. Wait till you see one that catches your eye and you think, 'I want this one.' "

One did catch my eye—a long white organdy dress with stand-up ruffles along the side seams down to the waist and around the hem back and front—a grownup version of the dress I wore to church when I was five years old. "This is it!" I exclaimed.

The saleslady beamed as she said, "Young lady, you have good taste. It was my choice all along, but I wanted you to have some to compare it with. Yes, you knew what you wanted, didn't you? Now, let's try it on you."

I always asked the cost before buying, and I wondered why Aunt Mary didn't. Instead she said, "Before she tries it on, get everything she needs to wear under it so we can see how it really looks."

Off the saleslady went to select the undergarments, and I had a moment to hold the heavenly dress up to me and swirl around in front of mirrors that showed me back, front, and sideways. *I see myself as others see me—all over*, I thought.

It was almost noon when we left the store after a shopping spree that left me tingling all over. As soon as the graduation outfit was complete Aunt Mary said, "Now she needs an outfit for the baccalaureate service."

We went to another department, and this time I did get to look for myself. Aunt Mary and a salesgirl helped me look, but finally I found the one I knew I wanted. Next, we bought shoes, hose, purse, my first hat and gloves—oh, so many things—I could hardly wait to get home and show Mama.

How will we carry all these packages? I thought as Aunt Mary paid the full amount. Then I heard her ask, "Can you deliver them today?"

Just as I thought our day was finished, Aunt Mary said, "Let's go to Frankie's Cafeteria and eat lunch."

A cafeteria may not sound like dining out in style today, but Frankie's Cafeteria in 1939 was not just a serving line. You knew you had dined in style after a meal there. I felt like a Queen for a Day (long before the television show of that name), and it wasn't yet graduation day.

Mama was still in the dairy barn helping Daddy milk the cows when Uncle John brought me home in his new Ford car, a V8, he proudly told me when I sat in the front seat beside him. I didn't know what V8 meant, but the way he spoke made it sound important. All the Ford cars I knew around Dad's place were either Model T's or Model A's. Kenneth had a Model T that he drove around the dairy farm and to the swimming hole. Uncle John bought a new car every year or two, and it was always a Ford. Today, it was loaded to the top with packages. He mumbled as we began unloading, "I know Mary likes to shop, but what in tarnation did you two find to fill this many boxes?"

"Wait, and let me show you. I'm dying to see it again and to show it all to Mama," I invited.

"No, I'll take your word for it. Tell your Mama I can't stay for supper. I told Mary I would come right back and take her to some fool party." Then under his breath, I hardly heard his words, "When she's not shopping, she's partying."

I wanted to hug him; since hugs were not a part of our family, I just reached out and touched his shoulder as I tried to thank him. "Oh, Uncle John," I exclaimed, "you don't know how happy you and Aunt Mary made me today. I'm so happy I could . . . I could fly away!"

"Well, don't do that," he laughed. "Stay around and keep on being the daughter I never had." The worry lines left his face as he reached out and almost hugged me before hurrying out the door.

The back door slammed, and I called out, "Come here, Mama, and see what I have."

We ooh'd and ah'd together and sometimes squealed as I opened each package and spread my fabulous wardrobe out on the bed, trunk, washstand, chairs, all over the room. When the last box was opened I looked at Mama, and I caught a glimpse of almost envy in her eyes and in her voice. She felt of the fabric and inspected the seams of the dresses saying, "Ann, I could have made these dresses if I had had the pattern and material."

"Oh, Mama, I know you could, but aren't you glad Aunt Mary bought them for me?"

"Of course I am," she answered. "Why would you ask me that?"

"Mama, as wonderful as all this is, it doesn't outshine the outfits you've made me. Remember my first day in school and my first car date? I won't look one whit better in all these store-bought clothes than I did in what you made me. But even this, Mama, came from you. Aunt Mary and Uncle John did it for you, remember?"

"What's wrong with you, Ann? I know all that," she answered, but her eyes brightened at my words, and she was my fun-loving Mama again.

SPEECH

I marked a big bold *complete* in the box for *What will I wear?* The next big item was *Speech.* As valedictorian, what would I say? It was past my bed time, but the word *speech* jump-started my motor until sleep was out of the question.

I grabbed a pencil and paper. What would I say? There was just one thing I could say about my future, and graduation speakers always spoke about the future. I began writing. It went something like this:

Friends, parents, and teachers, we are here tonight celebrating a great event in our lives. You are a vital part of it. I believe every graduate here will agree with me that you made it possible for us to reach this milestone in our lives.

It is just a beginning. We are ready now to launch out and reach our goals. Mine is a vision I've had since I was twelve years old. You may call it a dream, but it's more than a dream. I see it in my wide-awake hours, and I dream about it in my sleeping time.

May I share it with you and challenge you to help me see it become a reality in my lifetime? This is a brief summary of my lifetime goal.

America is a land of the free and the home of the brave. We sing about it and brag about it, but not all Americans are free. A whole race of black people is still in bondage even though our forefathers fought a bloody war to declare them free.

Segregation laws deny them the freedom you and I enjoy. My goal is to work not to change the segregation laws, but to abolish them completely. Let's see that black people have the same opportunities and responsibilities, and the same accountability that we have.

I not only have a vision; I have a strategy. I plan to go to law school and not to remain a lawyer, but one day become a judge. By then the laws that separate white and black people today will be abolished, and I can judge each person and each case that comes before me by the law, and not by the color of his skin.

Will you work with me to make America truly a LAND OF THE FREE AND THE HOME OF THE BRAVE?

Thinking, *Now the cat is out of the bag; I've said it,* I carefully folded the speech and hid it under my pillow as I tumbled into bed dead tired.

Mama's voice roused me saying, "Ann, what's wrong with you? I called you before I went to milk. Get up or you'll miss the bus."

Opening my eyes, I caught a glimpse of the long white graduation dress hanging on the wall before me. A breeze from an open window moved its billowing skirt toward my bed. I raised my head, and as I did, the paper I hid under my pillow the night before rustled. The sound reminded me of my speech. I jumped straight up—wide awake—remembering the words I had written.

I shivered all over as I hurried to dress. My imagination ran wild as I thought of tales I'd heard about what happened to people who championed black people's rights. I knew little or nothing about a Ku Klux Klan. Apparently, there was no need of one in Pulaski County. Black people didn't have any rights, and no one, black or white, contested it.

I hid the speech again, this time in the back of my notebook. No one had to know until graduation night, and it was a week away.

A few minutes later and without breakfast I rushed out the door and down the gravel road to meet the school bus. *I won't be riding this bus again after next week,* registered in my mind as I hurried down the half-mile trek to catch it. *Life won't be the same again,* I thought, and for the first time I felt a sense of apprehension in facing the future.

I wanted to read the speech again as the bus moved faster than usual toward school. I sat in the back, but I didn't dare unfold it for fear someone would read it. What if someone grabbed it, teasing me, thinking it was my homework. Later, I clutched my notebook close to me as I hesitantly entered my homeroom.

Mrs. Stewart didn't look up from grading papers as I hurried by her desk. *What if she wants to read my speech?* jumped into my mind, and I held it even tighter. As I sat down, she looked up and quietly said, "Ann, here's your speech. Blake already has his. I want you two to practice giving your speeches and make Joe T. Robinson School proud on graduation night."

I stammered, "But . . . I thought . . . I mean . . . I wrote my own speech."

"Ann, you will not be speaking for yourself. Graduation is an academic ceremony. You will be representing your class, your school, and even your teachers. See that you do it well."

I took the paper she handed me without saying a word, but right then I didn't feel like doing anything well. My image of my beloved Joe T. Robinson School was blurred for the first time with unbelief. Had it prepared me for the future, or had it prepared a future for me that said, "Color within the lines"?

FUTURE ARRIVES

Graduation week was like having Christmas, New Year's Day, Fourth of July, and my birthday all crammed in seven days. It began with a fabulous shopping spree in Little Rock and continued each day with gift after gift. Along with a gift, some said, "Ann, we are so proud of you."

It humbled me to hear their words and I honestly answered, "I couldn't have done it if you hadn't helped me."

Beginning with Mama and Daddy in countless ways, but I especially remembered my hard-working, fun-loving Mama and how she used every means at her disposal to dress me for any occasion. Daddy helped by teaching me that honesty and hard work pay off, and he released me from farm work allowing me time to read and study.

Marie, my slim, long-legged, cartwheeling big sister, taught me life was more than studying when she had a baby girl as beautiful as the baby brother I almost had. When she named her Ann, I thought I'd reached the zenith in my personal life.

Then there was Kenneth, my big brother, who treated me like a princess until I proved I wasn't. After that I was his little sister whom he cared for and tried to shield from life's mistakes.

Grandpa adored me and let me be his teacher each day after school when I was in first grade.

Grandma Nancy shared her library with me, and how it changed my life course.

Aunt Fletcher was a special woman who reflected a God in her life that I did not yet know.

Mr. Walser, Aunt India's new husband, graded my algebra and geometry homework and made it possible for me to outrank Blake, and thus become valedictorian.

A parade of helpers marched down my memory lane, too many to name, but all a part of the honor I was receiving at graduation. Heading the list in my memory was Jay, always on the sideline cheering for me. In the last year he edged out most of his competitors for my attention, and he visibly moved to the front line with me. As that flashed in my mind I thought, *I must convince Jay there will be no time or place for marriage in my life plan.* My jubilance was sobered for a moment, but I pushed the thought back to deal with later, and I continued to bask in the pleasures of the week.

Valedictorian of my class topped the list of honors, but almost equal to it was receiving the Daughters of the American Revolution Good-Citizen Award. Mr. Hoggard's admonition while I was a truant junior high student flashed across my memory: "Make straight A's, Ann, in all your subjects and in citizenship as well." Then he said, "I hope you will graduate with honor from Joe T. Robinson School."

Where would I be today if he had not given me a second chance and opened a door for me to pursue it? He sure didn't color within the lines. With that thought, came the question: *Would Mr. Hoggard let me write my own speech if he were still principal? What about Mutt Jones who taught me to think on my feet in debating class? What would he say if he heard my speech?*

But the fact remained, Mrs. Stewart, who did color within the lines, was making the rules at Joe T. Robinson today. As I tore my speech to shreds I said in my thoughts to her, *I can't say it now, but you just wait. One day I will.*

And with that vow, my joyful spirit returned.

Daddy's bantam rooster crowed outside my open window. Half awake, I looked over the edge of my bed and saw him strutting on the window ledge. His ruffled red feathers and neck stretching upward as far as he could muster made him look twice his actual size. I wondered how anything so tiny could make such a loud noise and strut like he was the cock of the barnyard. I thought of Mutt Jones, my former debating teacher, no more than five feet tall, but what a racket he could stir up in any crowd. The comparison brought me wide awake.

The smell of boiling coffee and frying bacon filled the air, and I called out, "Mama, isn't it time for me to get up?"

Mama didn't sound quite like herself as she stepped in the doorway and answered, "I thought you'd like to sleep awhile longer today. Life won't let you sleep in much when you're grown up and have a family of your own. Now that you're out of school, first thing you know you'll get married and have babies and your sleeping-in days will be over."

I thought, *Why would she say that? But then, why wouldn't she? That's what girls do—grow up and get married.*

I wanted to jump and hug my dear Mama and tell her all about my life plan: "Mama, I'm not going to get married and have babies. I'm going to college and one day I'll be a lawyer and after that, a judge. I'm going to help wipe out segregation laws. You wait and see, Mama, and some day those black people will have the same rights and obey the same laws we do. What do you think of that?"

I honestly thought she would be proud of me for wanting it, but to hear me say it would scare her to death. The racial question, like sex, was never discussed inside our household. Young boys might talk about it outside on the doorsteps when they thought no one was listening. The only time I ventured a question about the subject I asked Aunt Fletcher, "Why can't black and white people sit together on the streetcars in Little Rock?"

She was sitting at her kitchen table, and she placed her hand on her Bible that was always nearby as she softly answered, "God said that is the way it should be—but, Ann, don't ever mistreat them. Remember, God loves them just like He does you."

That doesn't make sense, I thought. *I wish I knew God like you do. I'd ask him about that. He sure hasn't said anything like that to me.*

Since I couldn't share my secret ambition and neither could I hug Mama as hugs were not a part of my family, I jumped out of bed, and as I surveyed the bountiful table she had waiting for me, I lamely said, "Mama, you cook a special breakfast."

That was an understatement. Her breakfast was no micro-wave, toaster, electric coffeemaker, or gas stove accomplish-ment. It began at 4:00 a.m. when Kenneth built a fire in the wood cook stove before he and Daddy and Mama went to the dairy barn. At six o'clock Mama came back and rolled out the biscuits. She popped them in the hot oven when Daddy came in after he had finished the milking. Next, she fried bacon from hogs killed the past winter and eggs laid the day before. The well-worn coffee pot, brown from boiling hundreds of cups of coffee, simmered on the back of the stove. Wild muscadine jelly (made from the fruit Mama and Aunt Fletcher picked in the woods surrounding the pastures) sat on the table along with fresh churned butter.

This was the special breakfast Mama served her family seven days a week, varying it at times with big slices of home-cured ham or a heaping platter of fried quail. Cream gravy was a daily side dish except when she served ham, and then it was red-eye gravy. Mama expected everyone who sat at her table to be a hearty diner, and since dieting was unheard of and hunger stalked many families in nearby Little Rock, she had few picky eaters. The Great Depression took the money out of Daddy's pocket and left him almost penniless, but he boldly vowed, "There will be food in this house as long as I have my land."

I looked up at the roses in a painting over the kitchen win-dow as I sat down to eat and thought, *One day my life will be a bed of roses. I can feel it in my bones.* Grandma Nancy often said she felt rheumatism in her bones, but today I felt good things in mine as Mama and I had our first private coffee time together.

PITY PARTY

"Annie, where are you? The milk cans are ready to be cleaned." Daddy's call at the kitchen window interrupted my coffee time with Mama.

She jumped up saying, "Oh, my goodness, it's later than I thought," as she hurried out to finish her morning work in the milk house.

The back screen door slammed shut behind her. When I heard the familiar sound, a strange feeling swept over me as I sat alone at the kitchen table with an empty coffee cup in my hand. Unexpected tears trickled down my face, for just as hugs were not a part of our household, neither were tears.

I hadn't cried since Miss Martindale put me out of her Home Ec class in junior high school. Mama never cried openly unless tears were mingled with the sweat that flowed down her face as she cooked standing over the wood cook stove during the long hot summer months. Her cheeks looked as red as the tomatoes she stirred on canning days, and after every other stir with the long-handled wooden spoon, she stopped to wipe her eyes and face with her apron that stayed wringing wet. If there were tears, as well as sweat, she didn't admit it.

Men didn't cry, period. Or if they did, no one knew it. I remembered hearing Mama say, "Women cry, men cuss." There I sat, crying as my life plan suddenly appeared in my mind's eye. It was no longer a goal set for my future; the future had arrived.

Still, no one knew about it but me.

Mama thought I was going to get married and have babies. Aunt Fletcher assumed I was to be the teacher she had groomed me to be since first grade. Jay hoped I would marry him, go to college, and do whatever I wanted as long as it included him.

How could he ever imagine what I planned to do, and if he found out, what would he do? Whoever heard of having a lawyer for a wife, and one who planned to be a judge as well?

There I sat, a 17-year-old girl just graduated with honors from high school, with a desire and an aim burning in my soul to change the world. With all my well-made plans, I should have felt, *I'm on my way.*

Instead, tears flowed down my face and I had no apron to hide them under or to wipe them up. They dripped down in puddles, spotting the oil cloth covering the kitchen table. I felt like the only person in the world, and the loneliness seemed unbearable as I thought, *How do I begin?*

COLLEGE PLANS AND A JOB

All my plans for going to college had been on the academic level. I thought of it as a promotion to higher learning, and I worked hard to meet the challenge. Scholastically, I was ready. My valedictorian scholarship would pay for the first semester, but how would I get to the college more than a hundred miles away? I had my last six-dollar paycheck—big money in high school— but even in my inexperience, I wondered if six dollars would do more than buy a bus ticket to the college. What would I do when I got there without money? Where would I live? Who would feed and clothe me like Mama had? Aunt Fletcher said she would write and get me information, but she warned that I would need money besides the scholarship.

But where would I get money? I had borrowed a few dollars from Daddy from time to time when I needed it before my paycheck came, but I couldn't do that now. I remembered a few weeks before I had caught a glimpse of the bottom line in his pocket note pad. He sat squinting to see under the dim kerosene lamplight after supper as he wrote the number with his stubby pencil. From where I sat I strained to see what he seemed to want to cover up. It looked like less than ten dollars. All the years I had watched the bottom line, it never had been that low. I knew it reflected every cent my daddy had.

I thought of Uncle Charley, Grandma Nancy's brother, whose farm joined Daddy's. He was checking on mortgaging his land to get money to send two of his thirteen children to college. Daddy was horrified at the thought and said, "What if he can't pay it when it comes due? He will lose his land. And how will he feed his family?"

Uncle Charley had a strange solution. He said, "The Lord will provide." Well, Daddy's land, instead of the Lord, provided our food, and he guarded it with his life—and his shotgun if need be.

I remembered Daddy's troubled expression; he sat with slumped shoulders and downcast eyes, and he stared at the note pad he held in trembling hands. Another puddle of tears dripped on the table before me.

No, I couldn't ask Daddy. But who could I ask? Looking up from the tear-spotted tablecloth, I tossed my head to shake the tears from my face as I thought of Jay. He would help me. He wanted me to go to college and told everyone who would listen to him, "Ann is the prettiest girl you'll ever see, but don't let her fool you—she's the smartest, too."

Whoever said *love is blind* must have known Jay. Apparently, love doesn't make one blind to one's own faults, as I had good vision when I looked in my mirror. It shattered his claim for my beauty, and I knew full well what it took for me to make the good grades he boasted about. If I had been blinded as Jay was, it sure would have made a fool out of me.

The song Jay sang to me on our first date when I was four-teen began, "You're the girl I'm going to marry . . . ." He changed the added lines from date to date, but he always began with the same first line. Lately, he had begun to sing, "Marry me and I will . . ." and added whatever he thought I wanted at the time. I knew I could say *college* and he would sing, "Marry me, and I will send you to college."

If college was all I wanted, I had my answer. But college was just the first step toward getting my heart's desire and aim in life: *freedom for black people.* Jay wouldn't understand that, and even if he did, I couldn't do what I planned and have time to be his wife and have babies.

No, I'd just have to be an—I couldn't say the word even in my mind—but it was the only word I knew for unmarried women. *Singles* was unknown. *Old Maid,* I thought and Miss Martindale appeared in my mind's eye.

Silently I vowed, *I'll be one if that's what it takes to reach my goal, but I won't look like one,* and as an afterthought, almost aloud, *I won't act like one either.*

Learn to think on your feet, Ann. The words surfaced from my subconscious mind and jolted me out of my pity party. I jumped straight up out of my chair, and sure enough as I stood on my feet, I began to think instead of weep. *Get a job. Save your money. Then go to college.*

I raced to get a pen and paper. Mr. Hoggard's instruction, "Write it down, Ann," trained me to list what I planned to do. Journalism taught me to think: who, what, when, where, how. So I began my list:

> ### WHAT I PLAN TO DO
>
> 1. Who—Me *(That was easy.)*
> 2. What—Get a job *(?)*
> 3. When—
> 4. Where—
> 5. How—

I almost marked the whole list out as I read it back to myself. How could a seventeen-year-old girl get a job when men with hungry families were walking the streets in Little Rock and all across the nation begging for work? Businessmen may have been the first to lose their jobs after the stock market crash in 1929, but unemployment rapidly moved to factory workers and in domino effect by 1939 it had spread to salaried jobs of any kind.

In the midst of the national disaster, President Roosevelt created government projects to provide jobs for masses of destitute men. It was manual labor and minimal pay, but it kept families from going hungry. I wondered why they called it *man*ual labor. Just for men? I didn't see women working on any of the building projects.

Daddy remained smug in his self-sufficiency during most of the ten-year depression. But when the bottom line in his notebook dropped to almost zero, even he knew he needed help. I heard him tell Uncle Glenville, "I still say I can take care of my family as long as I have my land, but I have to have some money to pay my taxes, and kerosene for the lamps is eight cents a gallon—then there's salt, baking powder, and soda for Annie to cook with. Coffee won't grow on this land, and it's hard to wake up in the morning without a pot of coffee on the stove. Annie boils it to make it last longer, but the grounds she boiled today were so bitter we had to throw it out. There's no more left. I don't want that government money, but if I work, it won't be like getting it for nothing." Uncle Glenville nodded in agreement.

The next day Daddy went to Little Rock and applied for a Works Progress Administration (WPA) job. He qualified easily for work assistance as he had no income. He was giving away the milk from his dairy cows; no one had money to buy it. He fed his family and neighbors with real milk and butter and slopped his hogs with what was left. Access to extra food came with his work permit. Daddy frowned on that saying, "I told that fool city man who filled out those papers I didn't want food. I wanted to work, and I'd supply my own food. He didn't even call it food—called it *commodities*. When I asked him what that was, he said it was surplus food that wasn't selling."

We may not have needed it, but delicacies such as blocks of yellow cheese, big hunks of baloney, and jars of peanut butter appeared on Mama's well-laden table. I didn't let Daddy know it, but I thought that store-bought cheese tasted better than the cottage cheese Mama made; baloney was better than ham; and peanut butter was right out of heaven. Daddy raised peanuts by the bushels, and they tasted good roasted, but Mama didn't make peanut butter.

Since I couldn't apply for a WPA job and there were no *Help Wanted* ads in Daddy's newspaper, I left the question mark beside number two on my list. I moved on to number three, *When*. I hastily wrote *tomorrow* beside it. Number four and number five were *Where* and *How*. *Ask Doyle* almost wrote itself beside them.

Doyle worked in the state capitol. He was my cousin, and he could tell me all about Little Rock since he grew up there. He lived there until his daddy lost his good-paying job two years after the economy collapsed. They managed to keep their nice house and furniture for a year or so, but when they couldn't make the payments any longer, their mortgage was foreclosed. They lost everything they once owned, and finally, in sheer desperation they moved into a makeshift shanty, a lean-to on the farm that was part of Grandma Nancy's land.

I remember Daddy saying, "It's a good thing Doyle still has a job, or that family would starve to death. His daddy doesn't know one thing about farming. I told him he could use my mule and plow to raise a garden, and you would have thought I had asked him to raise the dead from the way he looked." Aunt Paralee knew more about raising flowers than vegetables, but she knew more about farming than he did. She was a good manager. They didn't starve, but I heard it whispered that they did get hungry before she would give up and move out on the farm.

Doyle liked to spend time at our house after he came home from work. There was plenty of food on our table at supper time, and afterward we had popcorn and roasted peanuts to snack on while we played poker, Daddy's favorite card game.

I read back over my list and thought, *At last I have a plan, even if it does have gaps in it. I'll ride with Doyle as he goes to work tomorrow. If he can't help me find a job, someone will.* I told myself, *You just wait and see.*

The roses in the painting seemed to affirm my optimism, and I smiled with gratitude that there had been no guests at my pity party. We could still be a family that had no room for tears.

Doyle readily agreed for me to ride to work with him and said, "Be ready by 6:30 in the morning. I'll be there bright and early as I have to allow time for car trouble."

5

Professional Lady

Graduation gifts had provided a whole new wardrobe for me, and I could choose what to wear to apply for a job. I dressed in a navy blue skirt and jacket to match, a white blouse with a touch of lace on the collar, blue suede pumps, and my first pair of silk stockings. I told myself, *I'm not a schoolgirl any more. I'm grown up now, and I want to look like a lady—an office lady.*

After taking one last searching look in the mirror, I hurried out to the front porch just as Doyle drove up in his shiny black 1932 Ford coupe. As I settled down in the front, I looked around and realized it just had one seat. The thought flashed through my mind, *How can couples double date in a car like this?*

As he backed down the drive, Doyle warned me, "This is a good car, Ann, and a good-looking one, but it doesn't have safe brakes. You'll see what I mean before we get home, but I haven't hit anything yet."

I didn't know much about a car, but I remembered hearing Daddy tell Kenneth, "A car has to do at least two things to be worth driving: start and stop." Doyle's car started easily, but was he saying it didn't stop?

Well, I'll think about that later. He always gets back, and it sure is a snazzy-looking little car.

I mentioned it having just one seat and Doyle corrected me. "Oh, there's another seat on the back. It opens up to a rumble seat." He laughed, and said it worked real well on a double date—neither couple could chaperone the other. But he added, "I haven't used this car lately for dating, but I will if I ever get the brakes fixed."

I knew Doyle hadn't dated any girls since they moved out of Little Rock because I heard him tell Kenneth that one night while they sat on our front door steps. I had a place on the end of the porch where I could sit in the dark, and the men or boys talking on the doorsteps didn't know I was listening. I learned a lot of things from hearing their conversations that girls didn't know, or didn't discuss if they knew. Anyway, it wasn't bad brakes that kept Doyle from dating. He said he didn't have a penny to spend on himself since his daddy lost his job. I thought he meant money to take a girl to a movie, but I guess getting his brakes fixed was part of the money problem too.

We rolled along easily on the narrow and curving West Twelfth Street Pike. Actually it was a paved country road with few cars traveling on it. There was no reason to have brakes until we got to Kanis Hill. It was a steep incline with a sharp cliff dropping down on one side and a shallow ditch on the other. At the bottom of the hill the road curved, and a narrow one-way bridge covered a swift-moving creek. Doyle cautioned me of danger. He said if he had to stop on the way down he would head for the shallow ditch and for me to hold on. I asked, "What if you can't stop for the bridge?"

He said, "I've been driving it all year, and the Lord has taken care of me so far. Help me pray that nothing gets in our way."

He didn't know that all I knew about praying was the time I asked God to let Daddy have money to pay his taxes. But that was a life and death matter as Daddy threatened to use his shotgun if anyone tried to take his land. As we started down Kanis Hill it suddenly struck me, *That may be what this is for Doyle and me (a life or death matter) if something gets in front of us and he can't stop.*

I sure was glad Doyle had a praying daddy who taught him to call on the Lord. I guess my daddy thought he could take care of himself as I never did hear him pray. I knew Doyle's daddy prayed because I was eavesdropping and I heard him talking to God. Daddy's watermelon patch was next to the spot where Uncle John and Aunt Paralee were trying to plant a late garden. I went after a watermelon, and I heard Uncle John talking all the way up and down the rows as he tried to plow with Daddy's mule. I thought he was talking to himself so I hid behind bushes in a fence corner anxious to hear what a man would say to himself if he didn't know anyone was listening.

What I heard scared me half to death. He was talking to God. "Lord, help me—Oh Lord, I need help. You know I don't know how to plow, and everybody else knows it, and I need food for my family. This ornery mule acts like he knows more than I do and won't start or stop when I tell him to. What am I going to do if I can't raise a garden? Oh, Lord, help me . . ."

He went on down the row begging for help, and as soon as he got out of hearing range, I jumped up and ran as fast as I could.

Eavesdropping on my family was almost an art with me. I vowed to myself the day my brother was born, and everyone but me knew a baby was coming, that nothing was going to happen again in our household without my knowing about it. I didn't feel guilty about hearing when they didn't know I was listening, but today was different—eavesdropping on God.

I revised my vow: *I'll still try to know everything that's happening around me, but I won't spy on people when they don't know I'm listening. It's not honest."* For the first time, I was ashamed of myself for doing it.

Hearing Uncle John talk to God didn't teach me how to pray, so it was up to Doyle to pray us safely down Kanis Hill. I closed my eyes before we got to the bridge, but nothing stopped us. Doyle finally said, "We're safe now."

We drove on to the state capitol building without any mishaps. Doyle reported for his work as an apprentice surveyor, and then took me directly to his supervisor. He said on the way, "If anyone can find you a job, Ann, this man can."

Doyle took me in and introduced me as his country cousin. He had a touch of pride in his voice as he told his supervisor about my background: "Ann has just graduated with top honors from Joe T. Robinson High School, and she wants to go to college. She has worked four years on an NYA program as the school principal's assistant."

The man interrupted Doyle saying, "I know just the place for her; the County Welfare Department needs a clerical worker. We can get her papers transferred there. Take her over there now, Doyle, and tell them I'll tend to the paperwork."

Within an hour I had a job—an office job in downtown Little Rock surrounded by state, county, and city officials. It was walking distance to the state capitol, the courthouse, and the city hall. I thought, *I'm on my way!*

I stayed wrapped in a security blanket of family protection—enclosed in a cocoon that unraveled bit by bit, sometimes slowly, even years at time, but other times changing with the speed of an Arkansas tornado. From a country bumpkin to a high school senior seemed a lifetime, but suddenly I emerged a full-fledged professional lady in a downtown office. Or that's how I felt as I sat at a desk following instructions right and left from my immediate director. My first day's schedule consisted of filing applications for scores of people applying for food to feed their families. The Great Depression was no respecter of persons—the former *haves* were sitting alongside the *have-nots.* Hunger erases all barriers when food becomes the common denominator.

College graduates, who held responsible positions a year or two before, sat alongside others who could not read or write. Black and white people sat across the room from each other waiting for the same thing—food—or the means of getting it for their families.

After three days on the job my immediate director, Mrs. Carter, said as she gave me my schedule, "Ann, you have a heart for these people and their need, and they recognize it. I want you to start making the preliminary interview and fill out their paperwork before you send them in to me to evaluate their eligibility."

Except for staff meetings which included the county director, the three case workers, and a secretary, I was an active part of the Pulaski County Welfare Department, and I loved every minute of it.

When a state office asked for a file from the county office, I was the one who delivered it. As I walked in that majestic state capitol building, I felt like an important link in the chain of government in our great state.

Within a few weeks I became known at the capitol as *the lit-tle lady from the Welfare Department*. I basked in their recognition of me, and I observed carefully the dress, manner, and conduct of each one I met. Working at the capitol seemed like a fertile field for the growth of a future lawyer, and I didn't want to miss anything it could teach me.

UNEXPECTED LESSON

All the women working in the county department were churchgoers. I listened intently to their discussions of church activities that they looked forward to on weekends. I tried to learn all I could about what would get them into heaven someday.

With all my desire to learn everything on the new job, an unexpected lesson came in mid-summer. Our office closed during the noon hour with one case worker staying to keep communication open by telephone. Mrs. Carter seemed reluctant to ask me when she said, "Ann, can you take my place at noon this week? It is my turn to stay, but I've been assigned to do something else."

I readily agreed and wondered why she was hesitant in asking. All I would be required to do was answer the telephone. I was still a novice with a phone, so I enjoyed the thought of having a whole hour to take messages.

The waiting room was cleared of people, and the door was locked before the workers left for lunch. I was sitting quietly at my desk waiting for the phone to ring when in walked a director from one of the other state departments. I heard his key open the door, and when I saw his oily, black patent hair, I recognized him from my trips through the state capitol. He came directly to my desk, handed me a folder, and said, "Miss, check your file on this name, please."

I stood at the file cabinet, and as I turn around to hand him the folder, he was right in my face from head to feet. Without saying a word he shoved me back against the cabinet and pushed his body hard against mine. My skirt was twisted tight around my body, and as he tried to untangle it, instinctively I slung down low, and my right knee jabbed upward. Catching him off guard, I slid out from under him and ran to the staff restroom.

Shaking violently, I bolted the door behind me. It was a flimsy bolt that a man could easily push through if he tried. There was no one to call out to for help, and I thought, *God, I need help. I wish I knew how to pray.*

I pushed against the door, shaking so hard I was afraid it would rattle and let him know where I was hiding. After awhile I hadn't heard anything, so I ventured to the washbasin and turned on a bare trickle and began splashing it all over me—my face, my hands, my arms. I felt dirty all over. The cool water revived me, and I was reminded again of Mutt Jones' speech class admonition: *Think on your feet, Ann.*

I struggled to put in perspective what was happening to me. *What should I do? Who do I tell when I get out? Or do I tell anyone? Is this the way of the city? Should I go home and be a country bumpkin?*

Finally, I heard doors opening and women talking. I rushed out and went directly to Mrs. Carter. I closed the door, and told her the whole story.

She looked nervous, almost scared, as she listened and was silent for at least a full minute before she said, "Ann, I wish I could help you—I really do—but this is out of my hands. I will tell Mrs. Sims (the county director) what you have told me. Go back to your desk and don't tell anyone else." Within an hour an after-work staff meeting was announced, and I was summoned to attend.

I remembered being summoned as a junior high girl to the principal's office for smoking, and I wondered if Mrs. Sims handled problems in the business world anything like the way Mr. Hoggard did in school days.

The conference room joined Mrs. Sims' office, and the other workers were already seated at the table when I arrived. I thought, *I'm on time, so they must have met earlier.*

"Sit down, Ann. We're ready to begin." Mrs. Sims began her lecture saying she felt a need to give us counsel on how a lady must guard against attracting men in the business world. She discussed first *the way to dress.* Surely I passed that test as I wore suits and blouses of proper length and fit. Second she talked about t*he way to smile*—men often take that as an invitation.

I thought, *What kind of smile is that? I am known for my smile—but what does that mean? What is she saying?*

While I was still trying to figure that out, she closed the meeting by saying, "Ladies, if you are going to work in the business world, you must learn to take care of yourselves."

The entire County Welfare staff of six ladies attended that meeting—the county director, three case workers, one secretary, and me.

With downcast eyes they filed past me and silently went back to their offices, gathered their belongings, and left for the day. I sensed a fear of losing their jobs if they said a word. For city people a paying job was the difference between eating and being hungry during the Great Depression. They chose to eat.

TAKE CARE OF YOURSELF

You must learn to take care of yourself, echoed in my ears as I stood on the street corner waiting for Doyle to come after me. *But how do I begin? I'm not afraid to speak out, but who do I tell? I may lose my job, but unlike the city ladies, I'll always have food to eat—as long as Daddy has his land.*

Tell Daddy. He will know what to do, was my first reaction. Then I remembered his response to the possible threat of the *government* taking his land if he couldn't pay his taxes. He boldly said he would meet them with his shotgun if that ever happened. So what would he do if I told him a *government* man tried to rape his daughter?

No, I couldn't tell Daddy. I remembered Mutt Jones' teaching again—*A free press is the best guard we have against evil in high places.*

Go tell the editor of the *Arkansas Democrat* newspaper; I had met him on a high school field trip in journalism. I thought, *He will gladly expose that man.* But then I thought, *I'll be exposed too and Daddy will know about it.* My thoughts began to ramble. Little Red Riding Hood and the Big Bad Wolf were not fairy tale characters any more, but real living people.

Sex became a reality. I had never used the word *sex*, or heard it spoken. Even the barnyard word for an animal's sex act was called breeding. I thought of Daddy's bull and once seeing a cow put in the pen with him.

Marital relations was the term used when it related to people. I wondered what that entailed as I read Grandma Nancy's classical literature, and later as I saw couples getting married at movies. Since I didn't plan to get married, it wasn't a big issue with me.

But today I was exposed to it—saw it, and felt it in a man's body. I escaped with my virginity intact, but I lost my innocence.

I thought, *There really is a big bad wolf, and he is out there ready to devour young Red Riding Hood. Is it a part of every man—some more and some less?"* My thoughts continued to ramble, *Do city people follow different rules to country folk? Maybe, maybe not, maybe just more people . . ."*

I thought of Randall, a city man, and with all his crazy kissing, I still felt protected when I was with him. And Jay—he's a city man, and he's never acted this way. And as Doyle's car pulled up to the curb, I slid in beside him thinking, *I'll tell Jay. I don't know what he'll do, but unlike Daddy, he doesn't have a shotgun.*

It was a comforting thought to my troubled mind, and I closed my eyes trying to blot out the picture that kept appearing, the oily black patent hair. I was home again before I realized I had fallen asleep.

Mama thought I was sick when I couldn't eat my supper. "I wish I had some potato soup, Ann. That would make you feel better."

"I'm okay, Mama. Really I am. Jay will be here in a few minutes, and we'll go drink a Coca Cola. That will settle my stomach."

I met Jay coming in the door and asked, "Can we talk for a minute?" He took my hand, and we drove to our special place. Couples met there so often while they were courting that it was known as Lover's Lane. Actually, it wasn't a lane but a fork in the road with a broad space for parking alongside. He held my hand as he drove, but he didn't question me until he parked the car.

"What is it, Ann? You look sick."

I began telling him what happened, but when I got to the part where I was shoved to the filing cabinet, I began crying—my first tears since it happened. It was the first time Jay had seen me cry. He took me by the shoulders, his strong hands pressing so hard it hurt as he struggled to speak, "Did he . . . did he . . . Ann, tell me, did he. . . ?" He couldn't bring himself to say the word.

"No, but he almost did." The pressure on my shoulders subsided, and he drew me tenderly in his arms, but not before I saw an expression I'd never seen on his face. He looked mean enough to actually kill somebody.

I dabbed my tears away and finished telling him the story. His expression changed from anger to unbelief and back again to anger when he heard how my supervisor handled the situation.

"I'm scared, Jay. What can I do?"

"We won't give him a chance to try it again. If you have to stay alone at lunch hour any more, I'll come and stay with you."

"I'm supposed to take Mrs. Carter's place all week, but after this I won't do it even if it costs my job."

"He's not apt to show up again this soon, but I'll come tomorrow and stay with you during my lunch hour. I'm going to talk to my boss. He has coffee with city officials and if he doesn't know anyone in the state office, some of his friends will. That varmint has to go—and the sooner the better."

I felt better all over. Jay would take care of me. "Now, let's go get that Coca Cola," he said, and a few minutes later he came out of the Ferndale grocery store with an ice cold bottle of Coca Cola, a Snickers candy bar, and a ten-cent package of Chesterfield cigarettes.

I preferred Camel cigarettes, but they only came in twenty-cent packs. Through the week, he slipped Chesterfields in my pocket and on weekends, Camels.

I didn't think it looked ladylike to smoke, even if it was fashionable. Beautiful women were pictured in magazines and movies holding a cigarette between manicured fingers. I smoked discreetly, almost privately, and I promised myself that one day I would quit; but when it came to naming that day, I never did.

Jay revealed two sides of himself that night I hadn't seen before—an anger that I didn't know he was capable of and a tenderness that only a mother's loving touch to a newborn baby could equal. Here was a man who wouldn't shoot a rabbit, a bird, or a deer (they were all Bambi to him), but looked like he would tear a man's body apart if he touched me.

READY FOR BATTLE

I was back at work the next morning feeling bright as a new dollar. The women looked surprised at my reaction, or rather my lack of reaction, to the problem. They didn't know I had an answer.

Noontime came and Mrs. Carter disappeared without saying a word. Apparently, she expected me to stay as no one else was assigned for the noon hour. I was looking forward happily to seeing Jay when the ladies all left for lunch. They looked at me with a puzzled expression as they locked the door behind them. The thought came to me, *Surely they don't think I'm happily looking forward to seeing Mr. Oily Hair again.* I dismissed the thought—it was unthinkable.

Whatever they thought, they locked up and left. Soon after I heard Jay's knock. I let him in, and we joyfully embraced for a moment.

He handed me a sack of the Shack's famous barbecue sandwiches. I felt like hugging him again as I smelled the delicious sauce, but it didn't seem the proper thing to do in my business office. Instead, he crossed the room saying, "I'll sit over here and you can go on with your work."

Just as I settled down at my desk, I heard a key unlock the door and in walked Mr. Oily Hair! I was too surprised to move or say a word as he started toward me, but Jay wasn't. He met him head on. Surprised, the man said, "This office is closed till one o'clock. What are you doing here?"

"I'm here to take care of Ann," and with the same expression I saw on his face the night before, Jay started toward him.

The man vanished with the speed of a cockroach when a light shines in a dark room. I likened him to a big bad wolf the day before, but he looked more like a slimy rat as he disappeared.

Breathless, I asked Jay, "What would you have done if he hadn't run?"

"I don't know. But I do know he wasn't going to lay a hand on you."

6

Marriage Proposals

Daddy called the closing days of summer from August until often the middle of September *dog days*. Whatever that term meant to him, it was his way of describing hot, sweltering weather with no rain or breeze to cool one's body. Home air conditioning was unheard of and there were electric fans only where electricity was available.

Daddy's dogs stretched out lifeless in the dirt under the house so maybe that is why he used that term. It may have made him want to find a place to stretch out and wait for the long, hot summer to end. There was no way he could do that since dairy farm work continued on both hot days and cold all year long. There was only time for short rests.

I didn't do farm work, but trying to keep cool was a major problem. I loved to ride in Jay's car with all the windows rolled down and feel the wind cool my skin which was moist with perspiration. Our movie dates were on weekends and the ten-mile drive to Little Rock was like a moving electric fan as the wind blew across our bodies.

Neither of us had a church background so we celebrated Sundays by eating barbecue lunch at the Shack back of the state capitol building and then going downtown to a first class, first run movie. On our way we saw people coming out of churches all dressed up in their Sunday best (even as we were), and I wondered what they had that we didn't have. Jokingly, I asked Jay if he thought they had a password to heaven. If they did, they didn't share it.

Jay didn't let me puzzle over it very long as we rolled along on West Twelfth Street Pike getting closer to the Shack. He liked to croon love songs in my ear as he drove. Most were originals. He made up the words as he sang, but always extolled my beauty (as he saw it) and added the line, "You are the girl I want to marry." The word *hyperbole* wasn't in his vocabulary, but he sure did use the strategy that Francis Bacon said should be limited in use, but permissible in love.

Since he never delivered an ultimatum or asked for any type of answer, I didn't have to tell him that marriage was out of the question for me. Instead, I enjoyed the exaggerated flattery he lavished on me, and as I knew what I really looked like (mirrors don't lie), it didn't do any harm for me to enjoy the songs he sang.

One day we were early for the matinee and Jay pulled in a parking place almost in front of the theater. I said, "Let's hurry in where it's cool."

As Jay opened the car door we heard the loud voice of a policeman shouting at the occupants of a car ahead of us. He was red-faced, sweating profusely, and his agitated voice reminded me of how Mama sounded the hot summer I was sick and she thought the heat was going to kill me.

"Yankee, you better head for home. Do it now and I won't write you a ticket."

The young black man bristled as he answered, "What did I do? They backed into us. Look what they did to my car. I was parked. Why would I get a ticket?" The "they" he referred to had left the scene.

"Well, you better not be parked any longer, or you'll find yourself in jail. You better get going while going is good," ordered the officer.

What could they do but drive off? They did go, onlookers cheered, and the policeman strutted with pleasure.

I felt condemned by the expression of four pairs of eyes as they left our city—a man's, a woman's, and two frightened children's eyes. It seemed they looked right at Jay and me with *help* written on their faces as they passed us, but they were gone before I could say a word.

I looked at Jay, and what I saw turned my whole world around. There were tears welling up in his eyes as he said, "Ann, how long will we stand for this before someone speaks out?"

I blurted out, completely unrehearsed or planned, "Why don't we get married?"

Jay's countenance changed instantly to the most ecstatic and revealing expression a man can have—looking at a woman he loves and picturing her as his wife. His full lips quivered as he reached to fold me in his arms right there on Main Street, Little Rock, Arkansas, in broad daylight.

Just as his lips touched mine, suddenly he drew back, slid back in the car, then jumped out again, stood up, flexed his muscles, jumped up and down a time or two, and getting back in the car he said, "I'll have to think about this."

But what was there to think about? Isn't this what he's been wanting? Or has he been just singing songs to me?

He looked dead serious as he said, "Let's go to the park and talk about this."

He didn't croon any love songs on the way, and I cringed at my brashness in asking him to marry me. But I thought that was what he'd been saying he wanted for four years since our first date.

Don't I know anything about how men think? I sure didn't know, and still don't know, what Randall thought, and is it true of Jay, too? I asked myself.

It was blistering hot when we got to Boyle Park. Jay took my hand as he opened the car door for me saying, "Let's sit down on that bench," pointing to one close to a small lake of water. A breeze blowing across the pond felt cool to my face that must have been flushed blood red with embarrassment.

"Why did you say that, Ann? Do you know what you just asked me?" he said as soon as we sat down.

My words rushed out like water from a faucet turned on full force. I tried to convey my secret obsession that I hadn't been able to share with a single person—my vow to myself that I would study and one day be a lawyer, work to abolish segregation laws, and later be a judge who would rule by the law and not by the color of one's skin.

Jay's expression showed no comprehension of what I was trying to tell him. He looked like a stranger as he searched my face that before had reflected beauty (in his eyes), but I couldn't tell what he saw now.

"Can't you see, Jay, that I would have no room in my life for a husband, marriage, babies, and accomplishing my goal? But when I saw tears in your eyes as you saw how that black family was treated, and heard your plea for someone to take a stand, I thought, *Jay and I can do this together*."

Jay looked at me in utter amazement, as though he had never seen me before. "And that's why you asked me to marry you?" was his reply.

Not understanding what he was thinking, I answered, "It's why I *can* marry you."

His head dropped down in his hands, and he sat silent a moment. Without looking up he said again, "I'll have to think about this."

Silently he led me back to the car and drove me home. No songs or words broke the silence as I sat huddled in the corner of the seat. He stopped in my driveway just short of the front porch, got out, and slowly came to open my door. He reached in, took both of my hands, pressed them tenderly between his two big hands, walked to my front door, and without looking me in the eye he said, "I'll be back tomorrow night." Off he drove.

I hurried in the house hoping to hide before I had to talk to anyone, but Mama detected something was wrong and asked, "Ann, why are you back so early? Are you sick?"

"No, Mama. Let me rest awhile," and I shut the bedroom door (doors always stayed open in our house) before she could ask any more.

JILTED AGAIN?

I flung my body across the bed without turning back Mama's homemade coverlet thinking, *Am I jilted again? And this time just when I was ready to go to the altar. All I lost when Randall jilted me after a few months special dating was a big slice of my pride, but what if I lose Jay?"* And suddenly I put in words to myself what I hadn't acknowledged before—*I love that man!*

As soon as I formed those words, a surge of energy flooded my body, and I stood straight up on my feet. I began to think, *Jay didn't want to look at me after I admitted my life's goal. He must not want to have a sympathizer with black people, especially one who wanted to be a lawyer and judge, as his future wife. I don't know how, but I'll convince him I'm still the girl he wanted to marry from the first time he saw me, but one with a call to change the world. He hasn't jilted me; he told me he will be back tomorrow night. I'll be ready to tell him I love him. Or should I do that? Maybe not yet.*

Anyway, I had a plan, and I hurried in to tell Mama, "I believe Jay and I are going to get married."

"What do you mean, you believe you are?" she asked. "Either you are, or you aren't."

"Wait and see, Mama," and my mind echoed, *and I will, too.*

I took special care dressing when the next night came. I wanted to see Jay's expression that would say again, "You are beautiful."

Finally, he came, but his eyes were not on me when he entered the living room. Instead, he talked to Daddy and avoided looking at me altogether. "Why don't we stay in tonight and play cards?" he suggested.

Daddy thought it was a good idea and answered for me, "I'm for that. The rain today has cooled things off. Usually, we have to wait till October to stay inside, but I'm ready to play a game." He picked up a well-worn deck of cards and began shuffling them.

After an hour or so and without once looking directly at me, Jay stood and took my hand saying, "Let's go out on the porch awhile."

The screen door slapped shut behind us, and without saying a word he led me to the porch steps. It was too dark for me to see his expression when he said, "Ann, Randall has been wanting us to come to Memphis and let him show us the big-city zoo he is so proud of. Why don't we go Sunday? I'll ask Doyle and his girlfriend to go with us." He stopped talking, waiting for me to answer.

It didn't make sense to me. *Why would he want to go see Randall, especially now?* I didn't know how to respond. I stood up expecting standing on my feet would give me words to answer, but instead I stammered, "I don't know . . . Jay, I don't know . . . "

When I didn't continue, he took the lead saying, "I'll be after you early Sunday morning. Let's leave by six o'clock."

He took both my hands and pressed them gently between his; then he jumped off the porch steps and left.

Almost a week later, from Monday night till early Sunday morning, I reasoned, *Surely Jay will be as anxious to see me as I am to see him. This is the longest we've been apart since our first date nearly four years ago.*

I rolled out of bed at four o'clock as Mama and Daddy went out the back door going to the dairy barn to milk the fifteen to twenty cows that required milking twice a day, seven days a week at 4:00 a.m. and 4:00 p.m. I got another glimpse of the hard work Mama did as a dairyman's wife as I pushed myself out of my bed at the early hour. I wasn't going to milk cows; instead, I was getting dressed to go with a good-looking man that I discovered the week before was going to be my future husband.

I thought, *Jay, you are twenty-four years old, and I'm not quite eighteen. Maybe your age is making you want to think about it, but I feel free as a bird—so here I come, ready to go to Memphis or wherever you say, as long as I am with you.*

Jay drove in the driveway right on time, 6 o'clock. He'd never looked handsomer in his suit, vest, tie, and with his shoes polished to a shimmer. I thought, *We're both looking our best today. Something special must be going to happen.*

Doyle and Mary Ann were in the back seat when Jay quietly led me to the car and seated me in the front. His eyes didn't directly look in mine, but I caught a glimpse of his seeing me earlier when I first came in to greet him. His expression was *Wow for* an instant before he averted his eyes, so I knew he still liked my looks—but did he like me?

He didn't offer to coax me over closer to him when he began driving. I wasn't seated by the door, but not close to him either— just barely off center of the seat. If Doyle and Mary Ann noticed anything unusual about our behavior, they didn't voice it. Instead, they were busy sitting close and enjoying each other in the back seat.

Jay hummed along as he drove, but didn't sing any words. I pretended I needed to catch up on my sleep from getting up so early, so I closed my eyes and the motion of the car along with Jay's humming lulled me to sleep.

RANDALL RE-ENTERS

We arrived at the Memphis zoo before I realized we were there. Mary Ann and I asked to find a restroom to freshen up from the trip while Jay and Doyle went to find Randall. He must have been close by as they were waiting for us when we came out of the pavilion.

Randall rushed toward me, took both my hands, stepped back and looked me up and down and finally full in the face, and exclaimed," Does Jay ever tell you how beautiful you are?"

"All the time ,well, except for today," I bantered back at him thinking, *Who taught these two men how to say what every woman wants to hear—even when she knows he's just flattering her?*

"Why don't we eat an early lunch before I show you my kingdom of animals?"

He was the same pleasantly arrogant Randall, only now he had what he looked forward to getting when I first knew him. Then, he wasn't letting anything get in his way of achieving his goal, and now he had it.

He escorted us to a lunchroom, stopping right and left, exchanging greetings to employees on his way. As we entered with Randall, a waiter hurried toward us and seated us immediately—Doyle and Mary Ann in a nook to themselves, and Jay, Randall, and me in a secluded spot.

Randall seated me, pulled his chair up close, and with his lips brushing my cheek he said in my ear, "Jay called me this week and said you asked him to marry you. Did you actually do that, Ann?"

I was furious! How could Jay do such a thing? But he must have or how would Randall know? Jay didn't deny it and I sat there looking at two men waiting for my answer. I forgot every debating rule Mutt Jones taught me and I spoke from my heart instead of my head.

Anger tinged my voice as I shot back, "I don't know what Jay told you, but I do know what he's been saying to me in songs from our first date—'You are the girl I want to marry.' Wouldn't you think that after four years of saying it, that it's what he wanted?"

And even louder I repeated, "Wouldn't you think that?"

"Okay, I don't have any doubt about that," Randall responded. "Jay has wanted to marry you since the first time he saw you. If you had been old enough, he would have asked you then; but he promised to wait until you were eighteen. What I want to know is why, all of a sudden, that you want to marry him so much that you asked him? Why? Is there something wrong, Ann?"

As perturbed as I was, I still felt relieved that Jay hadn't revealed my secret obsession.

"Why, Ann?" Randall repeated.

"Because . . . because I love him," I almost whispered.

But it was loud enough that both men heard it.

Jay jumped up out of his chair, pulled me to my feet, and kissed me full on the mouth right there.

I don't know what Randall did, or anyone else for that matter. The lines of an old song, *I only have eyes for you*, described Jay and me. We couldn't take our eyes or hands off each other.

I don't know how we managed to eat the bountiful lunch Randall ordered for us, or even if we did eat it. I couldn't wait till we were alone. I had a bunch of questions I wanted to ask Jay, but apparently he just had one question for me.

ANOTHER PROPOSAL

As soon as we left the lunchroom, Jay took my hand while Randall was signing the ticket, and we darted around the corner. Out of sight and sound Jay found a nook covered with greenery, almost like a chapel. He pulled me up close to him and with his mouth right over my ear asked, "Ann, will you marry me?"

Breathless, I whispered, "Yes . . . if . . . you promise to never tell another person that I asked you first."

Solemnly he vowed, "I never will."

Holding hands, we raced back happily and joyfully laughing to tell the others.

"I just asked Ann to marry me! We're getting married! Can you believe it? We're getting married!" Jay called loudly to Randall, Doyle, and Mary Ann as we approached them and before we were in speaking range.

"Well . . . uh . . . well . . ." Randall began, but if he finished the sentence, I didn't hear it.

Doyle congratulated us and Mary Ann squealed with delight, but Jay and I were oblivious to what anyone was saying to us. We were all wrapped up in our new relationship—engaged. We were going to get married. It was like new wine, or what I'd heard wine did to one's feelings and actions.

Randall soon lost interest in showing us his kingdom as he realized we weren't hearing much of what he was saying. After an hour or so, he said, "I need to get back to work, and I'll let you two lovebirds entertain yourselves."

He walked us back to the car, and just before Jay got in he jauntily slapped Jay on the back. Jay teasingly returned the gesture. Two grown men, twenty-four and twenty-six years old, were reflecting the camaraderie of friendship that began in boyhood.

Randall leaned forward as Jay got under the wheel, and just before we drove off said, "Jay, keep on taking care of Ann," and he marched back into his kingdom, the Memphis zoo.

If a theologian had heard the love songs Jay crooned in my ear traveling from Memphis back to Little Rock, he would have thought surely that Jay was quoting words from the Song of Solomon, but not so. He sang it from words composed in his heart.

ENGAGED

After we took Doyle and Mary Ann home, we headed for our courting spot. It truly was Lover's Lane now. Jay stopped kissing me long enough to say, "We have plans to make. If you're going to be a first-class lawyer—and I'm going to see that you are—it's going to take time, a lot of work on your part, and a lot of money on my part. Let's get started."

Stopping right in the middle of a passionate kiss, I pressed my index finger on his full lips and asked, "Tell me why you had to think about it when I, well, when we talked about getting married. I was afraid you couldn't bear the thought of having a lawyer who wanted to be a judge for your wife. What changed your mind?"

"Oh, I was surprised that you had all that bottled up inside of you, and you hadn't given me a clue of it, but I wasn't surprised that you wanted to shoot for the stars. I knew the first day I saw you that you were not only the most beautiful girl in the world, but you had something besides that. I knew it, Ann, and you were barely a teenager. I saw it."

"Then why did you have to think about it?" I persisted, "And why did you want to go see Randall?"

"Ann, I thought you wanted me to marry you just to help you reach the stars, and I was ready to do that. I wanted to make sure you didn't love anyone else."

"Who did you think I could love but you?"

"It doesn't matter. I know now you love me—you said so."

Interrupting another kiss, I asked, "Why did you keep putting the words in song instead of just asking me to marry you like you did today?"

"I promised, well, I promised myself I would wait until you were eighteen before I proposed to you, and I almost did. Now, I need to ask your Daddy before I start shouting from the housetops, 'Ann and I are getting married!' Let's go right now before he goes to bed."

We walked in the living room holding hands, and our body language probably shouted louder than Jay's words, "Mr. Thompson, I want to marry Ann. I'll be good to her . . . "

Before he could ask, Daddy quietly said, "Well, I believe you'll be good to her."

"You can count on that, as long as she will let me," Jay solemnly promised.

Jay and Ann
Wedding Day - 1940

PART II

Marriage and Family

Ann continues to seek the way to heaven, but does not find it in church attendance or through friends.

7

Mansion in the Sky

Beaming with excitement Jay drove close to the curb where I stood waiting for him at the end of my work day.

"Ann, I found us a house today—it's our *Mansion in the Sky*," he exclaimed as I was getting in beside him. "I wanted to wait and let you see it before I rented it, but I was afraid someone else would get it if I did."

My vivid imagination instantly conjured up a fairy tale mansion, and before he could say more I breathlessly asked, "Where is it, Jay? What does it cost? Can we afford it?"

My first reaction to a mansion was whether it would fit the budget we planned to get me in college.

"It's twenty dollars a month and we pay the bills. My boss says we won't find anything cheaper than that. It's right downtown here on State Street, close to my work and yours, too—just a few blocks from here."

"It's two months before we get married. Can I see it now?"

"Not yet, it's not quite ready, but they let me rent it early. I can show you the outside—let's go."

Parking across the street and looking up at a rambling old two-story house that reflected the nobility of an earlier generation, I could understand Jay's calling it a mansion . . . it had been.

"Tell me, Jay, what does it look like inside? I can't wait to see it."

"And I can't wait to move you in it as my wife," he said as his face revealed even more excitement at the thought of being married. "Just think, two more months and you will be mine—mine to have and to hold. Imagine, Ann, we've waited so long. You will be my wife."

"But now, Jay, tell me what our house looks like."

"Well, it's not the house, just rooms upstairs. The owners live downstairs. We have a living room, bedroom, kitchen, bath, and a glassed-in porch—she called it a veranda. See it up there? We can sit out there at night and look down on the state capitol building."

"How is it furnished? Tell me," I insisted.

"Partly furnished, that's what the newspaper ad said. Really not much, but we can manage. It has a gas cook stove, an ice box that makes ice, a table and four chairs, and a glider swing she called a sofa on the porch. It's a good thing we have our bedroom suite, isn't it?"

Jay saw to that soon after we announced our engagement the year before. He put it in the lay-a-way and paid it out weekly. (There were no credit cards then; you paid, and then received.) He insisted that I go with him to select one, but I was too embarrassed to go shopping for a bed before we were married.

The furniture store was in the same block as the generator shop where Jay worked. It seemed every businessman on that block knew Jay and liked him. If they knew him, they heard about me as he talked so much about me, especially after we were engaged. Jay selected a bed he liked and the owner put the full bedroom set on display in the window for Jay to walk me by and see it. A year later he still owed a few payments, but they assured him they would move it in on time—by December 24, 1940—our wedding date.

But for then, we sat looking at our dream house and built castles in the sky of our future:

— Jay would send me to college.
— I would be a lawyer—make big money.
— Jay would buy a generator shop.
— I would become a judge.
— We would make the world a better place, and
  live happily ever after.

WEDDING DAY

I dressed like a bride for my high school graduation, but I dressed like a lawyer for our wedding ceremony. I shopped for an expensive black suit that would keep me well dressed while I was preparing several years for my prestigious career. I selected one that an exclusive Little Rock shop put on sale the season before our wedding date and put it in the lay-a-way even as Jay did our bedroom suite.

The best shoe shop in town had a mid-summer sale, and I paid ten dollars for a pair of black leather pumps that set my suit off perfectly. The most I'd spent for shoes before that day was three dollars and ninety nine cents. I went home feeling like a lawyer who was already making big money even though I spent the last dollar in my pocket.

Standing before the family's tilted mirror on our wedding day, I dressed in that suit coordinated with a feminine white blouse, gorgeous black pumps, and appropriate accessories. The reflection I saw was, I thought, that of a prestigious lawyer lady.

Jay arrived on time dressed superbly for the occasion, but looking sick enough to be in the bed—as the doctor advised him to be the day before. He was carrying a huge corsage. As I pinned it on my well-planned outfit I thought, *I wish I didn't have to wear this,* but I knew I must or he would be disappointed.

Mama looked me up and down carefully and tearfully as I came out of the bedroom, but she didn't say, "You're cute, Ann." I don't know what she thought as I couldn't share our secret— only Jay and I knew that. I couldn't explain to her my solemn bridal apparel and why I hadn't asked her to make my wedding dress. I was too caught up with our plans to see or wonder why she would have felt left out.

Silently, she followed us out the front door, down the porch steps, and stopped abruptly behind us as we got in the car. My last glimpse of her standing alone as we left for our wedding ceremony was blurred by unexpected tears that welled up in my eyes.

I thought, *Mama, I wish I could tell you why, but I'm grown up now, and I am on my way."*

I left without looking back or waving goodbye.

Jay's voice was hoarse and raspy as he tried to croon love songs in my ear on the way to the courthouse where his boss had helped him arrange our wedding place. He held my hand and hummed most of the way, but the words, "You are the girl I am going to marry *TODAY*," came out bold and clear now and then.

I sat beside him feeling almost numb and wondering, *What will it be like?*

Finally, we stood before a judge and four witnesses (my brother Kenneth, my cousin Doyle, and their girlfriends) and pledged our vows "till death do us part." Before he pronounced us man and wife, and maybe even afterward, he prayed, and prayed, and kept praying. Over and over I heard him call my name and Jay's name out to God. He literally claimed our marriage all the way to heaven and I thought, *Maybe he is going to tell us how to get there.*

He ended his prayer by likening our marriage journey to a ship sailing on the Holy Sea of Matrimony, but he let us leave without a compass or an anchor.

AT HOME

Stumbling down the courthouse steps, almost blind with unshed tears, I held Jay's arm tightly as we made our way to the car. Speechless, he drove quickly the few blocks to our Mansion in the Sky and led me up the stairway to our new home. At the top of the stairway, he turned loose of my hand and hurried away to the bathroom. I got my first glimpse of the interior of our mansion as I stood there facing the open doors of our apartment. Whatever the owners had to do to make it ready to rent wasn't finished until the day before our wedding. Our bedroom suite was delivered and set up at the last minute, but Jay was sick with the flu plus an upset stomach and unable to supervise the procedure.

Startled, I looked out to rooms that overwhelmed one by their size and height—ceilings fifteen to twenty feet high and the tallest windows I'd ever seen in a house. Our bedroom suite with its modern 1930, low-cut design looked beautiful in the store window display, but appeared grotesquely small, like doll furniture, in its new surroundings. Musty, faded rose drapes covered the huge windows, and I drew back from touching them when a dust cloud erupted after I tried to fasten a tie-back.

I struggled to envision a better sight, but none appeared. Jay was in the bathroom so I couldn't wash my complexion, a nightly ritual since an early age. What could I do? Make the bed was my answer. Using my new sheets and the embroidered pillow cases with crocheted edging that Mama made me, I made our bed ready. I hurried into my gown and under the covers before Jay came in—but he stayed only for an instant and back to the bathroom he hurried.

Later, he appeared long enough to say, "I'd better sleep on the porch until I get to feeling better." All night I heard him going to the bathroom while I lay sleepless on our new bed.

Finally, morning came—Christmas Day. I reached for the housecoat Mama spent hours making to match my gown. One would have thought it was my wedding dress from the care she put in trying to make it beautiful. Wrapping myself in it, I ventured out to find Jay. He must have been raging with fever as he lay on the glider swing babbling apologies for being sick along with other words I couldn't understand. I wanted to call a doctor or get help, but he understood enough to say "No" with such feeling I was afraid to upset him and make him sicker than he was. Instead, I waited, hoping he would soon be well, and we could forget all about this.

He slept most of the day, and I had access to the bathroom. I washed my face, bathed, dressed, and suddenly I felt hungry. Mama always had my breakfast ready when she called me to get up, but I was on my own today.

Looking in the ice box I found eggs, ham, pork side meat (bacon), milk, and butter that Mama sent in the day before. Jay had brought coffee and other staple groceries. The cabinet was covered with fruit jars of vegetables, sacks of potatoes, turnips, onions, peanuts, and popcorn. I knew Daddy must have provided them. Seeing the reminder of home made me homesick, and I almost, but not quite, lost my appetite.

Breakfast was a big meal at Mama's house, but I'd never helped cook and didn't think I'd have to, or at least not so soon. Jay always said, "Don't worry. I know how to cook. I'll do it." But he wasn't able to cook today.

I put together the most ridiculous wedding breakfast that even I can imagine and sat alone eating it. (It remains a secret menu to this day.)

Being up, bathed, dressed, and fed made me feel better or at least curious about my surroundings. As I looked through some of our wedding gifts, the new radio caught my attention. I went back to bed and listened to Christmas carols most of the day. I pondered again, as I had each holiday season, *What is it about this day that the whole world celebrates?* I knew it was Jesus' birthday, but why was that such a big deal? I found no answer in what I heard and it continued to haunt me.

Jay felt better the second day, but he was too weak to stay up long at a time. I fed him my ridiculous meals—or tried to. He wasn't able to eat. He continued sleeping on the glider swing saying he would wait until he felt better before he joined me.

Boxes of our limited belongings cluttered the rooms, but I felt no inclination to unpack and begin setting up housekeeping. The third day I revived enough to explore every nook and cranny of our apartment space. A stack of books stashed away in one closet proved to be a gold mine for my sanity the next few days as I waited for Jay to heal.

My fertile imagination began picturing how these rooms and the people who owned them must have looked and lived. Had I been a writer, I would have spent my time well. Instead, my imagination did keep me occupied—a new bride waiting for her groom who was sleeping in an adjoining room.

MR. AND MRS. A. J. CURTIS, JR.

"Good morning, Mrs. Curtis. Happy New Year to you. I love you, Mrs. Curtis; wake up and love me, too." Jay crooned softly in my ear as he knelt beside the bed kissing the palm of my left hand and turning our wedding ring round and round on my finger. "Open your eyes and let me see you."

The perk-perk-perk of the percolator in the adjoining kitchen and the accompanying coffee aroma drifting into the bedroom had already signaled a wake-up call to me. But I lay still after Jay got up, not wanting to relinquish our wedding night to a new day.

"You called me 'Mrs. Curtis,'" I whispered before my eyes barely opened. "We've been married since Christmas Eve and this is the first time I've been called by my new name. I will have to get used to that—but I like the sound of it. Say it again."

"You want me to keep calling you Mrs. Curtis? It sounds good to me too, but let's let others do that. You are my wife—the wife I've wanted since the first day I saw you. You are mine, not like the judge said 'till death do us part,' but forever."

"Look at me, Ann. I want to see what your eyes tell me today. I'm so ashamed of being sick—the doctor told me to stay in bed and wait to get married. He said I might be sick a week or longer but I said, 'Give me something to stay on my feet and I'll make it.' I never dreamed I could ever get too sick to kiss you, Ann. No wonder you said you were lonesome and wanted to go see your mother by the middle of the week, and I was too sick to take you."

He sounded so embarrassed I opened wide my eyes, touched his full kissable lips with my index finger, and said, "Jay, I needed that week before I actually became your wife. You can't imagine how scared I was to get in the bed that first night. I didn't know it, but I still had my stockings on when I slid under the covers. Sometime during the night the garters began pinching my legs before I realized what I'd done. But after several nights alone, I wasn't scared and began getting anxious for you to be well again, and last night you were. We really are Mr. and Mrs. A. J. Curtis now, aren't we?"

"Well, I didn't need a week to get ready to sleep with you, Ann. I've waited four years, but you are worth waiting for. You are mine now, and I'll love you forever and ever . . ." his words faded away as his lips touched mine.

Slipping back in the bed beside me, he crooned:

It's New Years Day.
Let's keep on sleeping.
The coffee can stay.
We've waited too long.

Drawing me close to him, he continued to croon:

Let's start the day now.
Instead of good morning, Mrs. Curtis—
Good night, Ann, my wife.

"Good night, Jay, my husband," I answered, "and I don't have on my stockings."

NEW YEAR'S DAY—LATER

I woke up mid-morning when hunger pains popped my eyes wide open. Arousing Jay from his deep slumber I called out, "I'm hungry."

Shaking his head and rubbing his eyes, he responded in like manner, "Me, too."

"Let's go see Mama. It's New Year's Day—she will cook a big dinner."

Both of us bounced out of bed with Jay saying, "And we can eat supper with my Mama—whew, I need some real food." (Nothing more was said about my ridiculous menus.)

"Let's wear our wedding clothes, Jay."

"And you wear your flowers again, Ann. I put them in the ice box that night I was so sick. You laid them on the cabinet. They still look good—go see them."

Why didn't I throw them away? flashed in my mind. *I wouldn't have to mess up my professional look by pinning them on my beautiful tailored suit. Oh, well, Mama will think they're pretty.* We quickly dressed and went merrily on our way to Mama's house with Jay crooning a new song all the way.

Mama rushed out to meet us at the back door almost hugging me as she ushered us to the kitchen. Daddy was already seated at the well-laden table and he stood up to greet us. "Well, you did come. I asked Annie why she cooked all this food for just the two of us, and she said you would be here."

Before we were seated Aunt Fletcher, Uncle Glenville, Glenville M^c, and Kenneth came in the front door, and soon the table was full as we all sat down to eat. Daddy always asked Aunt Fletcher to bless the food when she ate with us. It seemed fitting to me that on this special day God wasn't left out.

Well fed and feeling good after celebrating the day eating dinner at Mama's house and later supper with Jay's parents, we started home—our home. When we drove in the driveway, suddenly the sight of it took on a new picture in my mind.

Jay took my arm and escorted me up the stairway as though he owned the whole house. His mood was contagious. I felt like the wife of a prominent judge instead of a "wanna be" one myself.

The large rooms with high ceilings and huge windows began to reflect majesty in my eyes. The once elegant drapes were now musty and faded with age. When pulled back, they revealed a beautiful panoramic view of downtown Little Rock with the state capitol dome as a centerpiece.

Jay found a broom and mop in a kitchen closet saying, "I'll clean this place up. Give me a few days and I'll have these rooms as clean as Mama's house." And he went to work sweeping and mopping.

Later, closing the drapes for the night, he said, "I'll take these down tomorrow and hang them on the clothesline out back. They will get such a beating and shaking there won't be a speck of dust on them. And Mama says there's nothing like sunshine and fresh air to make things smell good."

"If you get this place as clean as your mother's house, it will sparkle," I answered, thinking that my mother was known for her cooking and hospitality, but not for a sparkling clean house. Daddy had a rule: Everything has a place, so put everything in its place. What Daddy wanted, Daddy got if Mama could get it; so there was order in her house, if it was not dust free.

Immediately, I thought, *Jay and I make a good household team—he likes to clean, and I like to organize and put things in order*. With that resolved I couldn't wait to start making Jay's mansion our home, and I began putting things in place. Wedding showers, as did everything else in those days, reflected the Great Depression. Almost every gift we received was lovingly handmade—quilts, bedspreads, pillows and feather beds stuffed with goose down, pillow cases, towels, pot holders, crocheted or embroidered scarves of all sizes, jelly and jam. An iron, a radio, and a toaster comprised our electric appliances.

After doing all we could do for the first day, Jay said, "Not bad, is it? It's looking better all the time, but let's go to bed now. We have two more days to work on it before we go back to work."

Not saying it, but looking it over I thought, *This must be a far cry from how these rooms once looked.*

Even as I thought it, I caught a glimpse of a future home Jay and I would someday have when he would buy a generator shop and I became a judge—this was just our first installment.

But then we were Mr. and Mrs. A. J. Curtis, newlyweds, happily living in our first home—Mansion in the Sky.

8

Change of Plans

The holidays ended abruptly and work days began. We faced the challenge joyfully and began our pilgrimage hand in hand, almost skipping down the stairway on our way to work each day. We had a plan, not just in our minds, but carefully listed on paper that would allow me to enroll in the fall semester of college.

I was already taking non-credit courses three days a week at Peabody School. These were tuition-free. But this was not college; it was training me to qualify for a better job to help pay my way to college.

Jay got home before I did on the days I went to class and had our supper ready when I came up the stairway hungry and anxious to eat and be with him. On the other days we happily prepared our supper together, and I slowly learned how to cook.

Both our pay checks were budgeted to the penny, and using Daddy's method of keeping account we knew at a glance how much money we had. Watching our savings grow each week was more exhilarating than any recreation we could have found. It prompted us to figure ways to not spend money instead of how to spend it.

Six dollars a week covered our groceries and household supplies. We didn't budget entertainment—we already had that. We were in love and had each other—movies couldn't show us anything we didn't already have. Jay made good sandwiches and the Shack didn't tempt us with its barbecue. His boss gave him a *rolling machine* that made the cigarettes we smoked. On weekends he slipped a package of Camels and a Snickers bar in my pocket. Each time we found a way to save another dollar thrilled us more than spending one ever had.

Saturday noon found us headed for our parents' houses where we stayed till late Sunday. Eating their good food, enjoying their loving company, and going home with our car laden with enough farm food to feed us another week was the peak of our entertainment.

Daddy picked up on our thrifty lifestyle and beamed with pride in us. He had no idea what was prompting it and assumed it was to get our feet on solid ground financially. Land was his gauge to determine that goal. He offered to deed us a choice acre of his priceless land facing West Twelfth Street as a future building site. He pointed out a corner plot that had fascinated me as a child. Along the outer edge crystal rocks sparkled like diamonds—especially after a hard rain. Grandpa had helped me unearth them after heavy rains washed the top dirt away, exposing large crystal rocks buried beneath the surface soil. We selected the most beautiful rocks and carried them home for Mama to use in her flower beds.

My heart was touched by Daddy's remembering my childhood and offering the corner to me now as a gift. *I wish I could tell you, Daddy, about the Mansion in the Sky we will one day own. Maybe we will build it right on that plot,* I thought.

But for now, only Jay and I knew. Two people, deeply in love, with one purpose and one goal—it seemed nothing could stop us; we were on our way.

THE TONGUE IS A FIRE . . . (JAMES 3:6)

From December till May, except for Hitler and war clouds overseas that weren't apt to affect us with an ocean separating our shores, Jay and I didn't know of a problem that we didn't plan to solve. We sailed along on our "Sea of Matrimony" (as the judge described it) in heavenly bliss.

Then Mother's Day came. A schoolmate and her husband stopped in to see me at Mama's house. They married in December as Jay and I had, and she took me aside for girl talk. She confided, "Ann, we're going to have a baby—I never expected one so soon, maybe in a year or so, but not a few months. How do you feel about having babies?"

"I don't intend to, not for at least five years," I confidently answered.

"But we didn't intend to either, so what if. . ."

I interrupted, "Jay takes care of that, and he promised me it won't happen."

"Ask him to tell Jerry his secret as we sure don't want to have another one next year like my mother did. She had a baby every other year until she had five."

Later that night I stopped Jay in the middle of a loving kiss and asked, "Are you real sure we won't have babies until we plan to?"

"As sure as rain," he confidently answered. "Well, you know there's only one way to be sure, but my boss said I could be ninety eight per cent sure. That's good enough for me. Is it for you?"

"If you say so," I replied and accepted it as *gospel truth.* Somewhere I had heard that phrase as being a sure thing. Anyway, I relaxed in our good fortune as I thought of Mary and Jerry.

That was May, and by the first of June I had reason to wonder, but I told myself, *I can't be. There's no way we can have a baby now, or even in the next five years.*

I called out to God fully expecting Him to rescue me as he had my Daddy when he thought he could lose his life's treasure—his land. I asked Him to pay Daddy's taxes, and He made it possible. If He could do that, I reasoned, He can wait on giving me babies until the treasure of my life is won. I expected to see a sign every morning that He had. There was none.

I couldn't tell Jay my misgivings, as to voice them would make it seem true. Instead, I kept it to myself, and it must have changed my whole personality. Jay was distraught saying, "Ann, what have I done? Tell me. You don't want me to even touch you. Tell me what I did. Let me make it right. I will, I promise I will."

"There's nothing wrong with me," I vehemently denied, "nothing. I don't know what you're talking about."

This continued for the whole month of June. Our happy supper times together disappeared. I made excuses for not eating, saying I was tired after a long day at work, or I had a headache.

Jay didn't know what to do with me, but he kept trying to find an answer to my sudden transformation. "Ann, I'm sorry. I should have known better. Having you is all I need, but you need more than me. Let's change our budget and give you some money to spend. We both need to spend some—let's do something together tonight—go to a movie, eat barbecue at the Shack—have fun like we did before we were married. Come on."

The thought of eating barbecue sent me reeling to the bathroom. It was down the hall or he would have heard the regurgitating sounds that surely would have alerted him to my problem.

I returned later saying, "I don't feel good," and hurried to bed pulling the covers over my head.

July came and Jay tried to cheer me by making plans for the July Fourth fireworks display. We were both fervently patriotic, and he thought I would respond to the excitement of the celebration.

"Are you ready, Ann?" he asked when it was time to leave. "Let's leave early and get a parking space close enough to see the 'rocket's red glare and the bombs bursting in air,' " he gaily sang to me.

Sobbing uncontrollably, I rushed out of the bedroom and lashed out at Jay with a fury that must have come right out of hell (. . . it [the tongue] is set on fire of hell. James 3:6). "Jay, how could you do this to me? I'm going to have a baby."

If I had shoved a pistol in his face, he wouldn't have looked more shocked; if I had pulled the trigger, it wouldn't have hurt him more than my words did. His expression jolted me back to my senses. I ran to him and clung helplessly to his embrace sobbing, "How could I say that to you, Jay, when you love me enough to give me the moon if you could? How could I?"

He needed comforting more than I did at that moment, and we hurt together. All day we stayed home hurting and there was no *balm of Gilead* (a Biblical reference to a healing ointment) to soothe our pain—nothing but our love for each other. At last Jay shared the problem with me and we were one again; no, we were three. Finally, whimpering like a hurt puppy, I asked, "What can we do, Jay?"

Jay responded with more assurance than he probably felt. "Ann, we'll make it. Let's include a baby in our plans. It will slow us up, but it won't stop us."

But I knew even at that moment, I couldn't do both. I had counted the cost when I made becoming a lawyer and pursuing social justice my life's goal. I pursued it willing to give up marriage, having babies—whatever it took to accomplish it. Only when Jay was ready to make it his goal with me did I consider marriage. It was more than a childhood dream; it was an obsession that had filled my secret thoughts and plans all through my school days. To be deprived of it at this stage was a life-crushing blow, and I literally fell beneath the load.

MOM AND DAD

"Ann, it's Sunday morning; let's get up and go see your folks. You haven't seen them in at least three weeks. They must be wondering about us. Have you told your mother?"

I snuggled close to him, and feeling the first relief I'd had since my apprehension of a possible baby, I wanted to stay in the security of his loving arms and never get up.

"No, I haven't told her, but I think she knows. Mothers seem to know things about us before anyone else sees or suspects. Was your mother that way?"

"I guess so. We used to say she had eyes in the back of her head."

"Mama told me after my graduation I'd soon be marrying and having babies, but I wasn't supposed to do that, was I?"

"You may never believe me again, Ann. I honestly thought we were safe. I guess the only sure way is to stay single." Struggling to speak, he continued, "But we are married now. I can't give you up, Ann—what can we do?"

"We will have this baby. I will go to college, get a good job, and you will some day own a generator shop." My words sounded more optimistic than I felt, but saying them bolstered my courage.

"If you'll cook breakfast, I'll get ready, and let's get out of this house for the day."

He didn't need further prompting and soon we were dressed, eating breakfast together—a subdued, but still newlywed couple.

"Come along with me, Lucille, in my merry Oldsmobile," Jay crooned a popular jingle as we rolled along West Twelfth Street Pike on our way to Mama's house.

"I'm not Lucille, and this isn't an Oldsmobile," I bantered.

He laughingly answered, "Nobody knows the difference, but us."

Mama had that *I know what you've been up to* look and as soon as dinner was over and the men scattered, I told her.

"I knew it, Ann; I could see it on your face. When is it due?"

"January, Mama, and I don't know what we'll do with a baby."

"Oh, don't worry about that," she interrupted. "Babies have their own way of doing, and we just fit in their plans."

"That's the problem, Mama—my fitting in the plan."

She patted my shoulder saying, "Don't worry, Ann. You'll be a good mother. It will be as easy as pie before you know it. You just wait and see."

I thought of her assuring me with those same words when I couldn't tie my shoes on my first day of school. I remembered how long it was before it came easy to me. But calling me a good mother jump-started my thinking motor. Until then I had thought of a baby as upsetting my life goal. Suddenly I realized, *I am a mother. This baby is Jay's and mine, even if it isn't on our time schedule.*

Our way had come to a fork in the road. Instead of just Jay and Ann, like it or not, we were Mom and Dad, and that put us on a whole new highway.

DOCTOR'S VISIT

"Mama said I need to see a doctor. That sounds awful. I never have been examined by a doctor—a man."

"But you have to, Ann. Let me check and find a good one. I'm glad we have money saved and that hospital insurance policy I took out right after we married will come in handy now. Remember, we wondered if we could afford it, and my boss said we couldn't afford not to. He's been right about some things."

That was on our way home from Mama's house and at the end of the next day Jay said he had an appointment with Dr. Strauss to see me on Wednesday at 4:30 p.m.

I forced myself to go thinking, *Mama let a strange man examine her, and if she could tolerate it, I guess I can.*

"Honey, what's your problem?" the kindly doctor asked, patting my arm as I lay shivering on the examining table.

He looked like a good Daddy and I felt easier as I answered, "I'm going to have a baby, and I want to know how I can be married and keep from having babies."

"Well, let's take that one at a time. First, let's see if you really are having a baby. Then we'll talk about the other."

Later, he agreed that I diagnosed it right and said, "After the baby comes, I'll show you another way. There is a means now that is practically foolproof. I can fit you with one."

"Do it today," I interrupted. "That's what I want. Don't wait. One baby is all we can manage now."

"Honey, you don't have to worry about another baby until this one is born."

"Are you real sure?" I hesitantly asked.

"I can stake my life on it," he stated solemnly as though I had asked a logical question.

I liked him immediately and left his office thinking, *We won't have to worry about that till January, and then he will tell us what to do.* Foolproof sounded a lot better than the ninety eight per cent sure.

Jay was waiting for me when I left the doctor's office. "What did he say? Are we really going to have a baby?"

"Yes. And he knows more about having babies than your boss does. He's going to fit me with something that he says is foolproof. But I won't need it until after the baby is born."

"Let's celebrate, Ann, and have fun again. Can you eat a barbecue sandwich at the Shack tonight?"

"I feel like I could eat a dozen—let's go." And away we went.

A NEW NEST

October came, the beginning of my favorite season of the year. I was six months pregnant, feeling good, and looking forward to a newborn baby in January. Mama began sewing baby clothes as soon as she knew one was coming.

"I believe it's a girl—from the way you are carrying it," she predicted, and she made nearly everything pink. "I'll make some white just in case it's a boy." Her crocheted pink bootees reminded me of the blue ones she made for my baby brother— and he was buried in them. I shivered at the memory.

"What are you naming her?" she asked. I hesitated a moment. We hadn't given any thought to that, but the morning newspaper showed a picture of a popular singer named Brenda Lee. I thought when I saw it, *I like that name, and maybe our baby will sing.*

Without further thought I answered, "Her name is Brenda Lee Curtis."

On our way home from Mama's house I told Jay, "I named our baby today. She is Brenda Lee Curtis and one day maybe she will sing like you do—only she will sing for the whole wide world to hear."

He was pleased, but he teasingly asked, "What if 'she' is a boy?"

"Mama doesn't think so and she knows things like that. She thinks we need to move downstairs before the baby comes. She says carrying diapers downstairs every day to hang on the clothesline in the back yard and leaving the baby upstairs is not a good idea. What do you think?"

"I think she's right. I'll see what I can find. But are you sure you want to leave our Mansion in the Sky?"

"It's really not ours—we'll have one that's ours one day. It will be Jay and Ann's Mansion in the Sky."

Jay began looking the next day, and before the week was over he found a place. He waited this time for me to see it before he rented it.

"Ann, you may not want to make this big a change; there's not nearly as much room as we have here. It's just two rooms, and we share the bath with an older couple who own the house. It costs twenty dollars a month, same as we pay here, but we don't pay the utilities so it will be cheaper. It's located right on the streetcar line, and when I use the car, you can go anywhere in Little Rock for six cents. Do you want to go see it?"

"It sounds way too small, but let's go see."

I liked the looks of the house and the well-kept lawn as we drove in the driveway. A motherly woman answered our knock saying, "I hope you like this apartment. We never have rented before, but our daughter married and moved out of state. We live in this big house all by ourselves so we made two apartments out of part of it. Let me show you the one I like best."

I liked it immediately—the rooms were small compared to ours, but big enough and beautifully arranged. Our bedroom suite would fit perfectly in the décor. Everything else was furnished—comfortable chairs, end table, lamps. It had a modern kitchen, and the drapes and carpet were clean, as well as attractive.

A large nice bathroom opened off our apartment and she assured me they would leave its use mostly to us. Their telephone was available, and a clothesline stretched across the back yard entrance.

"Do you rent to babies?" I asked.

"Oh yes, we would love to have a baby in the house again."

"I want it—when can we move in?"

"Anytime you're ready," she replied.

"We can move in Saturday," I answered, and my mind began setting up a whole new schedule as we headed home.

"Jay, I'm going to cancel my after-work classes this week, and I'll turn in my resignation at work to be effective January 1. We'll move in our new home Saturday and be ready to have our baby daughter, Brenda Lee."

He grinned, and reminded me again, "What if she's a boy?"

I answered, "We'll name him Jay Kendall Curtis. After J. Kendall Hoggard gave me a second chance in Junior High I had secretly promised myself, *If I ever have a son, I'll name him for Mr. Hoggard.*

Boy or girl, our baby received a name that day and automatically became more than a baby in my body; the baby was now an active and loving member of our family.

WAR CLOUDS

War clouds overseas erupted into bloody war and disturbed the American feeling of safety enough that a draft law was passed to conscript young men for military duty. Kenneth was single, working on his first job after finishing high school, and he soon received his call to service. That was a wake-up call to our family that we might be affected by the war across the ocean.

Pearl Harbor came on December 7, 1941—a month before our baby was due. Our security vanished. In later years I tried to describe how shocked and frightened we were when the attack suddenly happened and plunged us into a bloody war overnight, but I could find no words to convey its horror. Not until September 11, 2001—when terrorists struck us right on our homeland and threatened to wipe us out as a nation—did I see anything to compare to our fear then. The nation plunged into World War II with a fury to conquer our enemy.

Troops were sent into battle after short periods of training. Kenneth barely finished boot camp at Fort Leonard Wood, Missouri, when he was shipped out the middle of January 1942. We were not told his destination or the length of service (as long as needed). It was two months before we heard from him, and he was in the jungles of New Guinea where he remained two years and three months before he came home.

Daddy crumbled under the impact. Overnight he became a man with no hope, and the result was devastating. He repeated over and over again, "I'll never see my son again." Each time he said it, he became a weaker man right before my eyes. He read the war news from the battlefield and imagined all degrees of torture or dying Kenneth might be experiencing. He could not eat or sleep with ease.

Mama boldly declared, "I'll see him again," and went almost calmly about her usual lifestyle. She didn't tell us what she based it on, but I liked her response better than Daddy's, so I adopted hers for my own.

I asked God to bring my beloved brother back, but with little belief that He heard me since He didn't hear my plea to wait on giving me a baby. I thought, *I wish I knew how to pray.* On second thought I decided that maybe He gave me something better than what I asked for, and I wondered, *How can we know what He will do?*

News of Kenneth's departure came the week Brenda was born. A snow and ice storm closed down most of the traffic to and from Little Rock, but Mama got to St. Vincent Hospital soon after Brenda's birth. Jay was there, and the three of us greeted the most beautiful baby girl in the world, and I never questioned God's not delaying her birth again.

The baby and I stayed in the hospital ten days before we were discharged, and I had to learn to walk again after being bedfast for ten days. I wasn't allowed to set my feet on the floor even to go to the bathroom. We went to Mama's house from the hospital, and she took care of us for a week until I regained my strength. Finally, Jay and I took our new baby daughter home and tested our parenting skills—which we had to learn. All babies look innocent, but Brenda had an almost ethereal expression, and she bonded to me with cords of love I could not fathom. I accepted it as a natural response until she was three weeks old. I had finished bathing her that morning and when I picked her up to dress her, she looked at me with pleading eyes that seemed to say, "Help me." As I clasped her to my breast, I was aware again of a *Presence* that I had experienced only once before when I heard distinctly the words, "Help me," in my inner being. It was so real I answered aloud, "Whatever you need—I will help you."

9

Heart Problems

"Ann, you're making too much of this baby; you need to let go, and she'll soon work out her own schedule. Crying won't hurt her. Let her cry at night and she will finally go to sleep. You've got to get some rest. You look like you are walking in your sleep."

Jay interrupted Mama saying, "I've been telling her that, but she won't listen. Ann has our baby so spoiled that she won't even let me stay up with her at night and let Ann sleep."

That was after dinner at Mama's house, and that night the conversation continued at Jay's mother's supper table. Mrs. Curtis said she knew what would take care of that problem—that she used it on all six of her babies and it worked every time.

"Let me get my bottle of paregoric. Let's give her a few drops now, and she'll be sleeping by the time you get home. You and the baby will have the best night's rest you've had since you left the hospital."

Jay was all for it, and she began measuring the drops. Uneasily, I asked, "Are you real sure this is safe?"

"I know it is," she assured me and continued with the procedure. "Once she sleeps tonight, she will stay awake tomorrow. It's just a matter of getting her days and nights mixed up. Let her cry, Ann. Crying won't hurt her."

I didn't try to explain that it wasn't crying she did at night; it was a plaintive sound that echoed *help me* through every fiber of my being. I had no words to explain even to myself, much less to another what I meant.

Jay's mother was right. We did sleep all night without stirring. It was my first real rest in four weeks, and it was nearly 10 a.m. the next day when I woke up. I jumped out of bed sensing Jay wasn't beside me, and when I saw the clock, I knew he had left for work without disturbing our sleep. I made a pot of coffee and sat down with toast and cereal feeling more like myself than I'd felt since I became a mother.

Brenda was peacefully sleeping in her bassinet when I picked her up to bathe and dress her, but she didn't wake up when I handled her. Suddenly, I realized something was wrong. I knocked loudly on my landlady's door screaming, "Help me—hurry!"

She rushed in, took one look at Brenda, and said, "Call your doctor—give me the baby. Come on, use my phone," and we hurried back to her bedroom.

I called Dr. Strauss' office, and they first said he wasn't available—that he was with a patient. I said, "Tell him Ann Curtis needs him for my baby. He promised me when I left the hospital he would see her any time I needed him. Tell him I need him now!"

He was on the phone immediately, and when I told him the problem he said, "Get her here as soon as you can."

We put her in Mrs. Winters' car, and her husband exceeded the speed limit, driving as fast as his car would go, saying, "Maybe a cop will stop me and escort us the rest of the way." An ambulance couldn't have got us there any quicker.

Dr. Strauss took one look at her when we arrived and whisked her away, leaving me standing in the waiting room. About thirty minutes later he called me in, and I never had such a lecture as he gave me.

"Don't ever do this again, never. Not just paregoric, but anything. Don't give this baby anything unless I say so. Do you understand? Nothing. Another few minutes and it would have been too late. I told you I would take care of her when she needed it, and don't let anyone change your mind about that— are you hearing me?"

"Yes, sir, but what if you're busy when I need you?"

"Ask for my daughter who works in the front office or my son, an intern here. They know to get me."

I went home with another genie in my pocket, but not one I'd ever want to use. Mr. and Mrs. Winters puzzled on our way home at our good fortune in having a doctor who took such a personal interest in his patients—especially one who was Chief of Staff at St. Vincent Hospital and such a busy doctor. I didn't puzzle over his interest in Brenda. She was a special baby; why wouldn't he be interested? But I did puzzle over what made Brenda so fragile, and whatever others said, I knew she was.

I tried to ask Dr. Strauss about it, but I didn't know how to explain my fears. He seemed to understand, but he offered no explanation. He just patted my shoulder and tried to assure me saying, "Honey, I'll take good care of your baby, and you are, too. Don't listen to anyone else. We will do what's best for her."

Sure enough Mrs. Curtis' antidote broke the cycle. Apparently it did turn Brenda's days and nights around, and she continued to sleep at night. Jay and both grandmothers rejoiced saying, "I told you so." Mr. and Mrs. Winters were the only ones besides me who had misgivings about the paregoric effect on her.

I felt better after a few weeks of sleeping at night, and Jay continued to encourage me to plan our budget and time for me to go to college—but I had no heart for it. I had made a vow to my baby daughter that whatever she needed I would help her. It was binding to me, and somehow I knew it was going to take all I had or could become to fulfill it.

I felt secure in our small apartment. Brenda was never out of my sight while I was cooking, cleaning, washing diapers on a rub board, or doing all the work a baby required. Jay began to feel dissatisfied saying, "Ann, I don't mind living in such a small place if it helps get you in college, but if you've lost interest in that I can't stay in these two rooms forever."

Both our parents agreed with Jay about wanting a different place to live, but I asked for a little more time before we considered a move. Brenda did seem stronger as long as she stayed on a regular schedule: bathing, resting, and eating a balanced diet at the same time each day.

I tried to encourage Jay to go back to school instead of me, but he wouldn't consider it. His dropping out of high school was a subject he wouldn't discuss. During the Depression years it was usually the means of helping the family financially, and I assumed it was his reason.

"I know you can't now, but when this war is over, you can. Let's plan our budget for you . . ."

"Not me," Jay interrupted. "I like my work, and I don't want book work."

"I can help you catch up. I helped several boys who had dropped out, and they graduated when I did."

"Forget it, Ann. I am not going back to school," and I could see he meant it.

Brenda captured Jay's heart, but the change in me overshadowed our relationship in various ways that neither one of us understood. His once happy countenance changed to an almost perpetual frown. I was caught in the middle of the struggle, and I guess he was, too. Brenda was spared our silent conflict, and she basked in our love for her and was the only bright spot in our daily lives.

Summer came and Jay was still badgering me to go to college in the fall. A nearby junior college offered night classes, and he insisted I enroll and let him take care of Brenda. Everyone but me thought it was a good plan; I had no interest. I knew how much studying college would require, and I couldn't separate my time from Brenda both day and night. No one understood my reasoning, even I didn't.

MOVE TO KANIS HILL

I didn't realize the power of my newfound genie until an unexpected crisis arose. I was peacefully rocking and humming baby words to Brenda after getting Jay off to work. Mrs. Winters opened the door without knocking and shouted, "Call that doctor—call your doctor—something is wrong with Al (her husband)."

She handed me the phone after we rushed back in her bedroom, and I called Dr. Strauss. I gave the message to the girl at his front desk, and in a few minutes Dr. Strauss was on our doorstep.

"Where is the baby?" he asked when I opened the door, and then I knew what made him come—he thought it was for Brenda.

I took him in to Mr. Winters, but it was too late. He was dead. Later, Dr. Strauss followed me to my apartment and picked Brenda up and held her on his shoulder for several minutes, gently patting her back. I thought, *He loves her too, almost like Jay and I do.*

He patted my shoulder as he was leaving and said, "You're taking good care of her. Call me if you need me."

I felt comforted by his words, and I sensed he was more than my doctor—he was my friend. I needed one as I hadn't made any after I married.

Soon afterward, a newly-married couple rented the apartment adjacent to ours, and I immediately had a new found friend. Mary Ann adored Brenda, and she became a built-in babysitter. Brenda cuddled in her arms and purred like a kitten when she rocked her.

Mary Ann laughingly shared what she had told her husband Carrol after seeing Jay walk by their window on his way home from work soon after they moved there. Jay was frowning and had such a scowl on his face that she said, "I bet that man beats his wife." After she met Jay and saw what a gentle man he really was, she laughed at her first impression. But I thought, *What's happening to Jay and me that even strangers see we are not our true selves anymore?*

The months rolled into years—Brenda was two years old with no major problems except extreme weakness at times and a bluish tinge to her usual pink lips. Often I took her in to see Dr. Strauss who immediately worked her into his busy schedule. He always encouraged me, but didn't prescribe any treatment other than to tell me to bring her in any time I felt the need of it.

In the meantime Mary Ann and Carrol had their first baby, a delightful boy they named Danny. She made plans for him and Brenda to grow up like brother and sister. It wasn't long after his birth that she complained that Dr. Strauss didn't work him in when they needed him like he did Brenda. She teasingly wondered, "Maybe he has a crush on you, Ann."

Jay picked up on that and afterward said, "Ann, maybe that's why Dr. Strauss is so interested in our baby and keeps you coming in—maybe he wants to see you."

I interrupted before he could say more. I was furious at the very thought.

"Jay, how can you say that? Just because you like to look at me doesn't mean anyone else does."

Jay broke in shamefacedly, "I was just talking, Ann. I know better, but sometimes I don't know what to think or say."

"Well, just be sure you don't say that again," I snapped back at him.

Mary Ann and Carrol began planning to move out of their small apartment soon after Danny was born. Finally, Jay said, "Ann, we've got to have more room. I can't stay cooped up like this any longer."

I knew he was right, and I said, "Find something and we will move."

Carrol and Mary Ann moved in a small new house built on top of Kanis Hill just outside the city limits. They encouraged us to rent the one next to theirs. Each house sat on an acre of ground providing the outside space that the men needed, but they were very limited inside—three and a half rooms and no bath. Gas and electricity extended that far, but not water. It was unfurnished, and all we had was a bedroom suite. There was no carpeting, drapes—nothing to make it comfortable, and certainly not attractive. I quickly figured the basic furniture we would need to purchase, and there was not enough money left to buy the niceties our present apartment provided—comfortable chairs, attractive lamps, tables, drapes, carpet, modern kitchen and bath. I shuddered at the thought of no water in the house, but Jay assured me he would be take care of that.

With a heavy heart I agreed to the move. Jay never knew how heartbreaking it was for me to leave my cozy nest of an apartment, or he wouldn't have considered the move. Somehow I knew Jay was getting to a breaking point, and space might be a release for him.

The first year was better for Jay, and even Brenda improved. She had a puppy that she named Cookie which she petted and talked to for hours, and she had a playmate with Danny next door. I had Mary Ann for a friend, and I enjoyed brief moments of happiness. *Gone with the Wind* came to town, and we took Danny and Brenda and had a holiday. We packed a lunch (the movie lasted more than four hours) and took a bus into Little Rock, and I had a rare good time. We talked so much about the movie that Mama and Aunt Fletcher (two women who never went to movies—television was unknown) went the following week to see it. They came back star struck over Clark Gable and talked for days about the people as if they were real people they knew.

The summer after Brenda celebrated her third birthday she began having severe nose bleeds—so much so that we had to rush her to a hospital. Dr. Strauss wasn't as available after we moved out of town, and a different doctor saw her each time. They began referring her to specialists, and it was a continuous cycle of medical care and doctor bills. We managed to keep them paid, but no money above a bare living was left. Jay's frown grew more pronounced as he struggled with the expenses. I lost weight from my usual 120 pounds to 99 pounds.

Jay's salary was frozen at the generator shop during the war years. It was barely a living wage without medical bills, but each month the bills multiplied.

Jay and I agonized as we saw our precious daughter getting progressively weaker. Her grandmothers admitted she was *sickly*, as they called it, but predicted that she would outgrow it. Her nosebleeds were almost nightly by the time she was four. Then came the eventful day when what I had feared almost from her birth became a reality.

Hospital nurses were trying to draw blood and were unable to reach the vein in her arm. They called in an intern to help. She spoke in Spanish and by her tone quickly lost her patience in dealing with the problem. She reached for Brenda's foot to try that area, and Brenda screamed and kicked her soundly in the stomach. The intern's anger exploded as she said in English, "Why don't they leave her alone? She isn't going to live anyway," and out she went.

Jay and I stood dumbfounded at what she said, but not for long. I began to think on my feet—for the first time in four years. I went to the top administrator of the hospital and presented my case. Action began immediately and a conference of specialists was called. After a short meeting they explained their consensus to Jay and me: her heart had not properly closed at birth.

If Dr. Strauss knew about it before that day, he didn't acknowledge it.

Weakly, I asked, "What can we do?"

He advised, "Keep her under a pediatrician's care," and he suggested Dr. Briggs who was in the meeting.

"Will she live?" I asked.

"She has already lived longer than would be expected, so who knows, just keep on expecting her to."

Dr. Briggs looked me squarely in the eye saying, "We are learning more about this every year. I will work with you in caring for her, and if there is a breakthrough in treating it, we will be ready. Are you game?"

"I am," I promised.

Jay and I took our precious daughter home, and after putting her to bed that night we held each other, hurting together. Sharing it was a comforting pain compared to our four years of isolation. It was a short-lived comfort. The next day Jay didn't come home on time. Supper was cold when he staggered in the door.

"What's wrong with you, Jay? Have you been drinking?" I couldn't believe my eyes. "After all you've said about what drinking did to your family—Jay, how could you?"

"Not wine or booze, Ann. Just a beer or two—men do that all the time—even my boss thinks . . ." his voice trailed off as he slouched down in a chair at the table.

"I don't care what your boss thinks. Get yourself up and go wash before you go to bed," I retorted. As I cleared the table I thought for the first time in my life, *How much more can I take?*

UNITY RETURNS

I was up early the next morning after a sleepless night lying beside Jay who fell asleep by the time he landed in the bed. A drunken husband was a problem I had never considered happening. Jay was afraid to be in a room where drinks were served. He said that wine or whiskey was more dangerous than a rattlesnake, and that it would never be found in his house.

What made him do it? Sometime during the night I reasoned that his boss must have been trying to help him, and that was his way of reaching out to him.

I felt alone in struggling with the thought of what Brenda's immediate future might be, and I had no one reaching out to me—not even with a beer.

After drinking almost a pot of coffee I went in to rouse Jay, but he was reluctant in getting up even after he finally opened his eyes. The glimpse I got of his expression alerted me that he needed more help in this than I did. In my secret heart I had already faced the possibility of losing Brenda long before the doctor's diagnosis, but it came as a sudden shock to Jay and he couldn't handle it.

Later, he slumped down in his chair at the kitchen table and said without looking up, "What can I do, Ann, if I lose you and Brenda, too?"

"You haven't lost me, Jay, and when I've done all I can for Brenda—even if it isn't enough—we will make it together, and we will still have our Mansion in the Sky."

Before I could say more, he responded, "Then I can wait. I waited before, and I can do it again. Ann, I won't do this again. You can count on me."

He raised his head, and we ate our breakfast together not knowing what our future held, but united in thought and purpose. The power of unity gave us courage for the moment.

Oklahoma

Finally, I had an answer to what made Brenda so frail. Although my mother's heart had detected soon after her birth that she was fragile, no one acknowledged it until now. In the midst of others' shocked and saddened response to the doctor's diagnosis, I instead felt a power surging within me that stood me up and on my feet again—both mentally and physically.

I bonded with Dr. Briggs as he and his staff bonded with Brenda. Our goal was to keep her as physically well as possible to be ready if there was a breakthrough in surgery that would correct her heart defect.

Jay and I had a common goal again, and we pursued it with a passion—our daughter's life.

Medical bills drained us of money, and welfare was the only option available. Dr. Briggs cautiously asked us about that possibility, but when we heard the restrictions involved, we refused. She would be taken out of our care and responsibility and placed in Children's Hospital with visitors' privileges granted at limited times—two days a week.

Strengthened in our unity, Jay and I still faced almost insurmountable hurdles. We struggled with our budget and with seeing Brenda getting weaker even with the best care we could give.

I had read aloud to Brenda almost from birth, and she responded to Mother Goose with glee by the time she was a toddler. Fairy tales caught her fancy when she was three, and she cried with Bambi, but wanted to hear the story again and again. After we moved out of town a bookmobile came from the Little Rock library, and the best of children's books was accessible to us. I spent hours by her bedside or lying down alongside her, reading aloud until she closed her eyes in sleep.

School started, and I saw young mothers secretly wipe away tears from leaving their youngsters in another's care. I wept silently wishing Brenda could join them and wondered if she would ever be able to go to school.

Night after night she was now waking us calling out, "My nose is bleedin'." When she didn't, I found myself reaching across her bed that was pulled alongside ours and feeling her body to make sure she was still alive. I knew no prayer to say so I composed my own. All I knew was a creator God; I was convinced of that fact. I called out to Him saying, "You made the world. Can't you show doctors how to do heart surgery in time for Brenda to live? And teach us how to budget our money to pay the medical bills." I added "Amen" as I heard that always ended a prayer. That plea became an almost constant playback in my mind and heart during my waking moments.

Just before her sixth birthday the first surgery for congenital heart defects was performed in Baltimore, Maryland, and Dr. Briggs rejoiced as he told us the good news. He advised us to wait until more was learned and then plan to take her to Baltimore to see if she would qualify as a possible heart surgery candidate.

We were elated, and Jay began exploring a means of financing the trip. A way opened—Marie's husband worked for S.E. Evans Construction Company on a dirt moving project in Tulsa, Oklahoma. Homer could get Jay a job with them that paid more than four times his present wage. We immediately planned to move. We sold our few pieces of furniture, packed all our worldly possessions in our car, and on a hot July day drove away from everything familiar to begin a new lifestyle for all three of us.

Marie had a comfortable furnished apartment located for us, and we moved into it the first night we arrived. It seemed luxurious compared to our house on Kanis Hill that had no water, no bath, no comforts, and certainly no beauty. In comparison I suddenly wondered, *How did I survive four years in that house on Kanis Hill?*

A kindergarten school was next door to us, and the head teacher suggested I enroll Brenda at least part time. I was thrilled at the prospect and called Dr. Briggs for approval. He said to bring her in for examination the week before school began, and he would evaluate the situation.

Brenda and I took a bus to Little Rock the last week of August excited about seeing our family, as well as hopefully receiving clearance for Brenda to go to kindergarten. The change in her schedule and in her surroundings had caused an adverse effect on her general well being. I welcomed the thought of taking her home to bask in the love and attention of her grandparents and extended family. I needed it, too.

Our appointment with Dr. Briggs was within an hour of our arrival at the bus station. Brenda was taken into the examining room immediately, and within a few minutes Dr. Briggs called me in saying, "We must do something now. There's no time to wait." He called St. Vincent Hospital to arrange to admit a heart patient for surgery.

"A surgeon, Dr. Henry Hollenberg, is there who may be able to help us. He has been a part of the team in Baltimore who has done this procedure. It's our only hope at this point. Is your husband here?"

"No, but I can get him here by tomorrow."

I left his office and took a streetcar to the bus station to take a bus out to Mama's house. That was my intent when I boarded it, but sometime later the conductor came back where I was sitting. He tapped my shoulder and asked, "Lady, are you alright? You've made two trips on my route without getting off—where do you want to go?" I jolted to attention and thankfully I knew where I wanted to go, and when I told him he kindly assured me he would see that I got off at the right place.

Brenda sat quietly beside me, unaware of my turmoil as she looked forward to going to Grandma's house again. Finally, we got there. What had started as a joyful trip back home turned into a nightmare. I felt like I was walking and talking in a dream as I shared the news. Later, Daddy took me to call Jay and then to tell his parents.

Jay said in a choking voice, "I'll be there, Ann. I'll leave tonight as soon as I can see my boss. I'll be there." He could say no more.

Jay's mother was at a revival meeting in a small Baptist church nearby. I walked in and saw her sitting down front and started down the middle aisle toward her. A young evangelist, not much more than a teenager, was pleading, "If you want to be saved come—come to Jesus."

I suddenly turned and walked directly to the evangelist. I thought, *That must be the way to be saved—the way to go to heaven.*

He asked, "What is your sin?"

I didn't know which one he meant, and I answered, "I guess it's because I don't know Jesus."

He answered, "Until you know your sin, you can't be saved."

He may have thought I was drunk by my coming in late and marching right down the aisle. Whatever, he let me leave without taking my name or doing any follow up.

I took Mrs. Curtis' hand and whispered, "Brenda is worse—Jay is on his way home. Come, go with me."

As we left the church, I thought, *"What is the sin?" he asked,* and immediately my smoking seemed to be the answer. I vowed *I'll never smoke another cigarette.* I stopped cold turkey that very day—never to smoke again.

Nothing happened. I still didn't know how to go to heaven, except I learned that Jesus was the *WAY,* but no one told me how I could know him. I did feel a difference. There seemed a power in the name of Jesus that I couldn't explain. I pondered the thought in my secret heart and filed it away to pursue at another time.

HEART SURGERY

Dr. Hollenberg, a tall thin man with a shock of white hair, sat across from Brenda and me after we arrived at St. Vincent Hospital the next day. She sat looking up fearfully at him, but he didn't raise his eyes to her face as he said to me, "I am not ready to do this surgery. I watched one performed, and I helped with another. I can't give you any odds of success—you surely don't want me to do this, do you?"

"Dr. Briggs says she has no chance without it. This is at least a chance—yes, we want it done," I firmly replied.

He stood up and running his long fingers like a comb through his white hair, he almost accused me saying, "Do you see this white hair? It didn't come from years, but from patients I've had to take care of like this," and out he went.

Jay arrived by mid-afternoon, and we agreed to the surgery for the next day. I was still walking and functioning as if in a dream. Brenda was used to doctors and nurses shuffling her about, and as long as they didn't come with a needle to take blood, she was fairly calm.

Time came for the surgery, and a team came in to get her. They asked me to go with her and stay until she was sedated. I looked up when they said it, but I could not make myself move. I vowed soon after her birth I would help her, whatever she needed, and up to this point I had. But I could not take my daughter in to face a surgery that even the surgeon thought was doomed.

Jay detected my hopelessness, and he leaned over her bed holding out his arms saying, "Come, go with me, Brenda."

She threw up both arms for him to take her, maybe thinking he was taking her home—but with a trusting expression that turned my heart to Jell-O.

He gathered her up in his arms and followed the team down the hall to the operating room.

Soon after the doors closed behind them, Jay stumbled back out and almost collapsed by the time he got to me saying, "I couldn't stay, Ann. When they took her from me, I couldn't let her see what it did to me."

"But you took her, Jay, and I couldn't—at the end, I gave up," and we cried together with no balm of Gilead to calm our souls.

Friends and people from all over the area gathered around us. Some said, "We are praying," but I didn't hear anyone pray.

Finally, they cleared the hallway of people huddling together in small groups waiting for the outcome. Jay and I were left alone in the room from which they had taken her. We had no words; we just waited—afraid of answers, so we didn't ask questions.

Suddenly the whole atmosphere changed. They rolled Brenda in, and before any explanation we knew by their body language and triumphant manner the surgery was a success. Jay and I backed up out of their way and watched in amazement.

We didn't ask questions—not because we were afraid of the answers—we saw the answer. No one seemed to notice us being in the room until Dr. Briggs came in. One would have thought the three of us formed the team that did the surgery by his exuberance in explaining the outcome to Jay and me.

"It was just what I diagnosed from the beginning. I knew it was, but to actually see it, and then to see surgery correct it—we kept her well enough to survive, didn't we?"

He kept on marveling, and as he left he said, "When you take her home, she can go to school—do anything a six-year-old normally does . . ." his voice trailing off as if in wonder. Jay and I were just rejoicing that she was alive, and we were speechless, not knowing how to express our gratitude.

Brenda came alive right before our eyes. By the second day her skin, her hair, her eyes glowed with new life as blood from her heart now carried oxygen to all parts of her body.

Then the third day she suddenly stopped breathing. We were put out of the room, and doctors from all over the hospital rushed in. I stood outside her door, not knowing what to do. Two of Jay's friends from a nearby Assembly of God church were in the room when the commotion began. They were pushed out of the room, even as I was, but they knew what to do. They stepped aside out of the way of medical attendants hurrying in and fell to their knees. I heard them pray. Soon the doctors filed out saying, "Everything is fine."

It was enough explanation for me, and I didn't ask questions. I rejoiced, but I pondered in my heart thinking, *I wish I knew that prayer they prayed.* I had a written copy of the Lord's Prayer that we prayed in school, but it didn't fit a crisis like this one. I wondered what they said that God heard them. I filed the thought away to pursue later. The words of Dr. Briggs saying that Brenda could do what six-year-olds normally do—go to school, play, LIVE—echoed loudly in my ears and heart. If I had been an emotion-driven person, I would have literally danced with joy.

BRIGHT FUTURE

Hop—skip and jump! Do what every six-year-old automatically does came like marching orders, but we did more of that than Brenda. It came slowly and painfully for her as she ventured out in a world of youngsters who had had a lifetime experiencing all those things.

Jay and I literally came alive again, and we rejoiced in the midst of staggering circumstances. Jay lost his job when he came home for Brenda's surgery. The company hired another man to take his place, but promised Jay when that job was completed in several months they would hire him back for the next one. The insurance company cancelled coverage for Brenda after paying her hospitalization for the surgery.

But the generator shop where Jay formerly worked hired him back on a temporary basis, and we moved into a one-room efficiency apartment in downtown Little Rock to wait for his new job to open again. Both our parents, his and mine, welcomed us to live with them, but we preferred making our own way as long as possible. It did help tremendously to live close enough to enjoy their loving care while we waited it out.

I began immediately encouraging Brenda to use her new-found energy. A small corner store in full view of our upstairs apartment window provided an outlet to exercise her independence. I sent her several times a day to get small items, and each time she went out alone, she came back with more confidence. Without her knowing it I watched carefully her entire journey. One day I saw her suddenly stop—hesitantly skip, haltingly at first, and then pick up speed. It was the most beautiful sight I could behold, and I said aloud to God, "I know you did it, God. You cured her. Won't you send someone to tell us how to know Jesus?"

Whatever that young evangelist didn't do, he did give me my first clue to how to go to heaven when he called out, "If you want to be saved—come to Jesus."

After asking God to send a messenger, I expected someone to appear any moment to tell me the way to heaven. No one came.

Christmas came and we were still in our one-room apartment waiting for Jay's construction job to open. Jay and I were almost like newlyweds again. We enjoyed being together, and the lack of space was no big problem. We had a promising future, a living daughter to enjoy, a job soon to be available, and each other.

We spent the holidays with Mom and Dad. The war was over. The economy was good again. Kenneth was home. The pungent odor of fresh pine and cedar along with the beauty of holly, mistletoe, and red berries reflected Mama's fun-loving heart for the season. She prepared a bountiful meal: chicken and dressing with all the trimmings, pies, cake, and homemade candy. The house overflowed with family members and friends stopping in to celebrate. Life was worth living again. (Even before Fort Smith Mayor Ray Baker coined that phrase.)

Except for Daddy's frail health and Kenneth's recovering from traumatic war experiences, we seemed the same family that celebrated the Christmas season six years before.

We still didn't know Jesus—the one whose birthday we were celebrating, but we rejoiced in having each other.

DEBT-FREE

Daddy, ready to offer help when we needed it, kept a check on our financial needs all through Brenda's ordeal. His farm food practically fed us throughout the six years and made it possible for us to eke out a way through our other expenses.

When the call came in March that a job was open again for Jay, we were ready and eager to leave. Daddy asked us again if we had been able to pay our debts. I assured him we had, except for the $500 surgeon's fee, but we planned to make paying it our top priority after Jay went to work. Rather than let us leave with any unpaid debts, he counted out five one-hundred-dollar bills in my hand. Next to his land and his word, his credit rating was his most prized possession, and he must have wanted that for me.

With tear-filled eyes of gratitude I said, "Daddy, we will make paying you back the top priority in our budget."

We did. Beginning with Jay's first paycheck we set aside ten per cent each week, and before the year ended we had the $500 saved. The following Christmas we joyfully handed Daddy a $500 check.

10

Life Is Good

Similar to Okies going west during the Dust Bowl, we were Arkies going to Oklahoma with a vision of a whole new lifestyle.

Jay and I embraced each other and our almost resurrected six-year-old daughter, packed all our possessions in our car again, and headed west with a pioneer spirit surging through our bodies. Jay was going to a better-paying job, Brenda was going to school, and I was planning a budget that would include simple pleasures we had once taken for granted. Gratitude swelled up in our hearts that we didn't know how to express except in delightfully falling in love all over again.

We bounced along Highway 66 going west in Oklahoma—a joyful adventure for all three of us. Stopping leisurely along the way for a hamburger or an ice cream cone was a simple pleasure we didn't take for granted.

Looking for a place to live after Jay reported to his work site was fun. It wasn't hard to find an apartment that pleased me, as I compared them to the one-room efficiency we just left or the house on Kanis Hill we lived in for four years before that. By bedtime I found one we all three liked, and we unloaded our car, moved in our few belongings, and almost instantly it felt like home to us.

Brenda and I delighted in our new surroundings, and before the week was over I enrolled her in first grade, even though there were only nine weeks left in the school year. I thought it could serve as training for first grade next year. She loved her exposure to teachers, students, books, and the whole atmosphere. But when school started the following year, she was passed to second grade. I knew she wasn't ready, but I could not convince the teachers. They marveled at her vocabulary ability. I knew that came from countless hours of reading to her, but it didn't fill other gaps that first grade would provide.

A cycle began that kept Brenda struggling all through her school years. I home schooled evenings trying to fill in the missing gaps as we moved from one town to another with Jay's work. No one would put her back a grade. They indicated I was an over-protective mother, and since I had been accused of that before, I wondered if I was in this case. I didn't fight the battle of holding her back.

We faced numerous problems as we constantly moved, seldom staying more than a year, if that long, in one place. When one dirt moving project was completed, we moved to the next one—with the same company, but in a different locale. No problem seemed insurmountable to Jay and me as we had each other and a living daughter.

ANOTHER BABY

My sister Marie and her husband Homer were our family away from home, and I loved our time together. Their two beautiful and talented daughters, Pat and Ann, were close to Brenda's age, and they welcomed her in their activities: playing paper dolls, marbles, skating, and watching their new television. Brenda came home from their house wistfully wishing she had a sister. "I wish I had someone to fuss with," was her way of expressing loneliness.

"Mother, can you have a baby?" she finally asked. When I answered, she replied, "Why don't you?"

I began turning the thought around in my mind, and the more I considered it the stronger the urge grew to hold a healthy baby in my arms. I could think of no more delightful addition to our family.

Jay was hesitant saying, "I can't stand the thought of losing you, Ann. What if it happened again—the heart problem?"

We had good reason to wonder as my first cousin's son, the age of Brenda, had the same congenital defect. When Brenda's surgery was successful, their doctor advised it for him. He died in surgery. Then there was my baby brother who died soon after birth with apparently the same problem.

Somehow I had an assurance we could have a normal, healthy baby, and without any logical basis for my belief I convinced Jay we needed another baby.

A year passed with no sign of an approaching baby so I toyed with renewing my ambition to go to college. A way opened, and I walked right in it. We had just moved to Claremore, Oklahoma, on an eighteen month job. Brenda's school teacher was enrolling in night classes in Tulsa to further her education. She suggested I go with her and have her mother keep Brenda along with her daughter while we were gone three nights a week. Jay's work was always at night, so it fit our schedule perfectly. We were all three excited about the arrangement—Jay, that I was finally going to college; Brenda, to have a girlfriend three nights a week; and I, ecstatic with the thought of studying again.

Then the week I went to enroll I discovered I was pregnant. Oh, what a difference to my reaction from my first pregnancy. "We are having a baby," I reported to Jay and Brenda, and we practically danced with joy.

The nine months' pregnancy went smoothly until I was treated for a bladder infection with a newly discovered antibiotic. I lost hearing in my left ear before they took me off it. The doctor didn't attribute the hearing loss to the antibiotic, saying it was probably not a sudden loss (as I knew it was), but a gradual one I had failed to notice. Losing the hearing of even one ear is a severe handicap, but not one that is insurmountable, and I faced the challenge. I was fitted with a hearing aid, bone conductor type. After six weeks of frustration and no hearing, I opted to train myself to function with one ear—and I did.

Nine-year-old Brenda walked every step of the way with me during the pregnancy marveling at the thought of a baby sister or brother on the way. Mama thought I carried it like a girl—whatever that meant—and she crocheted pink booties that were Brenda's favorite reminder of a coming baby. Brenda named her *Debra* for her school friend and finally on June 20, 1950, I went to the hospital and had a gorgeous baby girl—pink as a rosebud and with beautiful auburn red hair. Then I remembered Grandma Nancy who had white hair when I knew her, but family said it was red when she was young.

If Brenda came into the world with a plaintive cry of "Help me!" that could barely be heard, Deborah (as her name was spelled on her birth certificate) came with a triumphant shout everyone could hear that echoed, "I can do it." That heralded the story of her life.

Nothing could have pleased Jay or me more than having a healthy, beautiful daughter who wanted to conquer the world, and Brenda immediately became her press agent. We were the happiest little family you could find anywhere as we basked in our good fortune.

Jay called her "Tweetie" until she was six weeks old. As he came up the stairs from a night's work, she responded to his call with her eyes wide open and smiling to greet him. He placed her in a rocking chair while he was eating breakfast and gently rocked the chair with his foot. What Debbie wanted, Debbie got, if either of us could get it for her. Love didn't spoil her; it made her more secure and confident.

Even as Brenda showed an early indication of struggling to reach her full potential, Debbie showed the opposite—going far beyond the accepted normal and seemingly reaching for the star. She could have been a prime candidate for one of the first astronauts who arrived in a later generation.

Debbie revealed an ear and memory for music that was phenomenal even before she learned to talk fluently. When she was no more than nine months old, a Samson and Delilah opera scene was playing on a radio program. When Delilah sang the love song, Debbie repeated it note by note for several lines after her. Neither Brenda nor I knew a note of music, but we knew a duplicate when we heard it, and we sat in awe—speechless at what we witnessed. We decided right then we had a genius in our family.

Jay beamed with pride when we told him he had a daughter who was a genius, but he wasn't impressed with her musical ability. He said, "Shucks, I can do that."

"But could you at nine months old?" I asked.

"I don't remember. You'll have to ask Mama," he laughingly replied.

I kept the radio tuned in to classical music hoping to hear Debbie do it again, but she showed no response.

I made a mental note to myself, *I must expose her to good musical training. If Jay had received that, there is no limit to where he might be today.*

Brenda began teaching Debbie everything she knew, and it wasn't long till Debbie wanted to teach us instead. Before she was three years old, her favorite game was bouncing a ball and singing a little tune: "Bouncy, bouncy, ball-ee. When my Daddy gets home, I'll teach him how to bounce."

The *terrible twos* didn't affect her. Instead of the "No" reply for which two-year-olds are famous, she smiled answering "Okay" when admonished—but continued to do whatever she was asked to stop. She could have been elected *Miss Congeniality* in any contest.

Jay was contented with construction work and with the paycheck he received each week. It was hard work and long hours, but the overtime pay added up to a good sized check that he delighted in spending on his little family. I purposely fit my life into being a construction worker's wife. It was not an easy life moving from one job to the next and not staying in one place long enough to feel any roots, but it gave me time and motive to major on my family.

Our whole schedule had to fit in the mold of Jay's working hours. He always worked the night shift as he serviced the big dirt moving machinery after it was closed down for the day. I began to look for ways to fill my time and interest on long nights alone after he went to work and the girls were in bed (no television then).

I explored the idea of sewing, and wished I had taken that Home Ec class back in high school. It would have prepared me for my present lifestyle more than my lawyer aspirations did. I confided my interest in a letter to Mama.

"Get you a sewing machine, Ann. Have Jay show you how to operate it. Buy as simple a pattern as you can find, follow the instructions, and you can do it. That's what I did," she wrote back.

I replied, "But your mother was a seamstress—she must have taught you."

"No, I was like you growing up—I had no interest in sewing, and by the time I wanted to sew, Mama was old (in her sixties), blind, and not able to teach me," Mom answered.

I took her advice. Jay and I went out and bought a Singer electric sewing machine (Mama's was a foot-operated treadle type). Jay enjoyed showing me how to use it. An attachment came with it to make buttonholes, and he loved to use it. Rather than teach me he said, "You do the sewing, and I'll be your buttonhole maker."

I bought a sun suit pattern in Debbie's size and began sewing. It was so much fun she soon had a whole sun suit wardrobe. I discovered a skirt and weskit pattern that seemed simple enough to try, and before long I was brave enough to make Brenda an outfit. That venture expanded to making their clothes all through their school days. It served as a creative outlet for me, saved me money, and kept me occupied and happy while being alone at night.

THE VISITOR

Brenda was six years old when I asked God to send someone to tell me how to know Jesus, but she was thirteen—seven years later—before one came. One almost did. I went to a Baptist church with the wife of one of the company employees, and her Sunday School teacher came with her later to visit me in my home. After visiting awhile she asked, "Tell me, Mrs. Curtis, about your spiritual condition; do you know Jesus?"

Before I could answer, my friend stood and took her arm saying, "We must go," and had her out the door.

Later she said to me, "I'm sorry, Ann. I didn't know she would embarrass you, or I wouldn't have asked her to come."

For several years I continued visiting churches, the ones closest to us as we moved from job to job. Church members welcomed us, pastors visited us. Some invited us to join their church, but none asked if we knew Jesus. They seemed to assume we did. Finally, I thought, *Something must be wrong with me, and going to church is not curing it.*

I quit going, but I continued sending the girls each Sunday. Brenda began soon after her surgery and continued faithfully each Sunday and loved every moment of it. She took Debbie with her as soon as she was old enough, and maybe even before. Debbie embarrassed her teenage sister by some of her antics. She came home furious her first Sunday in Sunday School saying, "Daddy, that teacher grabbed my pennies" (the money he had given her for an offering).

On other occasions she embarrassed me. Once a Sunday School teacher visited her, and after talking a few minutes she asked, "Are you foreign, Mrs. Curtis?"

Puzzled, I replied, "No, why do you ask?"

"Debbie says you can't read."

Before she could say more I asked, "Debbie, why on earth would you say such a thing?"

"You can't read my Sunday School lesson—you said so!" Debbie flared back at me.

I remembered. She came running in from Sunday School the week before while I was preparing our noon meal saying, "Read my lesson, Mother."

"I can't—go ask your Daddy," I answered.

In another town after Easter Sunday Debbie's teacher came to visit. She marveled at how well-dressed Debbie came each Sunday, and said, "She tells me her Daddy makes her little suits."

Again, I confronted Debbie, "Why did you say that?"

Before I could say more, she defiantly answered, "He does; he makes them. When I tried my Easter suit on he marked the buttonholes, and I saw him make them."

She guarded me like she was a Secret Service agent when we were out at night while her Daddy was working or when we moved to a new location. Once I was watching Brenda skate at a local skating rink, and a young man came and sat along side me. Debbie hurried up to me, took my hand, and led me away. She looked back over her shoulder, tossed her red ponytail up and down, and said, "Mother already has a Daddy!"

Over the years I heard elementary teachers say you could count on children telling the truth about their parents, but I thought, *Yes, as they understand the truth.* When Debbie thought she knew what she was saying, she could convince the severest skeptic.

IS THERE MORE?

Stanley E. Evans Construction Company was based in Fort Smith, Arkansas, and in between job assignments Jay was sent back to the home base to paint or repair the equipment. This prevented any layoff and loss of pay, but was difficult for a family with children in school. We learned to adjust.

In later years a young mother who was divorcing her husband came to me for counsel saying, "No one can live the life of a construction worker's wife and stay married."

I thought, *Yes, you can, if you make it your purpose.*

Doctors were my best friends as we moved about. On our first move to Fort Smith, Dr. Briggs recommended a pediatrician, Dr. Waddell, for Brenda's care. She soon understood our pattern of life, and she not only was Brenda's doctor, but mine and Debbie's, too. She called me her gypsy patient, and afterward when she heard my voice making my first call on arrival in Fort Smith for a short term layover she exclaimed, "Oh, my gypsies are back in town. When can I see you?"

Life was good, and I sensed there was more to be found if I could just find the way . . .

Ann visits the
family home place.

PART III

New Life

Ann and Jay find the way to heaven and the power of the shared gospel changes their lives completely.

11

A New Beginning

Our family life changed dramatically with a teenager in the house, but it was still enjoyable. We were back in Arkansas, but this time on a long-term job. S. E. Evans Construction Company contracted to build a water lake for the city of Fort Smith, and we joyfully moved in to stay for the eighteen-month job.

Jay was forty and I was nearly thirty-four—in the prime of our lives. Brenda was thirteen, involved in church and school activities, member of the marching junior high school band, and a Rainbow girl (Rainbow is a non-profit service organization for girls). Boys were beginning to notice her and her personality reflected a mutual response.

Debbie was five. Kindergarten was not part of the school system, and I was figuring our budget to see if we could enroll her in a private school. All four of us wanted a television set, and they were expensive in their early days. We took a vote on whether to send Debbie to kindergarten or buy a television. Both girls voted for kindergarten, and Jay and I followed suit. I was surprised, but proud of the girls' vote as I knew how much they wanted a television. By then, it seemed everyone we knew had one except us. Their choice showed wisdom beyond their years, and Brenda revealed a generous spirit in choosing education for her little sister rather than recreation for herself.

Lutheran churches were well known for having excellent school systems, so I chose their kindergarten for Debbie to attend. She was challenged to her utmost by their teaching. She came home each day rehearsing her newfound knowledge. Soon she said, "I'm writing a book, Mother," and proudly showed me its content—mostly pictures, but some new words as she learned to print them.

She detected her first glimpse of culture shock in being a construction worker's daughter and revealed it by saying, "Mother, don't open the car door so wide when Daddy comes after me at school—the other daddies wear suits instead of work clothes." I knew what she meant as most of the kindergarten pupils came from professional parents. We honored her request.

I made sure her school clothes were equal to any pupil and exceeding some. I bought yards of corduroy material in colors becoming to her—gold, brown, beige, and green—and sewed a complete wardrobe of skirts, weskits, and jackets in interchangeable colors and styles.

Debbie memorized Bible verses at kindergarten and recited them to us while we all ate lunch together each day. She introduced prayer to our household by thanking the Lord for our food before we ate. I listened carefully to the scriptures she memorized—Psalm 23, Lord's Prayer, Ten Commandments, and others—but none told me how to know Jesus.

SORROW

Life was good for our little family, and we were enjoying being back in Arkansas and close to our parents again. It was the week before Thanksgiving, and we were planning a big weekend trip to celebrate the holiday with them when a call came that shattered our plans: "Homer died!"

Homer was more than a brother-in-law to me. He was my friend, and I loved him like a brother. Visions of seeing my baby brother put in a freshly-dug grave and brown dirt shoveled on top of his tiny casket came instantly to my tear-blurred eyes. Death was a monster seeking to destroy me even as it had when I was ten years old and had no hope beyond the grave—the time when I buried my baby brother.

I wondered, *Did Homer know the way to heaven?* I trembled at the thought, *What if that were me, or Jay, or one of our girls? One day it will be, and dirt will cover our dead bodies even as it did my baby brother's years ago.* With that thought I more than trembled, I literally shook.

I thought of Marie and the trauma she must be experiencing. Hopefully, she had some answers to this that I didn't have. She joined a Baptist church a few years before, and I remembered expecting her to tell me how I could know the way to heaven. Instead, she said, "Ann, you need to go to church." I didn't say so, but I thought, *I've tried that and nothing happened.*

Homer was kept on the job in East Texas when Jay was sent to Fort Smith. It was there, Linden, Texas, where he died. When he had the heart attack, Marie called her pastor, and he talked to Homer in the hour before he died. Hearing that gave me hope and I was anxious to hear what he said. Later, her pastor, Brother Claude Martin, came to Homer's funeral which was in Cane Hill, and Lincoln, Arkansas, the area where Homer grew up. On his way to the funeral he traveled through Fort Smith and came by to see Jay and me. I don't recall any comfort he gave me. Facing the burial of a loved one when you have no hope beyond the grave is a devastating experience, and I was feeling the dregs of despair. Again, I was offered no balm of Gilead. He must have sensed I needed more than comfort.

But after the preacher officiating at the funeral completed his sermon, Brother Martin gave a short testimony of talking to Homer in the hour before his death.

Brother Martin said, "Homer, the doctors say you may not live through the night. I've talked to you about this before. You're a good man, Homer, but you're not good enough to go to heaven. If you live to be a hundred you'll never be good enough. You need a Savior. You need Jesus.

Homer asked him, "How?"

"Ask Him, Homer." *(For whosoever shall call upon the name of the Lord shall be saved.* Rom. 10:13)

A CHILD OF THE KING

On our way home from the funeral we were traveling down Highway 71, and on top of the scenic drive of Mt. Gaylor, surrounded by the beautiful Boston Mountains, Jay turned to me saying, "I've asked God for a lot of things—not out loud—but I asked. I asked for you, but I never have asked Jesus to save me from my sins, have you?"

I managed to whisper, "No."

"Let's ask Him now," Jay answered, and without stopping the car and looking out over God's beautiful creation, we both asked—out loud.

The way to heaven opened! Our sins were covered, all of them, the penalty paid in full by Jesus. We asked and gladly received His gift of eternal life and He instantly made us his children. *(But as many as received him, to them gave he power to become the sons of God, even to them that believe on his name.* John 1:12)

What a transformation—beginning as a farmer's daughter, then becoming a construction worker's wife, and now being a King's daughter!

I always knew I was *somebody,* and it must have shown in my bearing. Even in youth total strangers sometimes asked me, "Who do you think you are?"

I innocently answered, "Ann Thompson," not understanding what they implied.

But now I really was *somebody,* and since I finally met my heavenly Father, I wanted to *know* Him. I remembered preachers calling the Bible *God's Word,* so I thought that must be the way He would talk to me. I couldn't wait until I got home to get a Bible to hear what He would say.

Brenda and Debbie were in the car with us when we made our life-changing commitment, but they were asleep and didn't hear our conversation. Our exuberance woke them, and they rejoiced with us when we told them what happened to us.

Brenda instantly responded, "Now you will go to church with us, won't you, Mother? Will you go Sunday?"

"Go with me, Daddy," Debbie interrupted, "I'll show you where to go."

Jay and I discussed it and agreed that was our first step to make. I knew three things that I thought all saved people did: go to church, be baptized, and pay a tithe.

That must have come from Aunt Fletcher's Church of Christ background. She practiced more than that, but those three points were indelible in her doctrine. She was a godly woman, and it left its impression on me. She was my earliest role model except in one point; she thought God taught segregation of races—but with love.

FIRST DAY AT CHURCH

We left home weeping the morning of the funeral, but came back rejoicing with new life bubbling up in our bodies as well as our spirits.

Immediately, I began planning what Jay and I would wear to church the following Sunday. We each owned one good suit which we seldom wore, so I checked our shoes and accessories to make mentally certain we would be appropriately dressed. I knew First Methodist members dressed fashionably as I had observed them carefully as they got out of their cars when I took the girls to Sunday School there. Since Brenda and Debbie were already enrolled, I assumed we would make that our church home.

As soon as we got home, I went directly to the bookcase and pulled out the Bible. After fixing supper I eagerly began reading. Starting with Genesis, I continued reading night and day, stopping only for sleep at night and basic needs during the day. It challenged me far beyond anything I had encountered before, but I was determined to know Him, and not just about Him. I soon discovered this would be a lifetime assignment.

In the meantime I must tell everyone I see that Jesus saves— just like He saved me. People were like I was—wondering how it can be and no one sharing the Way—except maybe some preacher. By midnight I was reading where God told Moses, "Go tell Pharaoh," and an inner voice plainly said to me, *Go tell people what I've done for you, I can do for them.*

Sunday finally came and we were up and getting ready for our first Sunday as new born-again believers to go worship in His house. Jay was in the bathroom splashing cold water all over his face trying to wake up after a night's hard work on the job. The girls and I were putting finishing touches to our appearances when the telephone rang. It was a former neighbor, Raymond Moody, asking for Jay. He had heard about our experience after the funeral, and he called to invite us to come to his church, Grand Avenue Baptist. I told him we were going to our daughters' church, but later when Jay came to the phone, I heard him discussing it with Raymond. His final words were, "We'll meet you there in a few minutes."

He turned to us and said, "We are going to Grand Avenue Baptist Church. Raymond and Margie are meeting us there."

We were stunned, and Brenda was in tears. Debbie was happy her Daddy was going to church with her, and it failed to upset her. I was in such a jubilant mood that it seemed nothing could upset me again, and away we went with only Brenda grumbling as she said, "I'll go today, but after this I want my own church."

Raymond and Margie were waiting to meet us when we arrived. They introduced us right and left as we walked in the building, taking us right up to the pastor, Brother James Pleitz, and sharing with him how we were saved earlier in the week.

He immediately asked, "May I come by a few minutes to see you this afternoon?"

Pulling a scrap of paper out of his pocket, he jotted down our name and address asking, "Will three o'clock be convenient for you?"

We assured him it was, and he was knocking on our door at three o'clock sharp. He celebrated our victory in Jesus with us and instructed us in believer's baptism and welcomed us in church membership if that was our desire. Jay and I heartily agreed, and when he asked Brenda she said, "I have my own church," and abruptly left the room.

Later, she said she would go with us on Sunday evenings, but continue going to hers on Sunday mornings. She said, "Don't try to make a Baptist out of me—they don't believe in dancing and I dance at the Rainbow parties."

I assured her we wouldn't try to make her a Baptist, but that I would pray she would read her Bible and become a more dedicated believer.

After the pastor left Jay and I discussed the arrangements we made with him for church membership, and suddenly it flashed in my mind, *We will need to tithe.* I said, "Jay, maybe we better wait until after Christmas—there is no way we can give one tenth of your paycheck each week and have any money for Christmas shopping."

"I can't believe you would say that," he replied. "Tithe or no tithe—we are going to be baptized next Sunday."

"In that case, we will find a way to do both," I consented, and both girls looked relieved.

FAMILY OF GOD

We felt bonded to the family of God at Grand Avenue Baptist Church on our first day to visit there, but the following Sunday we planned to become officially a part of them through baptism and church membership. Jay and I approached it with awe and wonder akin in a mysterious way to our wedding day—a fork in the highway of life.

Jay opened the car door for Debbie and me when we arrived, and I felt a jab of loneliness without Brenda stepping out with us on this momentous day. True to her word she went to her church instead. The jab was fleeting, and it seemed I'd never have another unhappy time in my newfound life.

As we walked toward the church entrance, Mrs. Gardner greeted me saying, "I hear you are being baptized tonight—may I invite you to come help me in Sunday School? I am director of the six-year-old children's department."

I was surprised at her request, but quickly assessed the situation. I thought, *Even if I know little about the Bible and have just met the Author, surely I can help take care of children.* I readily agreed. She took Jay and Debbie to their respective departments before we went to hers. The children hadn't arrived and I looked out on a large well-ordered and inviting room. Interest cubicles circled the outer area with the Bible teaching center as the focal point. She explained, "I teach the entire group here from an open Bible and on a six-year-old level. I use the flannel board to illustrate the teaching."

"You will be assigned a housekeeping unit," she said, taking me to a miniature, but fully-equipped kitchen and dining area with a table and seven chairs for six little girls and their teacher.

Handing me a card with the names and addresses of six youngsters inscribed she said, "You will be responsible for visiting in the home of each child and determining the spiritual condition of the parents. Bring your report back to me, and I will do any follow-up that is needed. Begin with one or two a week. Can you do that?"

This sounded like much more than I anticipated in taking care of children, but before I could answer the girls came in and she introduced me to them as their new teacher. They immediately began cooking a play dinner. Some cooked, others set the table, and I marveled. When they announced dinner was ready, they treated me as their guest. I was placed at the head of the table with six little girls seated around me with heads bowed and one said, "Teacher, ask the blessing."

What do I say? I frantically wondered and instantly Debbie's simple prayer of thanksgiving for food came to my mind. I repeated word for word what I had heard her say since she started to kindergarten, and I meant every word of it as I said it to my Father in heaven. The girls chorused, "Amen" at the end, and I felt comfortable being their teacher in the housekeeping department.

Later, I was a pupil alongside them when we moved to the Bible Teaching Center. Mrs. Gardner knew the Lord, studied His Word, and taught with authority—not Bible stories, but Bible truths.

Jay and Debbie met me after the Sunday School hour looking as happy as I felt, and we went together into the sanctuary for the worship service.

Pastor Pleitz explained to us the week before that the Bible said born-again believers are to confess before men their salvation and to be baptized. In baptism we publicly identify with how Jesus died for our sin, was buried, and rose again. Jay and I were not only willing, but eager to obey. When the pastor invited people to come forward at the close of his sermon, Jay and I were among the first ones going down the aisle to be introduced as new believers before a church family and for baptism that evening.

As we left the church later, Pastor Pleitz stood at the door shaking the hand of all who went out. After shaking Jay's hand, he reached in his pocket and pulled out a crumpled piece of paper with a name and address. Handing it to Jay, he asked, "Will you and Ann make a visit for me today? Go by this address and invite them to come to Training Union tonight."

Five-year-old Debbie stood by us looking up at him expectantly as if she wanted him to give her an assignment, and he quickly kissed her upturned face. For the next eighteen months we lived in Fort Smith, she was right beside us each Sunday as he shook our hands. She waited with an upturned face, ready for him to kiss her.

Jay and I made our first visit for our church that afternoon. We walked up to the door, and Jay boldly knocked. When a big jovial man appeared, Jay stepped back (he later said he felt tongue-tied) and left me standing right in front of him. The man greeted us warmly saying, "I believe I saw you dear people at church today. How good of you to come by . . ."

I interrupted by saying, "The pastor asked us to invite you to come to Training Union tonight."

He laughed and laughed, slapping his knee with each peal of laughter, saying, "He's my pastor too, and it sounds like he's been missing me on Sunday evening—I'm the Chairman of Deacons. I'll be there tonight. Can you come?"

We assured him we planned to come, and he was still laughing and slapping his knees when we left. We had no idea what was so funny, but we laughed with him.

BAPTISM

Coming home from church that night, I felt clean as a whistle, and I asked Jay, "I know that baptism water didn't wash my sins away, but don't you feel clean all over?"

"Do you feel it, too?" he answered. "I know my sins were paid for that day when I asked Him, but I don't know why I feel so clean either. Maybe we can ask Brother Pleitz." But it was years later before we heard the reason—it was the answer of a good conscience toward God. We had obeyed Him.

> *The like figure whereunto even baptism doth also now save us (not the putting away of the filth of the flesh, but the answer of a good conscience toward God,) by the resurrection of Jesus Christ* (1 Pet. 3:21).

While we were discussing the issue, Debbie piped up from the back seat, "When can I be baptized? I'm a Baptist now."

"I'm glad you are," Jay answered, "but it takes more than being a Baptist to have your sin paid for—when that happens, then you can be baptized."

Debbie turned to Brenda saying, "Your sins must not be paid for either. You haven't been baptized, have you?"

"You can be a Baptist if you want to, but I have my church," she answered, closing the subject for all of us.

FAMILY PRAYERS

The next day at lunch Debbie looked up when it was time for her to bless our food saying, "Daddy, you're a Baptist now. You say the blessing."

He looked as shocked as I had felt when my Sunday School girls asked me to pray the week before.

"No, not today, Debbie—becoming a Baptist didn't teach me everything. You go ahead."

But later, before he left for work, he said to me, "A man ought to be able to bless his family's food. Write me one and I'll start saying it."

I wrote a blessing before I went to bed and handed it to him the next morning as he started in the bathroom to shower before breakfast.

As we sat down to eat I said to Debbie, "Your daddy is going to say the blessing today." She smiled approvingly, and we all bowed our heads waiting expectantly to hear Jay's first public prayer. It seemed a full minute before he uttered a word, and when he did it was so jumbled and mixed up the girls giggled, and then all three of us laughed.

He stopped, looked up, and said, "I'll just say what I think," and he proceeded to thank the Lord for food, for his family, and for his salvation. When he stopped, he looked at each one of us saying, "Now you say what you think."

Thus began our daily prayer time as a family.

CHRISTMAS

We had our first real Christmas that year. We celebrated the earthly birth of Jesus coming into the world as a baby—being born in a manger, living a sinless life, and dying on a cross to pay the penalty for our sin. He was buried and rose again the third day. No wonder the whole world celebrates such an event. Now that I knew Him, the lights of the season shined like the stars, and the carols sounded like angels singing.

Jay and I worshiped our Savior with joy unspeakable and felt no loss in not exchanging gifts. Our tithing didn't alter the girls' gifts, and our house rang with joy and laughter.

A ninety-eight-cent cardboard nativity manger with miniature Joseph, Mary, and Baby Jesus cradled inside was the centerpiece of our decoration. Jay brought in fresh cedar, holly, and red berries from his job site along with a small tree for the girls to decorate. We stuffed a turkey and prepared a festive meal beginning a family custom.

After Christmas the cardboard manger was carefully packed away to be used year after year as we moved from town to town and from church to church following Jay's construction work. It continues to be the focal attraction nestled in the family Christmas tree each year reminding our children, grandchildren, and great-grandchildren of our first glorious celebration of the true meaning of Christmas.

SATAN

Satan reared his evil head in the midst of our Garden of Eden.

From November to January I wasn't aware of known sin in my life. It reminded me of *the genie in my pocket* of school days, except this was on a heavenly basis. It seemed as though He provided everything I asked; I was almost cautious to ask, for fear it wouldn't be what I needed (I might ask amiss).

I witnessed to people and some gladly received Him. All I knew to tell them was my personal testimony, and I ended it with, "What He did for me, He will do for you. Do you want to admit you need a Savior and ask Jesus to save you from your sins?" Some did.

Then totally unexpectedly I found myself exasperated over something so insignificant I can't recall the problem. I used a word that signified the dirtiest thing in a barnyard. Lest one think this came from being a farmer's daughter—not so. I never heard my daddy say that word, though he may have in the barnyard. As an adult when something was revolting and I wanted to express disgust, the word pictured the nastiest thing I could think of.

The moment it popped out I covered my mouth with shame. We were getting ready to leave for church on Sunday evening, and Jay stopped my tirade by saying, "It's time to go to church—let's go."

Instantly, I came to my senses, and thought, *I can't go in the Lord's house after what I said.* I covered my face with my hands saying, "I can't go."

Patting my shoulder, Jay said, "Aw, come on, Ann, you didn't mean it," but I felt dirty enough to contaminate my whole church family if I entered the door.

Jay then said, "Come on, girls, we'll go—your mother will come next time."

I was left alone with my guilt and shame. *How could a child of the King act like I just did?* I thought, *I am born again—a new creation, and I have shamed my heavenly Father—what do I do now?* I had not heard the promise in 1 John 1:9 *(If we confess our sins, he is faithful and just to forgive us our sins, and to cleanse us from all unrighteousness)*, so I just asked the mercy of God to forgive me.

After what seemed like an eternity, I heard our car pull in the driveway, and Debbie came bounding in the doorway exclaiming, "Brenda got her sins paid for tonight, and she's going to be baptized."

I rushed out to meet Jay and Brenda saying, "Debbie says you're saved, Brenda—and to think I wasn't there to witness it. Tell me . . . "

"She's a Baptist now, Mother," Debbie chimed in.

Jay rejoiced saying, "But best of all, she's saved and on her way to heaven."

I asked again, "Tell me, how it happened?" I knew it was Youth Revival week and a teenager was preaching. "What did he say?"

"He preached on hell," Debbie explained. "He named a lot of sins that I didn't do, but when he said 'liars,' I said, 'Jesus, I have lied and need a Savior.'"

"My Sunday School teacher in Linden told me Jesus loved me and that He died for the sin of the world, but I didn't know He died for my sin until tonight." Her face glowed with the glory of heaven as she told me.

I thought, *Oh, the grace of God! How can I ever thank Him enough? But there is one thing I will do—I'll rush to His house instead of staying home when I sin.*

I learned a bitter lesson that night. Even as a King's daughter, I was still a woman with clay feet and an unruly tongue—that I wanted to overcome.

"Help me, Lord," was my heartfelt plea. (That *dirty word* never surfaced again. It was gone—removed from my mind and heart forever, but the unruly tongue continued to be reined in again and again and again.)

12

Construction Worker's Wife

We were in an incubator at Grand Avenue Baptist Church for eighteen months, cradled in love, nurtured in the milk of the Word, and progressing to some meat when Jay's job was completed, and we had to move on. Jay was sent to Jacksonville, Arkansas, on a dirt-moving contract to build the Little Rock Air Force Base.

Leaving our church family was a wrench we hadn't encountered before as we moved from job to job, and I couldn't imagine ever finding another one like it—and I never did. I left thinking it was a perfect church, and the only imperfections I saw during the eighteen months I was a member there were my own.

We were thrust out of that cozy nest into a church family squabble at our next church home. A few months after we moved our membership there, the church body voted the pastor out during a business meeting. The accusations seemed flimsy and no evidence was presented. Before the vote I didn't know not to speak, and I held my hand up and asked, "Did the deacons unanimously agree to this?"

The chairman didn't answer my question, but he lectured me on my questioning his integrity in presenting the case. I remained silent, but I didn't vote. Two deacons said as we were leaving the building, "No, we didn't vote for this."

I was crushed spiritually and physically. Jay was working, and not with me to tell me what to do. Thankfully, I stayed quiet and asked the Lord to take care of it.

My heart ached for our pastor and his family. We had already bonded to him in the short time he was our pastor, especially after he baptized Debbie.

Soon after our move there Debbie had begun complaining with a stomach ache on Sunday night after church. The third time it occurred, Jay was off work for the night and was with us. I heard her sniffling after she went to bed, and I asked Jay, "Go see if you can tell what is wrong. She will tell you if it's something besides her stomach bothering her."

Later, he came out rejoicing saying, "Well, she finally got her sins paid for, and she's more than a Baptist now."

"Tell me, what did she say?" I asked. Debbie was up and part of the celebration by now.

"Daddy, do you have to tell her?"

"Yes, let's do—this is too good to keep. You know the pastor preached tonight on one day the sheep will be separated from the goats? She was crying saying, 'I'm not a sheep. I'm a goat.' Well, she's not any more—she's a sheep."

MOVE TO THE MISSION CHURCH

I went to church reluctantly when the next business meeting was scheduled, but it was conducted on a higher plane than the previous one. A new pastor was voted on, and the affirmative votes far exceeded the negative.

He came on the field with great enthusiasm, and I forgot about the previous turmoil in the church body. Then after a few weeks, he announced his resignation without giving a reason other than the Lord was moving him on. Several weeks elapsed before another vote brought a man to be our pastor. He stayed two weeks and resigned without giving a reason.

Jay and I wondered if we would have a pastor before we had to move again, and we prayed for guidance in what to do. First Baptist Church, Little Rock, had a mission church just out of Jacksonville, and we wondered if it could have a place for us to worship and serve. Both girls were happy in their Sunday School departments and didn't want to change. Jay and I said, "Let's go visit and see."

The pastor, Brother Boswell, greeted us with moist eyes saying, "I've heard about your zeal for reaching people, and I prayed most of last night asking God to send someone to help me here. I believe He has sent you dear people."

When the invitation was given Jay and I went forward to move our membership to the new church. Brenda and Debbie followed us, but with misgivings about leaving their former church. The turmoil in the church hadn't affected them, and it was not a subject we could discuss. It took some time for them to feel comfortable in a smaller church, but not for Jay and me.

Pastor Boswell was true to his word about asking for someone to help him reach people, and he assigned me enough names to visit that I was working full time on a voluntary basis, teaching an adult Sunday School class, and loving every day of it.

Rental property was scarce in what was then a small town, and we bought our first house at 213 Jones Street. It was the first house built in a new addition—small, compact, and ideal for us. The girls loved having a house of their own to call home. Once when we were looking for a place to rent a schoolmate asked Debbie, "Don't you have a home?"

She answered, "Yes, we have a home, but we don't have a house to put it in yet."

Mom and Dad were ecstatic; probably thinking it would keep us living there close to them. Daddy seemed to like everything about Jay, except I could tell he was disappointed that Jay didn't put a priority on owning a home. Daddy had lived in one place all his life, and he couldn't imagine the nomadic life we lived.

FAMILY TIES

When the dirt-moving project for the Little Rock air base was completed, Jay was sent again to Oklahoma. We rented our house to an Air Force family and left with it tugging at our heart strings. The girls were in tears as we pulled out of the driveway on our way again.

Several job assignments later the company won a bid for laying a waterline to Little Rock from Lake Maumelle, approximately 25 miles away. We moved back in our house at Jacksonville, and Brenda graduated from high school there. She met her husband, John O'Neal, and Brother Boswell married them in Berea Chapel.

The two stints Jay worked at Jacksonville gave us time to be with our parents and extended families again. From the day I received a new life I wanted it for my Mama and Daddy, and I went immediately to share it with them. Mama said she was saved when a teenager, but after marrying Daddy she waited for him to go to church with her. When I gave my testimony Daddy responded, "Well, I always thought you were pretty good." This fit his thought pattern—If a man lives as good as he knows how, it ought to be enough for God or anybody.

Jay's parents were already saved and members of a Primitive Baptist Church. They believed so strongly in the doctrine of predestination that they didn't dare witness to another—not even their own children. His mother was such a godly woman that if a life could show another how to be saved, hers would have. But, alas, that wasn't the case. Jay had to *hear* the gospel, and another person had to *tell* him how he could receive the Gift.

Mama moved her membership to a local church and began growing spiritually overnight. I welcomed living close to them and fully expected Daddy to respond to the power of the shared gospel as I had seen many others do; however, he saw no need of a savior.

OKLAHOMA NOMADS

The hardest move I made was leaving Jacksonville the second time—not our house, or our parents, but our daughter Brenda. We expect our daughters to marry and leave us, but this meant our moving away and leaving her. It was a bitter pill to swallow and it affected my physical health, even my hair turned white almost all over. Women were just beginning to have their hair frosted, and people who may have thought I looked too young for it to be natural asked, "Who does your hair? I love that color."

It took a year for me to adjust emotionally, physically, and spiritually to the problems that arose in our once close family. The continuing struggle kept me on my knees seeking guidance to deal with it. The Lord didn't remove the troubles, but he kept reminding me His grace would be sufficient. I handed the problem back to Him over and over, only to pick it up again. Finally, I was able to leave it in His hands, but I continued to live with a broken heart.

Again Jay was sent west in Oklahoma—Chandler, Holdenville, Okmulgee, McAlester, and other towns where we only stayed a month or two. No matter the length of the job, if we relocated, we moved our membership to the First Baptist Church in the area. Sometimes our membership papers had not arrived before we moved on to the next project. My reputation for trying to reach people for Jesus preceded me, and I was plugged in almost immediately to teach, reach, whatever the need; each church had a need and welcomed me.

Debbie had a harder adjustment than I to make after leaving Jacksonville. She had become an accomplished twirler there and was looking forward to twirling later in the junior high marching band. A senior student who was widely known both as a twirler and also a teacher of twirlers instructed Debbie. She formed a team of young twirlers and entered them in local, area-wide, and even state contests. The group began dressing in skimpy, suggestive costumes that I could not approve, and I had to take Debbie out of it. I encouraged her to continue taking the lessons and to be ready for the school band which dressed in suitable uniforms. She rebelled and refused. It created an issue in our fellowship as mother and daughter that surfaced in various ways throughout her teenage years and on into her young adult years.

Communities have differing personalities, and as we moved from town to town following Jay's work each one laid another step in our path of life. Chandler, Oklahoma, opened its heart and doors to meet our need. Brother Jackson (our pastor), Mr. Near (Debbie's school principal), and a local doctor, who treated me with loving care, were all part of a ministering team during our stay in their midst.

Oklahoma schools had excellent music programs that encouraged the God-given talent Debbie had showed at an early age. We immediately sought a good teacher, and she began voice lessons. Even as she had excelled in twirling, she soon became a star pupil in voice. A summer opera at Chickasha Women's College highlighted the school music program. Debbie was chosen for a solo part in the two week opera summer program. Jay and I beamed with pride and joy. We had visions of her becoming a world-renowned opera singer.

Soon afterward, she went to Falls Creek Baptist summer camp and returned with a mission call tugging at her heartstrings. That stretched our worldwide vision for her to a higher level.

OKMULGEE, OKALAHOMA

Our move to Okmulgee, Oklahoma, introduced us to a different culture. Wealth was prevalent in the town and naturally showed up in its First Baptist Church family. I was asked to teach a class of women approximately my age; they were wealthy, educated, and fashionable ladies. It was a good thing I was young and didn't know any better, or I may have felt inhibited by their education and wealth.

They were members of a Great Books club and met regularly to discuss their assigned books. Quotes from Socrates, Aristotle, and others were as common to them as quoting Paul in our Sunday School class. Quickly surmising the situation my first Sunday as their teacher, I said, "Ladies, you have knowledge I have only heard about. I will learn from you, but as your teacher, all I can do is teach Jesus—I do know Him, and I want to know Him more and more. Will you join me, and let's be a team with that as our goal?"

They assured me they would, and I've never had a group love and respect me more than those wealthy ladies did while I was their teacher.

Debbie didn't fare as well with her peer group. Sororities in that wealthy town extended down to pre-teen age, and she was not voted in one. It made her feel like an outsider even in her church family. I tried to explain it was because she had just moved there, and they hadn't had time to know her, but the stigma remained during the entire school year.

Jay took the action personally—that somehow Debbie was slighted because of his work status and our being a *renter family* and not a homeowner in the community. Remembering how he could make her happy when she was a little girl by building her a swing, he put one up in a huge tree at our front entrance. She spent hours after school swinging as high as it would go, as if she wanted to go all the way to the sky. That and a basketball hoop inadequately filled the gap that girlfriends once supplied. My heart ached for her as I cried secret tears while lifting her up in prayer and asking our Lord to fill the vacuum in her young life.

Christmas came and she showed little interest in the festivities, or the gifts under the tree. We purchased a tiny black puppy, tied a big red bow around the neck, and put it in a basket on Christmas morning. Jay set it at the front door, rang the doorbell, and disappeared around the house. I sent Debbie to answer the door.

Joy bells rang in our household, and we celebrated the true meaning of Christmas again.

Dr. Bill West was our pastor. I had less contact with him than my previous pastors, but he must have had an eye on me that I was unaware of. After we moved away, he came to preach in a revival near our new church home. He called me saying, "The church I am preaching at this week is seeking prospects to invite to the revival, and I told them to contact you—that you made it your business to find lost people and to witness to them."

McALESTER, OKLAHOMA

As was our custom, we moved our membership to First Baptist Church our first Sunday after arriving in McAlester, Oklahoma.

Dr. Charles Meyers, the pastor, welcomed us warmly, but that night during his message he explained that it was a church requirement there for a new member to attend one year before being used in teaching or any leading position.

I thought, *I won't be here long enough for this church to use me. Lord, what do I do?*

Before the week was over, he knocked on our door and during his visit said he was breaking the rule—would I teach a group of young women in Sunday School? McAlester was called *Little Dixie* by reputation, and one man called the shots in political matters; Dr. Meyers apparently held the reins in First Baptist Church.

Soon afterward, he announced that he would be teaching a Bible class on the church campus. The class was out of Oklahoma Baptist University—*The Heart of Hebrew History* (a study of the Old Testament) and *The Heart of the New Testament*. I had studied my Bible for seven years, since the day I was saved. The cover was worn beyond repair, and the pages tattered with edges almost shredded from hours of reading day and night. But I did not know historical facts and overall background knowledge. I studied to know Him, and not about Him. Teaching required both, and I knew I needed the course.

Jay had already warned me not to count on spending his Christmas bonus for shopping, as he had his own plans for using it. One of the few bones of contention we had was over my spending most of our extra cash on the girls and not leaving enough for him to spend. He said, "A man likes to give his wife special gifts, and seems like it always goes to the girls instead."

When Brenda married, he said that I was to start going to a beauty shop weekly and wear something besides one good suit. If I didn't buy something, he was going to buy it for me. I convinced him that I wanted that Bible course more than any gift he could give me, and that his bonus would pay the tuition fee with some left over for him to do some Christmas shopping.

Other class members, all professional people, seemed to take the course as a survey of the Bible. I took it book by book, verse by verse, and read every word of the Bible as we studied the textbook. Dr. Meyers was criticized for giving hard tests, but I was ready each time. He began standing and watching over my shoulder while I wrote the answers—as if he thought I might be copying the answers. Not so, I took that course to learn, not to get college credits, and I had plenty of time to study.

At the end of the first semester just before Christmas, he handed my tuition check back to me saying, "I can't take your money—it's been a blessing to teach you."

Jay took me to Tulsa and bought me a beautiful fur-trimmed coat for Christmas.

WICHITA FALLS, TEXAS

From McAlester, Oklahoma, we moved to Wichita Falls, Texas, to do the dirt-moving for a city water lake. First Baptist Church was large, beautiful, and had a powerful pastor, Dr. Landrum Leavell. He hadn't been there long, and his preaching woke up a slumbering congregation. I can still hear the sound of his voice when he began some admonition to us with the words "My soul" resounding with his heartfelt fervor before proceeding to elaborate his point.

I received great teaching, as well as training to teach, and an opportunity to use it during the nearly two years we were there. Several years after we left Dr. Leavell went to be president of the Baptist seminary in New Orleans. I remember thinking I had Seminary 101 under him at Wichita Falls.

I taught a large Sunday School class of eleven and twelve year old girls. Most were saved before they promoted out of the department; some of their parents were saved as well. The Lord provided a godly woman to help me in the class. She served as chauffeur, taking us to visit and minister in the homes of the pupils, as well as church prospects that Dr. Leavell consistently reminded us to visit. She was my prayer partner, and we shared good times together. She marveled at the size of my small living room when we knelt to pray. We lived in the upstairs area of a lovely home and the living room was long and narrow—probably had once been a hallway. When we moved away she assured me she was asking the Lord to give me a larger living room in my next home to bring more women in to pray. Everything seemed bigger in Texas and I learned to pray for bigger things.

Debbie flourished in her school activities, as well as her church. Music was still her God-given talent, and she was soon soloist in the Sunday morning worship hour. Boys were attracted to her, but it was the older ones who were beginning to notice her. The Shepherd military base was close by and many of the young men attended First Baptist Church. Debbie's beautiful red hair and overall comeliness, along with her vivacious personality, attracted their attention—but she was still too young.

When the Wichita Falls water lake was nearing completion, we received wonderful news. Jay was being sent back to Fort Smith, Arkansas. The company was laying the pipeline from the water lake at Mountainburg to Fort Smith. Jay and I rejoiced thinking, *Now we can go home to Grand Avenue Baptist Church.*

But for Debbie it was a long stretch between being five years old and a teenager. About all she remembered about Grand Avenue Baptist Church was Brother Pleitz kissing her upturned cheek each Sunday. Her music teacher and the church Minister of Music recommended the Fort Smith First Baptist Church music ministry so highly to her that she was looking forward to going there. We tried to reason with her saying, "You don't pick a church home for its music ministry."

She replied, "But do you pick one because you were baptized there?"

Jay and I had no room for doubt about where we would go to church, and we secretly prayed that Debbie would willingly follow suit.

13

Return to Fort Smith

Rather than having to change her school in a few weeks, Debbie and I planned to move ahead to Fort Smith, and Jay would join us later. I drove and Debbie was the navigator as we made our first move without Jay at the helm. Crossing the Garrison Avenue Bridge into Fort Smith was an exciting moment for me. I recalled episodes in the journey upward of our path of life since our departure nine years before, and I quivered with anticipation of what this move would bring. Debbie was more apprehensive than excited, but she was not unduly upset with the move.

We checked in a motel, bought a newspaper, marked the rental ads, and made a list to canvas the next day. Jay usually did this part, and Debbie and I made the final decision. We were on our own this time. Debbie welcomed the challenge, and we were up early armed with a city map and a list of possible rentals. Our choice was restricted by two major requirements:

> 1. No apartment buildings—must be a furnished house, duplex, garage apartment, or an apartment in a family home

2. Rent—not to exceed $100 a month

The first requirement Jay made. He refused to consider living what he called *packed in* by other apartments.

The second requirement came voluntarily on Jay's and my part. We prayerfully committed to it in order to have $100 above our tithe to use as an offering to the Lord. In our reaching out to people with the gospel we often found they had material needs, and we wanted to have extra money to provide a limited amount of support to others. Often food was their need; it was hard to share Jesus with a hungry family, and leave them with an empty stomach. We didn't realize it at the time, but living below our income kept us living in humbling circumstances.

After checking out every possible lead on our rental list Tuesday and Wednesday, I was ready to go back to Texas and let Jay do the house hunting. I called him saying, "If we don't find something by mid-morning tomorrow, we are coming back."

It was Wednesday and Debbie knew we would be going to prayer meeting that night. She asked, "Mother, can't we just visit First Baptist Church?"

I was looking forward to going to Grand Avenue Baptist, but her plea touched my heart, and I thought, *Maybe I should take her—if we are going back tomorrow, I can wait till we get moved to go to my church.* So I agreed to go for one visit.

I discovered soon after our arrival in Fort Smith that we were not coming home to the same place we had left nearly a decade ago. I called my home church and discovered the entire leadership had changed. I wondered if many of its members would remember our short stay with them. I realized this was going to be an adjustment for all of us, and agreeing to one visit with Debbie at First Baptist might help make the transition to Grand Avenue Baptist easier for her.

I felt like we were entering a cathedral as we approached First Baptist Church. The outer structure with beautiful stained-glass windows witnessed to God-loving people of earlier generations who built this house of worship. The inner sanctuary was dark and dull compared to the elegant red and white décor of our Texas church, but plans showed that this church family was looking forward to refurbishing the sanctuary. Churches, like people, have differing personalities, and first impressions are important. First Baptist Church passed the test; it was a house of God.

The pastor, Brother Dan Cameron, was not in the pulpit that Wednesday night. The Minister of Education, Brother Bill Taylor, spoke instead. I don't remember a word he said but sometime during his message an inner voice spoke to me with authority, *Stay here and share the gospel.*

I questioned it thinking, *Surely this must not be the Lord, or maybe He means stay in Fort Smith.*

I called out to the Lord with my inner voice, *Is it you, Lord, or is it Satan counterfeiting you? Surely you don't want me to stay here. Show me if it's you.*

There was no answer and I went back to the motel troubled.

ANGEL IN DISGUISE

Before I opened my eyes the next morning the thought of not having a house to live in or a church home either made the motel room that Debbie and I were sleeping in seem more transient than ever.

I called out to Debbie, "Let's get up—we are going back to Texas today and wait till your daddy can come with us. He will have to take care of this."

She didn't argue the issue and began packing the car. Just before we checked out to leave I said, "Let's pray."

"O Lord, you said once when you were here that foxes have holes and birds have nests, but you didn't have a place to lay your head—so you know how we feel today. Help us, Lord," I prayed.

On our way to eat breakfast before heading back to Texas, Debbie saw a *For Rent* sign on a house and said, "Mother, let's stop and see if it is furnished."

She knocked on the door, and when there was no answer, she climbed up to a side window to look inside. The gruffest voice you can imagine thundered out, "What do you think you are doing? Get down from there before I . . ." and a large burly man carrying a big stick stomped his way into view.

Before he could finish or get to Debbie, I was out of the car shouting, "We don't have a house to live in. She is checking to see if it is furnished."

His entire demeanor changed, and he asked almost compassionately, "What do you mean? Why don't you have a house to live in?"

When I explained our predicament he said, "This house isn't furnished, but I have one that is," and he pointed to a beautiful home next door to his. "How long are you going to be here?" he asked.

"Close to a year," I said.

"That's just right," he said. "My daughter's marriage broke up, and she and my granddaughter both are leaving for college. The house will be empty until May. Do you want it?"

"I doubt that I can pay what you can rent it for."

He interrupted, "How much can you pay?"

I said, "One hundred dollars a month is our limit."

"You've got it. Come—let me show it to you."

He marched us right over, and when his daughter heard his plans, she emphatically said, "No way am I going to rent my house . . ."

He interrupted her saying, "It's my house, and I'm the one who will have to take care of it while you're gone. These people need a house to live in, and they just now got one."

I stood there amazed listening to their arguing back and forth. Finally, crying, she acknowledged defeat and said, "Go ahead and give it to them," and bolted for the door.

I stopped her for an instant in her flight, trying to explain that I understood her feelings—that I wouldn't want to leave a beautiful home in the hands of total strangers either. I looked her right in the eye and solemnly vowed, "I will take care of it, and I will move out in time for you to move back in on May 1."

For an instant she looked relieved as she went out her door and left us to take care of the arrangements.

I wrote him a one hundred dollar check for the first month's rent and asked if we could move in on Saturday after she moved out.

He answered, "You can move in now, and she can stay with her mother and me."

"No, we want to go to Little Rock and see my parents, but we can be back by noon Saturday," I explained.

He looked at our car packed from top to bottom and said, "Let me unload your car before you go," and he proceeded to store our things away in the garage.

While he was unloading all my earthly goods, I looked through the house I was moving into before the week was over. She left everything intact—her fine linens, china, crystal, silver— all the luxuries a construction worker's wife couldn't have moved around from job to job if she had owned them. And the living room extended across the front of the house—bigger than the entire floor space of our living quarters in Texas. I remembered my prayer partner there asking the Lord to give me a larger living room than the *hall* I had there. The owner handed me a key to the house as we left. I turned it over in my hand thinking it was almost like a key to one of the rooms in heaven— a beautifully furnished home.

I learned later that my benefactor was a former active deacon of First Baptist Church. Young boys in the neighborhood called him the *cussin' deacon* and they didn't dare go across his property with their bicycles. I never heard him actually *cuss*, but he rumbled around at all hours of the night carrying a big stick, stomping and yelling, as he worked in his beautifully manicured yards. There was no need of a burglar alarm system on any of his property—no burglar would have risked entering.

I was aware that I entertained an angel sent from the Lord that day.

A CHOICE

Debbie and I rejoiced with joy unspeakable and full of wonder knowing that our good fortune came right from the hand of God.

We stopped at a phone booth on the corner of Greenwood and Grand Avenue and called Jay to tell him the good news. While waiting for the call to go through, I scanned the walls of the booth; notes scrawled by earlier callers caught my eye. Some conveyed happiness, others sadness—some, made by army boys from Camp Chaffee expressed differing emotions—but when Jay finally came on the line, if our sentiments had been recorded, they would have expressed sheer joy.

Describing a miracle is difficult to picture in words, but Jay caught a glimpse of the grace of God showered on us in hearing my account, and we thanked Him audibly for his mercy on us. Just before hanging up the receiver I said, "I'll call you Saturday when we get back from seeing Mom and Dad. Something happened in church last night that you need to pray about and tell me what it means."

"What was it, Ann—is everything okay?"

"Yes, I can't discuss it now, but begin praying for wisdom. It concerns whether we go to Grand Avenue Baptist or First Baptist Church."

"That ought to be easy. We're going to Grand Avenue Baptist—Debbie will like it once she gets there," Jay confidently replied.

INNER VOICE

Debbie and I drove in the driveway of our new home at 12 o'clock sharp on Saturday. It was not the Mansion in the Sky that Jay and I dreamed of owning as newlyweds, but it sure was our mansion in Fort Smith, Arkansas.

Debbie immediately began unpacking the boxes as she brought them in from the garage. I called Jay and after *oo-ing* and *ah-ing* over describing the beauty of our surroundings, I shared with him the inner voice I heard at the Wednesday night prayer meeting. I asked, "What do I do?"

He was silent for what seemed a full minute then said, "Well, if the Lord said First Baptist, we don't have any choice."

"But how can we *know* it was the Lord?" I questioned.

After puzzling over the situation, he counselled, "Go back tomorrow, and let's see what happens."

Debbie came in with the last box ready to work all night if it took that long to make it our home. I said, "Let's stop and rest. We need to decide what we'll wear to church tomorrow and have it ready. Debbie, your daddy thinks we should go back to First Baptist tomorrow and . . ."

"I knew you would, Mother," she calmly interrupted.

I never knew what gave her that confidence, whether it was believing we would give her anything we could, or whether she had prayed, and expected God to answer. Hopefully, it was both.

I warned her, "Remember, Debbie, we are only visiting so don't get false hope."

Whatever she may have lacked, moving from place to place, Debbie always had plenty of clothes that I made to fit her in size, color, and style. Without answering my warning, she began happily hanging them in her new closet. Sunday morning found me sitting in the middle section about eight pews back from the front in First Baptist Church. I positioned my deaf left ear in an area where I could hear best with my right ear. I especially wanted to hear every word of the message, and hopefully, the Lord would speak to my inner ear as well.

The pastor, Dan Cameron, was in the pulpit. I don't remember what he preached, but when he gave the invitation a distinct voice moved in my inner being saying, *Go.*

I held on to the back of the pew and argued, *I can't go; Jay's not with me.* Trembling, I left the building feeling I had disobeyed the Lord.

Later when I called Jay, he said, "Well, it looks like we have our answer, doesn't it?"

"But I can't go until you get here. How long do you think it will be?"

"At least six weeks. Don't wait. We always move our membership when we move our belongings. You and Debbie go ahead, and I will join as soon as I get there."

Debbie was hilarious, but I was troubled. Jay's membership in Texas and mine in Fort Smith, even for six weeks, didn't seem what we should do. I prayed for counsel on my way to church that night. Brother Bill Taylor greeted me warmly as I arrived and asked about our membership. I shared our predicament, and he immediately offered a solution. "You and Debbie come, and we can present your husband by proxy."

It wasn't a perfect solution, but I agreed to talk to Jay about it. We did talk and pray about it every day by telephone, and before the week was over we concluded it was the path we would take. I couldn't imagine being idle for six weeks waiting for Jay before I could begin serving the Lord in this new location. Little did I know then that it would be several years before I would be given the opportunity to follow my calling in First Baptist Church.

The following Sunday Debbie and I went forward during the invitation, and Jay was voted in with us by proxy. I left expecting to be plugged in to some place of service before the week was over as I had been in all our former churches. Not so. I found outreach and evangelism were guarded carefully.

A former member who was saved under the *hell fire* preaching of the renowned J. Harold Smith witnessed everywhere he went. Later he said, "First Baptist couldn't use me after J. Harold left—some must have thought I might get someone saved who wasn't one of the elect."

I asked Lyn Boen if her husband Ken Boen, the World Champion steer-wrestling cowboy, was the one who said that, and she couldn't remember if he did. He is in heaven, and I can't verify it, but if he was the one, his soul winning didn't stop. His tracts are still pointing people to Jesus, and Lyn faithfully shares the Gospel each week with new members and with people she meets in her daily life.

Whatever the reason there was no ready opening for me. Brother Bill Taylor, a godly man, tried to plug the gap by involving me in a form of outreach he called a "100 Club." His goal was to enlist one hundred members to visit newcomers in their immediate neighborhood and report back the information they discovered. The church office assigned the prospects to the proper channels. First Baptist had mission churches planted all around the city, and they seemed to be the evangelistic arm of the main church.

I volunteered to be one of the 100 Club members and immediately received two names in the mail to visit. As soon as I mailed the report back I received another assignment, and before long I was visiting almost every day. I followed the instruction for visiting. There were survey questions to ask—with no mention of witnessing.

My evangelistic fervor popped up in Training Union discussions, and I wondered if that limited me for Sunday School teaching. But when our pastor left First Baptist, Brother Bill Taylor asked me to teach the class Brother Cameron's wife had taught. The first Sunday's lesson was in Matthew 24–25, and I made the fatal error of exposing my ignorance in teaching the millennium doctrine.

First Baptist Church is strongly premillenial in interpretation of scripture. I was also premillenial in view, but I wasn't qualified to teach the subject with clarity. Nothing I had studied prepared me, and I hadn't pursued the subject thinking pastors and theologians should take care of that. I remember thinking I would stay safe and follow the teaching in the Sunday School quarterly which explained the three main beliefs concerning the millennial reign. I was transferred the next week from teaching that class.

Without a pastor people tend to begin doing what is right in their own eyes, and I tried not to even drive by Grand Avenue Baptist Church for fear I would be tempted to go back. Brother Cliff Palmer was pastor, and I saw his outreach tracts all over the city in my newcomer visiting. I knew the church was reaching people for Jesus. Often I questioned God, *Why did you send me here?"* But I never questioned that He did, and that I was to stay.

LITERACY EVANGELISM

The WMU (Woman's Missionary Union) welcomed me to serve with them both in studying and involvement in foreign mission promotion. They strongly supported local missions through Mission Action projects. I became actively involved by working, but not in sharing the gospel.

Then a window opened that replaced the evangelistic door I had been seeking. Dr. Frank Laubach, world-acclaimed educator, author of *Forty Years with the Silent Billion*, came to Fort Smith. Dr. Laubach had spent his life in a battle against illiteracy. He traveled the world in his aging years recruiting and teaching volunteers to continue the work to which he had given his life. The WMU ladies engaged him to speak in our Sunday worship service.

"Teach them to read. It is the Jesus way to save our age," Dr. Laubach said with authority. "You hold the key." In that instant he recruited another prayerfully concerned volunteer in his mighty army against illiteracy.

Four years later when I heard of his death, I wrote an account of my reaction to his appeal that day as well as to the news of his death. [See Appendix A, p. 328.]

On the day when I was miraculously recruited to evangelize the *silent billion*—or my portion of them, I immediately formed a plan to set my new life mission in motion:

LITERACY EVANGELISM PLAN

1. Be available to teach half a day five days a week
2. No charge
3. Pupils must agree to
   —Be on time for class
   —Do homework
   —Be willing to receive Bible teaching
4. Evangelism—when reading ability progresses

My first pupils were from a Mexican family living in a shanty with dirt floors. They could not speak English and could not read or write in Spanish. Mary Gonzales, the oldest at twenty-five, her teenage brother Pete (fourteen), and sister Tommie (sixteen) came seeking help.

The Laubach phonic teaching equipped me to teach them to speak English. In a few months they spoke almost fluently before I started the reading schedule. The teenagers learned to speak rapidly, but dropped out soon after the reading classes began. Mary stayed; she came faithfully for three years—studying, doing her homework, and applying it to her lifestyle. A furniture company employed her and made a room available for me to teach her at the plant. By the time she progressed in reading to *Stories of Jesus* by Dr. Laubach, First Baptist Church finally had joined an evangelistic outreach program called Evangelism Explosion. I assigned her to a team who would share the gospel with her. She was the first of my eleven pupils, and the first to be saved.

Slow evangelism—but I remembered reading about some missionaries spending a lifetime on a foreign field without seeing results. When the Lord calls one to a particular task or place, He provides a way. At that time I honestly thought the story of my life would be teaching and recruiting others to teach the silent billion who can't read or write.

Soon I had more seeking help than I had time to teach. Since the Laubach method was taught on a one-to-one basis, the number I could take was limited. The Concord Baptist Association began asking me to speak at their associational meetings and give demonstrations of the teaching and material. My name was referred to serve on the State Board of WMU, and it seemed that literacy evangelism would truly be my life's mission until Jesus comes. One missing part troubled me—Jay wasn't called to this mission. He didn't object, but he didn't feel a part of it, and it hindered our prayer power.

INTEGRATION

Segregation laws were abolished, and black people had legal rights, but it takes more than a written law, or even an enforced law to give freedom. Fort Smith schools were first integrated in 1966.

Christians as well as other law-abiding citizens had no camouflage to hide behind to keep the races segregated. The blight was fully exposed. I was swept into the almost silent upheaval it stirred. My first encounter was returning from taking a school choir group to a state contest. I had Debbie, two black girls, and another white girl in my car. While stopped at a red light in downtown Fort Smith, a car pulled alongside us. The driver looked me right in the eyes and snarled, "You are not in Texas now—and if you know what's good for you, you will go back where you came from." (My car tag revealed my former address.) Two other men were in the car, and their glowering expressions reinforced his warning.

That was the beginning of continuing harassments. Later, it showed up in our church family where I was reproached for inviting black people to First Baptist Church. A strong leader both in our church and in the community stood firmly in the gap saying to fellow members, "If you bring one, I'll stand with you." When he took that bold and precarious stand, it led the way for others to follow. It was a slow process, but it continued to grow.

Civic as well as church leaders throughout the area stepped on the bandwagon and led the way in implementing integration. Fort Smith became a model for any city to emulate—contrary to the case in Little Rock nine years earlier where integration was forced by military power and left a bitter dividing scar on that city.

We were living in Jacksonville, a short distance out of Little Rock, when it was invaded by U.S. troops in full battle armor and became a war zone overnight. It was as close to a scene out of the Civil War as one can imagine, except outwardly it was a one-sided battle.

Even with my lifelong obsession to see freedom for black people, I could not agree with President Eisenhower's action. I didn't belong to any group—Integrationist or Segregationist—but I stood for freedom that requires responsibility for all races. I wrote President Eisenhower, pleading with him not to use force, but to negotiate.

White high school students, as well as young adults, were grappling with the brutal injustice they witnessed growing up in a segregated society and were ready for a leader to help them change it. I believe that if one strong civic leader, along with at least one Christ-led church, had stepped forward with the backing of the authoritative power of the President and the Law of the Land, the younger generation would have followed.

The dream of Martin Luther King seemed to breathe his longing for peace even in his battle cry: *We shall overcome.* Fort Smith continues to prove integration can work, and the pockets of segregation that continue to blight this great land of freedom have no excuse for remaining in darkness.

Jay and Ann
Fiftieth Wedding
Anniversary

Ann
At her desk

Part IV

Ministry and Going Home

Ann and Jay share the way to heaven.

14

Kingdom Assignments

Detours came in the path of life that kept Jay and me on our journey, but we longed for a highway. As a child on the farm, I enjoyed a path as it led me through the cool shaded woods on my way to the swimming hole, but only as it led me to the main road of my destination. Finally, Jay's and my path led to a junction, and we found ourselves sailing down a highway instead.

First Baptist Church was without a pastor. We had no undershepherd, and the path was rocky; living water did not bubble forth from every fountain. In the midst of the drought, Dr. Bill Bennett became our pastor.

As I sat among hundreds of fellow members listening to his first sermon in our church, I received a startling, life-shaking message from God. Unlike the inner voice I heard when the Holy Spirit spoke to me through Dr. Laubach and launched my literacy teaching mission, this time it was a *vision*.

When Dr. Bennett gave the invitation at the end of his message, *I saw scores of people filling the aisles rushing to the altar to be saved. I even heard the rustle they made in getting out of the pews.* It was so real that when I opened my eyes from praying, I fully expected to see them with my eyes wide open. Not so, but I knew they were coming.

As I filed by to meet Dr. Bennett following his message, I don't recall our saying a word to each other. Instead, he took my hand, and we looked deeply into each other's eyes, and I remember thinking, *He sees it, too!*

Dr. Bennett not only had a vision, but a burning zeal to see evangelism come alive in First Baptist Church. He was mighty in scripture, and he preached with the eloquence of Apollos. He witnessed with the consuming passion of Paul, and soon the gospel turned Fort Smith upside down and later the entire area.

My witnessing zeal that had been lying almost dormant fanned to burning heights again. Dr. Bennett opened so many doors for me to evangelize that they crowded out the good, but lesser projects that took my time. Soon he was giving me so many assignments that my literacy classes were limited to one pupil, my WMU projects eliminated, and I was at his disposal seven days a week. Some of the men said of him that he not only asked for your coat—but your shirt, your shoes, your *all*—when it came to getting the saving gospel out to lost people. They were quick to add that he never asked more from them than he gave of himself.

In the midst of this Dr. Bennett called me in with another assignment—go to the home of every newborn baby in the city with a gift for the baby and the gospel for the parents. I was already going to newcomer families, and I could see no way of adding this, but he believed in going by faith instead of by sight.

I responded, "Let me pray about this."

He answered, "I need to put you on my staff, so I can hold you accountable. Come in tomorrow and we will talk about it."

When we met again, I learned the gift I was to take to new babies was a comb—pink for the girls and blue for the boys. I flared back, "I would feel like an insurance salesman knocking on a door with a package of needles—but if you get me Bibles—New Testaments in pink and blue, I will do it."

"Well, I'm not sure I can do that," he hesitated, "but we will see."

He did it. I think that must have been my last chance to negotiate. Later, when he put me on staff I just took what he assigned, and surprisingly witnessed the impossible happening.

I discovered immediately the baby visitation was a fertile field for evangelism, and I prayed the Lord of the harvest to send forth laborers in the field. Naomi Williams, a high school math teacher, was facing retirement, and she came to me asking how she could use her last years on earth serving the Lord. She began going with me to visit new mothers, and soon she offered, "I can do this."

She not only did, but recruited others to go, and the ministry continues to this day thirty-five years later. Many new parents were saved over the years and are active members of local churches—two came on staff here at First Baptist Church (Bob and Jan Dyer).

EVANGELISM EXPLOSION

Dr. Bennett agonized in prayer as he sought to lead the First Baptist Church family of God in evangelism and outreach. The Lord answered his prayers by sending him to Coral Ridge, Florida, where he trained under Dr. James Kennedy in an

Evangelism Explosion (EE) Clinic. He came back and is credited with beginning here in Fort Smith the first EE School and later EE Clinic in the Southern Baptist Convention.

He began pouring his heart and time into six men through scheduled classes and going out with them to homes for on the job training. When the six men finished weeks of extensive study and training, they each enlisted two trainees and the school began. We soon realized why it was called Evangelism Explosion—that is what happened. The EE School eventually trained 3,000 people from both Fort Smith and around the world to share their faith. Nearly 10,000 conversions resulted.

The first class began with six men plus one woman. I wasn't in the class, but Dr. Bennett assigned me the lessons in the office, and I went out alone for my on the job training. After several weeks of lessons, he looked me right in the eye saying, "I want you to be my assistant and set this evangelism school in motion. Janey can do the secretarial work. You do whatever it takes to begin the school and keep it moving—the assignments of prospects for the teams to visit, the lessons they study. You follow my instructions and . . ."

I interrupted, "But I am not qualified to do that—I can share and I can train others to share, but I . . ."

He closed our discussion with, "Haven't you read Philippians 4:13?" and left me sitting there. (*I can do all things through Christ which strengtheneth me.* Phil. 4:13)

I hadn't shared it with him, but a door was open for me to pursue a college degree at the University of Arkansas in Fayetteville. The opportunity was not to become the lawyer I once aspired to be, but to pursue a degree that would qualify me to lead in whatever field the Lord placed me. (I best not share the humiliating words some spoke to me who thought I was not academically qualified to be a leader.) Debbie was away at college, planning to get married, and our nest was empty. Jay never lost sight of his goal to send me to college. He bought me a new car and encouraged me to commute the short distance and to begin the following semester.

All this flashed through my mind as I looked at the scripture Dr. Bennett challenged me to answer. I knew now what the men meant when they accused him of asking for not only a coat. He was asking for an ambition I had paid a high price to delay—but was it Dr. Bennett asking or was it the Lord?

I thought, *I must get home and pray.*

Our home truly was a house of prayer, and even when Jay was away at work, his prayers surrounded me when I knelt to pray. I hurried in and fell to my knees and poured out my heart to the God of heaven:

> *O Lord, you know what college means to me— and to Jay. It has been a lifelong goal, and now you've made it possible. From the day you saved me, I've said, "Yes, help me," to every known request you've made. Are you saying, "This too," and taking away my one earthly desire? Why did you make it possible if I can't have it?*

I struggled. I cried. I reminded Him how my heart's desire had been to follow Him and that He promised to give me the desire of my heart. My earthly desire is a degree—what do I do? Finally, in the midst of my turmoil I surrendered: *Not my will, but yours, and I will take it from your hand whatever you say.*

What then happened, no words can translate the encounter I experienced. Instead of being in the language of the soul, it seemed to be in the language of heaven. It was not an inner voice, or even a vision. It was a revelation. I had no afterward comprehension I could articulate, except I got up from my knees with a new mission and title: Evangelism Assistant to Dr. W. L. Bennett. It began with no pay—just an incredible offer to be used of the Lord in reaching people to hear the gospel.

When Jay came in from work the next morning he exclaimed, "What happened to you?"

Not knowing how to answer, I asked, "What do you mean?"

"You don't look the same," and coming closer as if to examine me he said, "I don't know, but keep it whatever it is."

His was the beginning of others' reaction, and I found myself drawing apart—seeking to recapture the *experience* again. Finally, I mustered courage to try to share with Dr. Bennett and to seek his counsel. I'm not sure what he understood happened, but he gave me wise counsel: "Don't dwell on it. Don't share it. Just keep your eye on Jesus and the gospel."

That is what I did. What I have disclosed here is more than I ever shared again. Satan would have gained a foothold and stopped my evangelistic witness right there if I had kept my eye and expectancy on an experience.

Whatever happened, the main thing I can vouch for, I sensed a supernatural power to step out on faith when Dr. Bennett gave me an impossible task in evangelism.

For the nearly twenty years he remained our pastor, he never ran short of assignments for me. He continued making them until I was almost as full of assignments as he was, as I sought to lead others to help carry out his instructions. A few times I balked—one time in particular.

A dear elderly widow of a former preacher lived alone with a huge unbathed dog. She called and asked for transportation to church. She was unable to keep herself hygienically clean, and her odor was so offensive that Jay, who could not smell, became her chauffeur. Soon members sitting on her pew complained to Dr. Bennett. He instructed me to go on Sunday morning, bathe, and dress her before bringing her to church. Apparently, he had no idea how many other assignments I filled before church time, or he would have referred this one to a ministering group.

My unruly tongue took charge, and I blurted out, "Dr. Bennett, you don't have any common sense," and when I saw his stunned expression I stopped, scared of what I had said. The Lord rescued me by giving me my next words, "All you have is supernatural sense," and then he looked pleased, but not with me.

He asked, "Don't you have a servant's heart, Mrs. Curtis?"

I didn't answer, but I still balked. I heard a speaker once say that men tend to formulate their expectancy of women by what they perceive in their mother or wife, or a combination of the two. I didn't know his mother, but if he expected women to equal his wife Doris, he was certain to get disappointed.

Doris—one of a kind even as he is, college educated, with a servant's heart, and called to missions—was Educational Director in a Baptist church when she met and married Dr. Bennett. She would have stopped whatever she was doing to go minister to that dear lady. The Lord knew what he needed in an evangelism team when He matched these two in marriage. I remember hearing my daddy explain to farmers the importance of matching a team if they were using one to work their farm. Each must be headed in the same direction, and what one lacked the other must be able to supply. Even more so, the Lord teamed these two choice saints to plant, water, and harvest His crop as He gave the increase—right here in Fort Smith, Arkansas.

Within a year after the first EE School began, the vision I saw during Dr. Bennett's first sermon here became a reality—the aisles were filled each Sunday with people coming to publicly profess their faith in Christ during the invitation. First Baptist led the state in baptisms.

When the job that sent Jay back to Fort Smith for one year was completed, it was replaced with numerous other contracts in the immediate area. We began to feel like residents. I was working night and day in the greatest cause on earth, *EVANGELISM*, and I expected it to last until the Lord carried me home.

Alas, it didn't. Leading members (not involved in the EE School) convinced Dr. Bennett to bring in a new staff member to take over the schools and give him more time for the entire church family. I was replaced, and a secretary filled the gap of an assistant.

I was baffled, hurt, and even angry at Dr. Bennett's decision. Jay and I thought the Lord had released our commitment to First Baptist Church, and we could go back to Grand Avenue Baptist. We did—for one month. No one called, or made any follow-up to our visits, and I wondered if any church wanted our membership.

I went to my knees—not just in posture, but in submission asking, "What do I do, Lord?" And as clear as a bell the answer came. He didn't call me just to be Dr. Bennett's Assistant. The initial call was *Stay here and share the Gospel.*

Jay and I were in our pew at First Baptist the next Sunday, and I went down the aisle during the invitation saying to Dr. Bennett, "I have sinned, and I want to come back."

He didn't look surprised and didn't ask any questions—just gave me some new assignments.

The day he removed me from being his Assistant in Evangelism was a bitter pill to swallow, but later he opened a far better assignment (*And we know that all things work together for good to them that love God, to them who are the called according to his purpose.* Rom. 8:28). He made sure I was used as a Trainer in every EE School and International Clinic held thereafter.

Evangelism Explosion was taught in three stages: Class Work, Home Work, and On the Job Training. The third and most important part was on the job training. Two trainees went out with a trained individual and listened as the trained person endeavored to lead someone to Christ. Learning in this capacity along with their class and home work continued for several lessons before a trainee was assigned an active role in the home.

As a trainer I was an integral part of the training of scores of preachers, missionaries, staff members, and laymen from here and around the world as they came to be trained in the EE Schools and International EE Clinics held for nearly twenty years in First Baptist Church, Fort Smith, Arkansas.

I took comfort from the words of Charles Spurgeon who said that the one who converts a soul draws from the fountain, but he who trains a soul winner digs a well from which thousands may drink eternal life.

BONNIE

Often I am asked, "How many people have you shared Jesus with who accepted Him?" I don't know; I don't keep count. But I always remember the last one, and I am looking forward to the next one. Jesus compared the harvest to the farmer's planting— he who sows much reaps much. During the Evangelism Explosion years, I was sharing day and night fully expecting to bring at least one each Sunday with whom I had personally shared.

There were also scores who came from EE teams who were assigned names to visit.

I know the results are in God's hands, but I believe He holds us accountable to share and that He delights in letting us see fruit in proportion to our obedience to His Great Commission. Jay and I fasted and prayed from Saturday morning to Sunday noon week after week, and we fully expected the Lord of the harvest to bring some in to confess Him as Lord and Savior—and He did.

I felt ashamed of my week's work the times I came on Sunday without knowing of at least one with whom I had personally shared who planned to come that day. Time and time again, one showed up just in the nick of time. One was a prostitute. She appeared seemingly out of nowhere as I stepped out of my car.

"Do you go to church here?" she asked. When I assured her I did, and before I could ask her, she continued, "May I come with you?"

I hugged her saying, "You're an answer to prayer—I just asked the Lord to send someone to go to church with me."

I took her hand, and she began pouring out her life story as we crossed the street. A neon sign couldn't have advertised her wares more vividly than her appearance, but she tearfully confessed them as well.

Her doctor in California had given her a few months to live, and she was staying at the Goldman Hotel while making her funeral arrangements to be buried near her birthplace about fifty miles out of Fort Smith. "I bought my dress to wear when I die—it's a long white party dress—do you think that will be right?" she blubbered. I cried with her as I hurriedly took her to my office to share the Good News.

I asked, "Do you know what Jesus said to a woman who was living your lifestyle?" She covered her face sobbing, obviously thinking He would condemn her. As soon as I closed the door behind us, I read the eighth chapter of John to her and hope filled her eyes. She prayed for forgiveness when I shared the gospel message, and she gladly asked Him to make her His child.

"Bonnie, Jesus is saying to you what He said to that woman—'Neither do I condemn you, go and sin no more,'—and he meant the sin you confessed as we were crossing the street."

"I won't," she solemnly vowed. I saw the meaning of *He that is forgiven much loveth much* and the transformation of that dear woman was as beautiful a sight as I have seen.

After instructing her in confession and baptism, I seated her in the sanctuary assuring her I would be right back to sit beside her and go down the aisle alongside her. My last minute words were, "I want you to meet my husband, and we will go to lunch together after church."

Later, when the invitation was given, I walked down the aisle with her. This was a street walker dressed in her flashiest attire. She wore high rise heels on her stockingless feet, and her long blood-red toenails curled like birds' claws. But even in that garb her face glowed with a Shekinah light (the light of God's presence) as she took Dr. Bennett's hand. His eyes rolled round and round at the sight of her, but when he looked in her eyes and saw the reflection of Jesus, he responded with joy unspeakable.

I stood aside thanking the Lord for a church family showing such unconditional love as they came by to welcome her. I spoke softly to Jay, "We are taking her to lunch."

"No, you're not, Ann. You can't take her looking like that," he responded and out he went.

When the last one filed by her, I said, "Bonnie, something has come up, and I can't take you to lunch today, but may I have you for lunch at our house next Sunday?"

Later, little was said as Jay and I drove to a restaurant. When our food was served, Jay bowed his head to bless it, but stopped and didn't utter a word. Then with tears trickling down, he asked the Lord to forgive him and said to me, "Believe me, Ann, it wasn't that I didn't want her. I didn't want you to be out with her looking like that, but I was wrong, and I'm sorry."

We had that lunch together in our home the next Sunday, served with the best china and silverware I owned. She was baptized that night and went back to California the next week.

A few months afterward her obituary came out in the local newspaper giving the time and place of her burial. The day it was scheduled I was given a full day of assignments to cover, and when I asked Dr. Bennett, he said, "Let the dead bury the dead, Mrs. Curtis, and continue taking Jesus to the lost." Lest that sound unmerciful, it's the very words Jesus spoke to one of His disciples who asked to go back and bury his father (*And another of his disciples said unto him, Lord, suffer me first to go and bury my father. But Jesus said unto him, Follow me; and let the dead bury their dead.* Matt. 8:21–22).

Bonnie was buried in more than a white party dress—she was covered with the righteousness of Jesus.

DAVID

Jesus ended His Great Commission with the promise to those who obey it *". . . and lo, I am with you alway"* (Matt. 28:20). I continue to marvel when he reveals Himself almost visibly as we seek to obey His marching orders.

Jay's and my zeal for witnessing limited our fun time with our grandchildren as both daughters began having children— Brenda with four and Debbie with one. His promise covered it all; as each one arrived and on through their lives, His presence was visible.

When Debbie's son, David Curtis Cowan, was nearly three years old, he often spent the weekend with us. Once after eating Sunday lunch he slipped outside and stood on a rock in the midst of a flower garden unaware of our listening ears. Holding my EE Soul Book in one hand and thumping it with the other, he preached Dr. Bennett's morning sermon word for word for a paragraph or two. We knew he was called to preach long before he was saved.

Another time he was with us when my EE trainees were meeting to pray in my home. We were kneeling at a long striped ottoman in my living room when a call came that Jay's mother had just died. As I was taking the call with tears flooding my face, David jumped up on the ottoman. Holding my EE Soul Book and thumping it soundly he proclaimed, "God give you peace." We were too stunned to speak, and he continued saying the same words more compassionately two more times, "God give you peace."

Later, when he was seven years old, Debbie came home to Fort Smith to begin a new life as a single mom with a son to raise. My three-ring card index containing the scriptures and illustrations of the EE lessons was David's main attraction. He held it like another might hold a TV remote control, and listened carefully to trainees practice. He longed for the family life he had once known, but I saw the Lord fill the vacuum with Himself.

When he turned eight, Debbie encouraged me to feel free to share the gospel personally with David, but I wanted to wait until he knew he was lost and needed a Savior. Christmas came and I thought he was missing his former family life as he seemed troubled. It was Saturday night, and he had been in bed several hours before I finished calling a long list of people to invite to church the next day. As I went by his open door and saw he was still awake, I asked if he would like to get up with me while I read the Bible and prayed before I went to bed. He gladly jumped up and as it was the Christmas season, I opened to Matthew's account and asked him to read the scriptures. He read, *". . . and thou shalt call his name JESUS: for He shall save His people from their sins"* (Matt. 1:21). With tears rolling down his cheeks he looked up at me almost accusingly, "Grandmother, can't you tell *ME* how I can go to heaven?" Heaven came down and joy filled our souls!

MOTORCYCLES AND MIRACLES

During the time Debbie and David lived with us, David witnessed miracles—people being saved from the penalty of sin and others from earthly dangers. On one occasion even David himself was spared. It was his birthday and I took him up on Mt. Gaylor, the holiest earthly spot I knew (where Jay and I were saved) to celebrate and eat lunch on top of the beautiful mountain. We found the restaurant closed, so I drove back to a Mountainburg drive-in for sandwiches to take to the lake area for a picnic lunch. We had finished eating and were sitting at the table while I was reading the Bible to him. Suddenly it sounded like all hell broke loose.

The thunderous roar stopped instantaneously as if a director had raised a baton, and we were encircled by a motorcycle gang. Their character was etched indelibly on their faces—the elite of their group were young, intelligent, strong, and capable of atrocity. They surrounded our table standing militarily at attention; their eyes were on their leader apparently waiting for him to give them their orders.

David looked up at me with the same question in his eyes—*What are my orders?* I picked up our stacked leftovers, stood with my open Bible in my hand, and pointed to the trash can right in front of the leader saying, "David, it's time for us to go—put this in the trash."

David didn't take his eyes off me and the open Bible in my hand as he stood and then walked unhesitatingly toward the trash can. As he did, without a word they fired up their motorcycles and with a deafening noise they roared out of the park. The roar now rang like bells of heaven to our frightened souls and left David and me standing *amazed*. I suddenly remembered the verse that Dr. Bennett quoted when EE teams came back celebrating victory over demon powers as they shared the gospel. Jesus said, "Nevertheless, do not rejoice that the spirits are subject to you but rejoice that your names are written in heaven" (Luke 10:20). I shared that with David adding, "We must keep our eyes on Jesus and His saving power—not on his miracles," but that didn't erase the joy bells ringing in our souls as we knew we were miraculously spared.

SHARING THE LOVE OF JESUS

Jay and I never had the bittersweet joy of having our other grandchildren—Johnny, Timothy, Shannon, or Shawn—live in our home as David did; there was never a need. But we shared high moments, as well as low times, that come in all our lives. Above all, they shared with us our love for Jesus and for each other. [See Appendix B, p.331, "The Positive Influence of Godly Grandparents," by Shannon Terry.]

15

Beyond Evangelism Explosion

I thought the miraculous, glory days of Dr. Bennett were over when he turned the helm of the EE Schools over to another staff member, but I drastically underestimated the power of God working in a man obeying the Great Commission.

Inspired by the Action Program promoted throughout the Southern Baptist Convention, Dr. Bennett began the Pastor's Class with no enrollment. He called members of First Baptist Church who were not enrolled in any Sunday School class and invited them to the Pastor's Class and asked them to bring others. Eighty-eight came the first Sunday, April 11, 1976. He immediately launched out to the entire city and surrounding area inviting people to the class. He issued invitations by telephone, by letters, through advertising in local newspapers, and as he met scores in his daily walk. He used every opportunity as it presented itself to invite people to hear the Word of God.

Again, he enlisted me as his Assistant in the class as he had in the EE Schools, but this time with a recognized position on his church staff and an adequate salary. The first two years I visited seven hours a day—two hours in the morning, three hours in afternoon, and two hours in the evening. I knocked on doors and invited people to come to a Bible class with no denominational strings attached.

Dr. Bennett honored the promise to maintain a class that was strictly a Bible class. Some members came for years to the Sunday morning Bible class, but continued going to their church for worship. As the weeks went by I visited briefly in the home of every enrolled member and registered visitor. I welcomed them and sought to discover their spiritual needs. I also visited newcomer families as a prime source of prospects for the class. The visitation made up a full week's work, day and night.

Our Goal Is Souls was my mission statement. I claimed *Faith cometh by hearing and hearing by the Word of God* (Rom. 10:17) as the scripture. I fully believed that saving faith, living faith, and dying faith all come from the Word of God.

My assignment was *Outreach* and I made Fort Smith my target. Every household in the city must get an invitation to come hear the Bible taught verse-by-verse by as gifted an expositor of the scripture as they could ever hear. It was not as exciting as one-on-one evangelism, but Jay and I knew it was God's assignment to us. We put our heart, mind, soul, and strength into reaching people to come hear His Word.

The Lord gave Dr. Bennett the vision, and he transferred the mechanics to me to put it in motion. I used the same method he used when he drafted me. I sought out spirit-led members in the class and challenged them to give their coat—their shoes, their *all* if need be—whatever it took to reach people for Jesus. Often I heard one say to another, "When Mrs. Curtis asks you, there is no way out—you just do it." But they wouldn't have continued doing what they did because of any person's request. It was the Lord Himself drafting them into His mighty army.

The class enrollment escalated dramatically from zero to more than a hundred—then two hundred—then four—five—then one thousand. At its zenith nearly three thousand were enrolled, and it required two and three classes to accommodate the numbers. Average attendance hovered around more than one-third of its enrollment through the years.

OUTREACH STRATEGIES

Over the next several years we employed various outreach strategies. They revealed the extraordinary power of the Lord working through the lives of ordinary people who sought to reach people for Jesus.

In the first year of outreach twenty-five class members each took six telephone directory pages and hand addressed, stuffed, and mailed 35,000 personal letters from Dr. Bennett to city residents.

The second year sixty-two class members took two directory pages and called residents tabulating results according to instruction. Two thousand people indicated enough interest to be put on the regular mailing list.

In the third year we took our vision from Habakkuk 2:2 in the Living Bible: *Write my answer on a billboard, large and clear, so that anyone can read it at a glance and rush to tell the others.* The focus for that year was outdoor advertising. A huge sign displayed an artist-drawn picture of Dr. Bennett inviting motorists to come hear the Word. The same week that the sign was posted more than seventy-five members mailed a reproduction of the sign to 42,000 homes.

That same year the class rented a booth by the ticket gate at the annual rodeo grounds. The booth featured a large picture of Dr. Bennett teaching the class. A huge television screen continuously projected a film of the Pastor's Class (made the week before) as the crowd entered. Sixty-eight class members kept the booth open from 3:30 to10:30 p.m. for six days. During that time 13,000 invitations were handed out, 3500 long, inflated balloons imprinted with *Pastor's Class* were given to children entering the gate. The following Sunday 1,338 people attended the three sessions of the Pastor's Class to hear Art Linkletter as the guest speaker.

Once masses attended to hear famous guest speakers, many came later to hear Dr. Bennett. Each week scores of class members took up-to-date invitation cards and placed them behind windshield wipers on parking lots all over Fort Smith and Van Buren. They covered the area so well that it caused an uproar. A city ordinance was finally passed forbidding the use of windshield cards citing them as a litter problem.

Ten class members served as absentee callers. Each was given twenty names weekly to call, to let them know they were missed, and to encourage them to come hear the exciting lesson the next Sunday.

Key leaders emerged for each need in the class. Jarrel and Jewel Page, a holy man of prayer and his wife with the gift of helping, became my right and left arms. She became my bosom friend that I shared my innermost struggles with—some beyond revealing in this book. They came to First Baptist in 1997 bringing their four children and were followed by twenty-four family members in the ensuing years—two serving as deacons (one as chairman of deacons), two going out as pastors, and two more called to ministry. Jarrel and Jewel stood beside me in each humanly-impossible venture I proposed under Dr. Bennett's direction.

The administrative details grew larger for each massive mail out. The Lord moved Don and Anita Shafer to Fort Smith, and they became active members in the class. Anita helped with a mail out, and when the next one was scheduled she offered, "Mrs. Curtis, I can oversee this if you want and give you time for other outreach." She used her full vacation time in doing it. Later, Shelby Ezell did the same and continued for five years. That began a pattern—the Lord raised up someone each following year to voluntarily lead in this tremendous task.

LESLIE

Year after year the attendance grew in proportion to the outreach. When the enrollment passed one thousand I found myself working beyond my physical limit; I was overseeing all the volunteer help, handling a multitude of other assignments, and doing the paperwork at night. When I told Dr. Bennett it was as far as I could go, he looked puzzled, and quoted scripture to claim for power. I balked saying the only way I could continue was to have a secretary. I asked him to call in the wisest man we knew, a leader of the church, to appraise the situation. Without hesitation he called him on the spot. He came right over and after looking at the situation said immediately, "Get her a secretary."

We put an ad in the local newspaper and a young mother came to apply. Her résumé showed her more than qualified for the workload, but her appearance, her manner, and her conversation revealed she was not a born-again Christian. Before closing the interview and dismissing her, I held up the Bible from my desk and asked, "Leslie, do you believe the Bible is the Word of God?"

Drawing back in her chair and looking as insulted as if I had suddenly slapped her, she answered, "Of course I do, what do you think I am?"

I retraced my thoughts and asked, "Why do you want this job to work at First Baptist Church?"

With trembling lips but direct eye contact she responded, "I have two babies—Christmas is coming, and I have no money. I need a job. . ."

I interrupted, "Do you like typing—your résumé shows your speed is phenomenal, but do you enjoy it? Most of this work will be typing, and isolated from others except me. Can you handle that?"

"Typing is what I like most to do and . . ."

I handed her an open letter from my desk and asked her to type it. She sat down at a typewriter she had never used before and handed it back to me in a brief time—typed letter perfect. I then said, "Leslie, I want you to be my secretary, but you will need to meet with Dr. Bennett and get his approval."

He met her the next morning and after she left he buzzed me exploding, "Mrs. Curtis, have you lost your mind?"

I waited until he stopped sputtering, and I said, "Let me try her, Dr. Bennett. She won't be on staff as a church secretary—but could be my secretary. Our goal in the Pastor's Class is souls—what if the Lord sent her to us?"

He then said, "Well, go ahead. She won't stay a week." She came. She stayed seven years and didn't leave until her job ended when Dr. Bennett moved from First Baptist to another assignment that surpassed even the EE Schools and the Pastor's Class for carrying out the Great Commission.

Ruth Johnson, a godly Sunday School teacher in our midst, once said to a group of young wives, "Living with your in-laws may seem like a bitter pill at the time, but I can tell you from experience it will guard you from having word battles with your husband. Imagine accusing him of bad things in front of his mother."

In a similar manner, having a lost secretary looking over my shoulder day after day kept me trying to keep a short sin list as I dealt with all the complexities of the needs in the class and outreach ministry. She watched my every reaction, and the lost have a higher standard for church members than Jesus does—He knows we have clay feet.

Even Jesus said the lost world is wiser in some areas than the children of light (*And the lord commended the unjust steward, because he had done wisely: for the children of this world are in their generation wiser than the children of light.* Luke 16:8). And Leslie was wiser in one area. She remembered she learned as a child in the Episcopal Church that Jesus came to seek and to save the lost (Luke 19:10). She thought the church's main business should be reaching lost people, and she made her top priority recording the names and addresses of every person visiting the Pastor's Class, as well as the person's attendance record. It was computerized before her tenure ended, but the first years she typed and kept accurate files of the full Pastor's Class enrollment.

At the onset, I gave her two rules she must obey if she continued working for me: no foul language under any circumstances and no criticism of Dr. Bennett.

She was loyal to me to a fault, and she thought Dr. Bennett asked too much of me. She voiced her dislike of him the first week. After I convinced her I would not tolerate it, she bit her tongue and said no more. But often when he was instructing me, I could hear a hissing sound like a family cat makes to show its disapproval coming from her desk—in the adjoining office.

Midway through her seven-year tenure, Leslie gave her heart and life to Jesus, and she was a new creation. She thought Dr. Bennett was right out of heaven. She loved it when he gave me an impossible assignment knowing she could be an active part of it.

Afterward, one by one, her entire household was saved.

Ezra

The Lord works in mysterious ways to involve us in His Great Commission. I took his marching orders from Acts 1:8— *But ye shall receive power, after that the Holy Ghost is come upon you: and ye shall be witnesses unto me both in Jerusalem, and in all Judaea, and in Samaria, and unto the uttermost part of the earth.* Jerusalem, which to me meant my own hometown, was my target, but He amazed me by expanding it to Jerusalem itself.

A shabby-looking man approached Jay and me at the city mall witnessing to us about Jesus. After assuring him we knew Him as our Lord and Savior, I asked what church he attended. He said he had gone to the Assembly of God with his wife, but after her death he was not attending. I immediately asked him to First Baptist, and since it was Wednesday, I invited him to midweek prayer meeting for a fellowship meal beforehand.

Ezra Amos, a converted Jew, met me in the Fellowship Hall that evening. When we sat down to eat the whole atmosphere changed—*ham* was the meat served. He was a converted Jew, but pork was still an abomination to him. He lashed out at me as if I had tricked him into coming to the unholy meal. Finally, he stopped and looking disgustedly at me, he asked, "How can you call yourself a Christian and eat what He calls unclean?" Jay was at work and couldn't answer for me.

I looked him right in his eyes and said, "If eating pork keeps you from coming to this church—you're looking at one who will never knowingly eat another bite of it."

He took me at my word and continued coming and claiming First Baptist as his church. Often he brought gifts of appreciation to me—flowers and fruit that supermarkets discarded. Later I learned he was a millionaire, yet he lived and looked like a pauper.

When he died, he left all his money to the Southern Baptist Convention to be spent for converting Jews in Jerusalem. After his death some, aware of my vow, said, "Now you can eat pork again," but I refused saying, "My vow was to God—not just to Mr. Amos."

Some have asked if an experience of that nature prompted me to always wear a dress and not pants. This decision came in an entirely different manner. In the 60s, before the term *same sex* became common language, I saw a movement emerge that seemed to have an agenda of erasing the differences in the dressing of men and women. I was troubled.

Without sharing it with Jay or our daughters, I vowed to myself, *I won't be a part of it—I will dress like a lady—not a man.*

I owned a striking white sharkskin slack suit that I loved to wear to appropriate places, but I immediately disposed of it. From that day, I have continued wearing a skirt—at the risk of being labeled *legalistic*.

16

Alzheimer's

Himself

A thief crept in
Not once, but time and time again.
No entry or exit could be traced;
Each time a little more was missing.

Elusive, as if from outer space,
Invisible, with no identity—
The tracks it left were like
A calling card without a name.

We clung to each other
Not knowing what it was
Or from whence it came.
We shuddered at the consequence.

Seven years we battled it alone
Until the day a doctor said,
"Your brain cells are deteriorating;
Nothing I can do will stop it."

At last the enemy was unveiled.
It leaped out baring every fang.
Instantly, I knew its name:
ALZHEIMER'S.

You sobbed and trembled at his words.
Then you bowed your head—I heard you pray:
"Lord, I won't have any brains . . .
Be my Master Mind; Ann can be the other."

Ten more years we walked together
The trails Alzheimer's people tread.
No charted paths—we carved out new ones,
Not heeding what the seminars said.

You didn't wear easy clothes or shuffle along as others do.
You wore your suit, your tie, and favorite shoes.
I became your caregiver, but not your mother.
I was your wife—you were my husband.

Cell by cell, Alzheimer's stole your brain away.
Each time the Master Mind moved in to fill the vacuum
Until one day all your brain was gone—
Replaced by the Master Mind, *Himself*.

SEVENTEEN YEARS WITH ALZHEIMER'S

After twenty years serving our Lord faithfully and joyfully, a thief crept in and cell by cell stole Jay's brain away.

Slowly, relentlessly it stalked our pathway, and before we knew its name, we battled it together on our knees. At first there were subtle changes in his memory, and then no symptoms for weeks. Just when we thought it was our imagination, it appeared again in a more drastic form. His doctor gave him a clear bill of health. I knew his wasn't a physical problem, but the doctor refused to discuss Jay's prognosis with me. Even our daughters wondered if I was imagining it when I shared it with them.

The last two years that Jay was able to work, another had to work alongside him—as he often left the machinery motors running after he serviced them. A new superintendent came on the job and the first time he found that Jay had left a big machine running after his night's work, he fired him on the spot.

Jay came home crushed physically, mentally, and spiritually. He bowed his head at the table, but he could not pray. For the first time I prayed in his place at our family meal time.

The next morning I said, "Jay, talk to the Lord about this. He will see us through."

"I can't. I can't even tell you, Ann, what I called that man—much less tell the Lord."

"Yes, you can tell Him—whatever you said. Why don't you go apologize to the man? He may not forgive you, but our Lord will."

Jay stood up, and went out the door without eating the breakfast set before him. Later he came back subdued by apologizing to his boss, but on praying grounds with his Lord. In retrospect, I rejoiced that his memory had not deteriorated to a point at that time that he could not recall the incident from the day before with clarity.

Even on praying ground a child of God can face trouble beyond the bearing—but not beyond the Lord providing a way out (*There hath no temptation taken you but such as is common to man: but God is faithful, who will not suffer you to be tempted above that ye are able; but will with the temptation also make a way to escape, that ye may be able to bear it.* 1 Cor. 10:13).

Later that day I saw Jay slumped over in his chair looking so forsaken that I rushed to our bedroom, fell on my knees, and literally stormed the doors of heaven, pleading for them to open and pour out mercy on Jay. *In my distress I called upon the Lord, and cried unto my God: he heard my voice out of his temple, and my cry came before him, even into his ears* (Ps. 18:6).

The telephone rang. A contractor in Western Oklahoma asked Jay if he could come to work as soon as possible. Jay assured him he could come immediately. He did, and it was the last job he was able to work, but it paid the best wages of his work history, and thus set the amount that Social Security paid him later when he was sixty-five.

Jay was sixty-two and eligible for early retirement with disability benefits, but he refused it saying, "Ann, the Lord is going to heal me and let me work again." I couldn't argue with that, but I am glad he never knew the financial struggle I battled the next three years before he began receiving Social Security checks—but then I never would have known how the Lord provides for His own.

Seven years we battled the condition, not able to share it with others, until it hit a peak of no return. With no thought of his being my boss, I went to my pastor, Dr. Bennett, asking for counsel. Again, he called the wisest man in the membership, a leading dermatologist in the city, and asked if he could see me. He replied, "Have her come right over."

He didn't mince words and plainly told me what it seemed to be—Alzheimer's. He knew and loved Jay and had seen his symptoms before I told him. He looked me straight in my eyes saying, "There is no treatment for it. It gets progressively worse."

Interrupting, I cried out in fear and helplessness, "What can we do?"

"Who is your doctor?" he asked.

"He won't discuss it with me, and Jay can't remember what he tells him. I need someone—who would you get if it were for you?"

"Dr. Pruitt is my doctor."

Interrupting again I said, "If he's your doctor, that's good enough for me. Can you get him for Jay?"

He did. Arrangements were made for Jay to be hospitalized that day for observation and testing. The next morning Dr. Pruitt came in, and after briefly greeting him said, "Mr. Curtis, your brain cells seem to be deteriorating, and there's nothing we can do to stop it."

I thought, *How can you say that to him? Why not to me— but not to him?*

He assured us he would take good care of Jay's physical needs, but he had no treatment for Alzheimer's. Jay didn't respond verbally, but the impact of the words was written visibly on his face.

I was speechless from shock, and Jay didn't say a word as we left the hospital. I fixed our noon meal, and when Jay started to bless it, no words came forth. I had none either. Finally, Jay sobbed saying, "Lord, I won't have any brains. Be my Master Mind, I'll let Ann be my 'other mind.' "

We raised our heads and with tears streaming down our faces, we ate our lunch. The doctor's words seemed ruthless at the time, but they proved to be the turning point in our battle with Alzheimer's. He was not only Jay's doctor, but his friend throughout the continuing ordeal. A caring doctor has healing power beyond the medical realm, and he provided that for Jay—always treating him like the gentleman he was. Jay responded with a dignity that Alzheimer's never destroyed.

It is a humbling assignment to be the *other mind* for another—especially for your husband. I fiercely guarded his dignity as I was forced to take the reins in our marriage, but I took them one step at a time and only when it was required.

Jay was in submission to the Lord when his memory loss began and continued to digress steadily. The transaction he made with the Lord when faced with his prognosis remained valid. Even when his memory seemed erased—he looked to me to be his *other mind*. The Holy Spirit was his Master Mind and continued to abide, lead, comfort, and supply his every need.

Jay's construction work days ended, but not his labor for the Lord. He continued working alongside me for eleven more years, praying with me, riding with me on house visits, staying in the outer office with Leslie while I was in my office. He could not be left alone as he might walk away and not know how to return. We made a joke of it saying he would wind up in a Lost and Found column. He laughed with us, and seemingly felt no stigma to our watchcare.

Seminars for Alzheimer's caretakers were offered, and I went seeking help. I found I was breaking every rule; I was doing almost everything they advised not to do. I only went to two sessions since Jay responded better to my treatment, than the individuals whom I observed in their care.

Early on I learned that Jay knew far more than he could communicate, and I refused to treat him like a child—he was a *man.* I saw the difference in ones cared for as though they were children. They shuffled about in loose clothing with no aim or purpose, no dignity. Jay continued to wear his usual clothing with shoelaces, buttons, zippers, and especially his tie. He walked up and down the stairway in our home (seminars made that a number one *no-no*). I regularly walked beside him on the escalator at the mall not letting it escape his memory. He went out to eat, handling his knife and fork correctly, until the last month he lived. Home Health attendants helped me care for him his last two years, and my first rule to them was, "Don't use the word *diaper* around him. Call it *underpants*." They took care of him as well as I did—releasing me to continue working in the church outreach through the Pastor's Class.

The Alzheimer's path was not charted. We had no map to follow. Instead of detours we faced roadblocks in our path of life. But for fifteen of the seventeen years Jay was often a silent, but always a powerful partner alongside me.

I am asked, "Did you ever feel like giving up in the midst of it?"

Yes, and I almost did at one point. I heard about, read about, and witnessed depression in other people; I did not identify with it until it swept over me.

It began getting harder and harder to get out of the bed each morning. I did well during the day—slept all night, but when the alarm sounded to begin a new day a panoramic view of the future unfolded before my opening eyes, and I could not face it. Covering up my head, I closed my eyes wanting to never wake up again.

Finally, realization came to me that if the Lord didn't rescue me I was doomed to despair. I was praying back to Him Psalm 143:7–8:

> *Hear me speedily, O Lord: My spirit faileth: hide*
> *not thy face from me lest I be like unto them that*

*go down into the pit. Cause me to hear by thy lov-
ingkindness in the morning for in thee do I trust:
cause me to know the way wherein I should
walk."*

I fell prostrate before Him when I read the word *walk*. It
seemed He said it to me rather than my saying it to Him.

I called out to Jay, "Let's start walking in the morning," and I
put our walking shoes out, set the clock forty-five minutes
earlier, and went to bed.

When the alarm sounded the next morning, instead of the
previous panoramic view before my waking eyes, I heard as clear
as a bell one word: *walk*. I jumped out of bed and woke Jay. We
put on our walking shoes and out the door we went—not jog-
ging, but walking briskly for two miles. We both came back
renewed and ate a hearty breakfast. That continued to be our
morning schedule. My depression disappeared—replaced by a
deeper trust in the Lord. Later, I read that walking activates a
hormone in the body that affects mood swings. Whatever, it
came from the Lord to me (*There hath no temptation taken you
but such as is common to man: but God is faithful, who will not
suffer you to be tempted above that ye are able; but will with
the temptation also make a way to escape, that ye may be able
to bear it.* 1 Cor. 10:13).

We lived in a comfortable duplex at 5414 Free Ferry. Caring
church members, who were not aware of our self-limitation in
our housing expenditure, made it available and even at $100 per
month. But years later new ownership raised the rent overnight
to $200 per month. Since First Baptist had a benevolence fund
available, we didn't need the $100 we had pledged to set aside
for that use in our outreach ministry. It posed no hardship. I
thanked the Lord for His watchcare, and He did more than

watch—He acted. He provided a specially designed house for Jay and me.

His plan began several years earlier with First Baptist purchasing a house adjoining the back parking area. The outer structure was credited with being one of the oldest in the city, a carriage house in its early form. A young architect bought it and designed the interior to reflect its original motif. Later he sold it to a chiropractor, and afterward it came to First Baptist ownership. It began to be used for staff housing. It was currently unoccupied, and Dr. Bennett offered it to me asking if living closer to my work would help me in caring for Jay. I responded with joy at the offer, but my next words were, "It's not furnished."

Dr. Bennett puzzled, "You mean you don't have any furniture?"

Jay and I never shared our pact we had made after we sold our house and furnishings at Jacksonville. We sensed the drawing power ownership had on our wanting to stay in one place, and we agreed to sever the tie that might keep us from going wherever the Lord would lead us. If we were really pilgrims in this world, we would travel lightly. But with Jay being unable to move to another job site, it seemed Fort Smith was our final earthly move.

All this flashed in my mind and with it came this thought, *We don't have any furniture, but we can get some—that's why Daddy gave me that Christmas check soon after we were saved.*

We had just moved to the Jacksonville Air Base job, close to my family home site west of Little Rock. Daddy gave me a $2000 check for Christmas. As I tried to express my appreciation, he was curious to know what I would use it for. He sensed our lack of interest in settling down in one place, and he attributed it to our new church life. He had no concept of tithing or giving to the Lord. He thought it was giving to preachers and to churches. He followed us to our car as we started home, and as we said goodbye and thanked him again, he asked directly, "Anna Mae, what are you going to do with it?"

"I don't know, Daddy, but right now I'll give the Lord one-tenth of it and invest the other. One day I'll either want or need something, and I'll get it thanks to you."

He looked pleased, and that is what I did. Now, I not only needed, but I wanted to furnish a house.

Dr. Bennett called in his youth minister, Eddie Graber, and gave him an assignment. "You and Linda use what time you need to help Mrs. Curtis and Jay furnish and move into the staff house."

It was like having a business manager and a home decorator at our disposal. Joyfully and carefully they took Jay and me and shopped piece by piece. With the money we allotted them they guided us in selecting furnishings that set the framework for later additions. People marvel today when they walk in and view its simplicity and Godly beauty.

Jay never lost his appreciation for beauty. He loved the feel of good fabric, and he admired Ralph Freeman's suits that he wore to church. Later, when his inhibitions were affected by Alzheimer's, he reached out and felt the sleeve of Ralph's suit jacket. Ralph sensed his eye for beauty and the next week he told me to take Jay to the best men's store in the city and get a suit as a gift from him.

Jay had a captivating saying as a young man: "A woman ought to be pretty, and if she isn't, she should at least wear something pretty." His construction work covered him with grease and dirt, but when he came home from a night's work he went directly to the bathroom and came out spotless and fully dressed to eat breakfast. He expected me and our two daughters as they were growing up to do the same, and we did—no curlers in our hair and no bathrobes. In other words, "Don't come to breakfast looking like an unmade bed."

PETI

Moving in the staff house at 1408 North C Street was a memorable day. Jay and I walked up the staircase hand in hand and at the landing just under the skylight Jay embraced me, and for an instant all his dots were connected, and he joyfully exclaimed, "Our Mansion in the Sky, Ann" (the title he gave our honeymoon apartment in Little Rock years before).

As suddenly as it came—it was gone, but such rare glimpses were priceless to me. I wondered how often he had them, but could not communicate them, and it kept me talking to him as though he understood every word I said.

His countenance continued to reflect contentment and even moments of sheer joy as he felt at home in our new surroundings; I rejoiced in the grace of God. Then out of the blue—with no warning—he came down for breakfast and stood before me with an indescribable expression for guidance in his eyes. I responded by talking to him, but no words came from him. I looked into the heart of a man who seemed to have no anchor, yet I knew he did. It was not a blank expression, and was more than a pleading one, but I could not identify it. I wondered, *Has he forgotten how to talk?* My heart shattered in a million pieces as I faced the new roadblock—he could not speak. And his voice was all that had remained the same to me.

Hindsight revealed that the Lord had already prepared Jay a lifeline for this hurdle. Two years before I had visited a newcomer to the city, Marge Pope, whose husband had recently died. She brought her teenage son and moved from Memphis to Fort Smith to be close to other family members.

In my visit I asked her the two questions that Evangelism Explosion is well-known for asking. She assured me she knew for certain she would go to heaven if she died that day because she was trusting in Jesus' payment for her sins to get her in. She whispered her answers to me explaining, "My teenage son is not saved. He's in the next room—can you tell me how I can go to heaven and speak loud enough for him to hear it? He won't go to church or let me talk to him about it since his daddy died."

I nodded in agreement and proceeded—thanking the Lord that the EE training equips one to share the gospel in any circumstance. I left afterward, assuring her I wanted to stay in touch as she planned to put her membership in a local Presbyterian church.

A few months later her teenage son was killed in a car accident. She never knew if he was ready to die, but the fact that he heard the way gave her hope. Our sharing the gospel in an unorthodox way bonded us together, and the Pastor's Class brought her to First Baptist. Later she became a member of the church.

When she was diagnosed with a terminal illness, our friendship deepened. One day she called saying, "Come see what I bought myself for Christmas—and bring Jay. I want him to see it."

It was a tiny Yorkie puppy, no bigger than Jay's hand. He bonded with *Peti* immediately. Each week she called to invite me over, reminding me to bring Jay because Peti needed someone with whom to play.

Eighteen months later Marge went to heaven. The day before she left, she couldn't talk, but she wrote, "Can Jay have Peti when I'm gone?" She had already bought me a new car "to visit people for the Lord" she said.

Jay lost his voice a few weeks before she died, but when I brought Peti home and placed him in his lap, he cupped Peti's tiny face between his two big hands and almost crooned, "Oh, you pretty little Peti." He continued talking from that day on. I never doubted that the Lord created Peti for Jay as surely as He prepared a gourd for Jonah (*And the LORD God prepared a gourd, and made it to come up over Jonah, that it might be a shadow over his head, to deliver him from his grief. So Jonah was exceeding glad of the gourd.* Jon. 4:6). The only difference was that He let Peti remain to minister to Jay.

The story of Peti and how he took care of Jay like a nursemaid would fill a book, and one day I may write it.

EARTHSHAKING CHANGES

Unexpectedly, like a sudden strike of lightning on a sunny day followed by a thunderbolt of life-shaking magnitude came the realization—Dr. Bennett was leaving First Baptist Church for another assignment.

Every area of my life was affected. Church wide, it was the loss of a great and loved spiritual leader. But for me it was that, plus my ministry—even the house we lived in that was home to Jay and me. Where would the Lord lead us from here?

Brother Mike Harmon had come on staff as Associate Pastor a year before, and he took the helm when Dr. Bennett left. As I approached his office to receive my new assignment the words he used later appeared before my mind's eye as plainly as if they had been flashed on a neon sign before he spoke them.

"Mrs. Curtis, we are asking you to retire," and his heartfelt reluctance in saying it showed in his eyes. Later, in discussing it I was offered a new arrangement. Since I was retirement age, I could draw Social Security benefits and still earn a limited salary. I could stay on staff in outreach and keeping records of Pastor's Class (taught by a layman, Rex Terry). In order to meet the guidelines of Social Security rules rent would have to be charged for the house in which we lived. It was set at a nominal fee, $100 a month, and I would pay the utilities. My salary would be cut more than half, but it was a package for which I was grateful. I accepted it as coming from the very Hand of God (*But seek ye first the kingdom of God, and his righteousness; and all these things shall be added unto you.* Matt. 6:33).

It was not a path I would have chosen, but it was one I needed at the time. Jay was requiring more attention, and my pace was much slower without Dr. Bennett handing me new assignments right and left. I had no secretary, and paper work that I could do at home filled a big gap in my time. I continued to go out on evangelism visits to mothers of new babies, but I longed for a pastor to come shepherd the flock.

In the midst of this I was struck down with a heart attack, then two days later with another. The first one was misdiagnosed as a gastric ailment likened to what the first President Bush had at a state dinner in Japan. The next one was called severe bronchitis. Then a third one sent me to the emergency room where Dr. Pruitt, a cardiologist, immediately put me in intensive care and warned me I was in grave danger.

I asked, "What do I do with Jay?"

He firmly replied, "Make arrangements—you may never be able to take care of him."

I interrupted, "Will you sign for him to be admitted to a nursing home until I can go get him?"

He assured me he would, and the hardest decision of my lifetime was consenting to such an arrangement. Don and Anita Schafer, who loved Jay like a brother, took him that very moment and did what I could not do and had prayed I'd never have to do. Both our daughters were here before the night was over facing a dilemma that shattered their hearts. If ever a family needed a pastor, we did.

The Lord Himself met our needs by surrounding Jay and me with ministering angels—our brothers and sisters in Christ, as well as our immediate family. Dr. Bennett arranged to speak to me by phone even in intensive care and flooded my cubicle with scripture and prayer. Angel Martinez came and before leaving each time he prayed Psalm 23. No one ever quoted that Psalm quite like Angel. He said once if David hadn't written it, he believed he could have.

Carl Riggins, our media minister, was a holy man of faith—not a pastor, but with a pastor's heart. He was a prayer warrior and our friend who stood beside Jay and me in every need we had before, during, and after this calamity.

Jewel Page kept watch over me while Anita Shafer and Maida Godwin, along with Brenda and Debbie, tried to comfort Jay. He had no comprehension of what was happening and kept asking for *Ann*. Then he wouldn't remember their answer. He must have thought I totally abandoned him, and he quit calling my name—never to speak it again until the week before he went to heaven eighteen months later.

I was kept in intensive care a week and later sent home to complete rest for two or three months. I followed to the letter the instructions I received at my discharge. My aim was to bring Jay home as soon as possible. For two months I wasn't allowed to go see him.

The third month I went every day, and if a broken heart could have killed me, I would have died right then. I finally told Dr. Pruitt I must go get him. He indicated it could well be the end of me. I replied, "If I don't, I know it will be."

That day a caregiver, Beulah Acorn, said she felt led to take care of Jay, and with misgivings Dr. Pruitt gave his approval.

We brought Jay home and he cradled his little dog in his big hands and marveled, "My pretty little Peti." For an instant, I was jealous. But when he turned and looked at me, I saw that love has a universal language even though he didn't call my name.

That began eighteen months of sheer joy in the midst of agony. He opened his eyes slowly when I woke him each morning and gradually looked around as if to see if he was really home again. I felt like I was traveling on hind's feet, and Peti jumped every hurdle with me.

Mama had left me an inheritance that provided the money to hire a caregiver, and when Beulah went home at night Peti helped me watch Jay. He knew when Jay was out of bounds and came scampering to get me. I teased Jay saying Peti was a little tattletale, and he was.

Usually Jay slept like a baby at night, but once Peti woke me with an urgent call. I jumped up and Jay was hanging straddled on the stair banister ready to plunge downstairs. I screamed, "Jay, stop!" on my way to him. He stopped, but said, "You're not my shepherd."

I threw my arms around him as I helped him down saying, "No, the Lord is your shepherd." I laughed and laughed at his way of expressing I was not his boss. It revealed how much he trusted in the Lord to be his Master Mind. He laughed with me as I put him back to bed, and Peti jumped up and down ecstatically.

THE FIVE THOUSAND

After months without a pastor, the Pulpit Committee brought one in to preach in view of a call. Brother Ron Herrod came, and we rejoiced as a church family. He had an evangelistic heart and a mission calling that was unmistakable when he came back from mission trips aglow with Shekinah glory. He preached with power the few years he served as pastor until he left with another assignment.

Alzheimer's didn't alter his fellowship with Jay. He talked to him like a fellow brother—teased him, laughed with him, and Jay loved it.

A high day during his ministry was November 20, 1990—the day First Baptist set aside for "Feeding the Five Thousand." His message to the crowd of needy people who came that day revealed his heart and concept of ministry. Both those receiving a bountiful Thanksgiving supply of food and those giving it were blessed. And most importantly one hundred professions of faith were made that day. Did 5000 come? No, but it was the biggest crowd I have witnessed attending one service at First Baptist Church.

Later, the staff members were asked to describe what happened that day, and I wrote an account of the event. [See Appendix C, p. 332.]

17

The Great Divide

When Brother Herrod left we were sheep without an under-shepherd again, and prayer warriors all through the church went to their knees.

Brother Dale Thompson came and preached in view of a call, and the church voted overwhelmingly for him to come. At first his response was negative, and apparently the Lord had to draft him; but he came and we rejoiced with joy unspeakable.

He was a young man, the age of my youngest daughter, and with a God-given gift of communication in the pulpit that captivated the interest of children, teenagers, young adults, senior citizens—all. His gentle, forgiving, and mercy-loving spirit was like the balm of Gilead to our mixed emotions throughout the church family. Slowly a unity formed that set the foundation for him to bring us the meat of the Word.

Again, my ministry was at stake. He began teaching the Pastor's Class immediately, and I thought, *Surely he will not want a woman the age of his mother to be his Assistant in that class.*

At our first meeting he observed me closely and asked, "How long do you intend to work, Mrs. Curtis?"

"As long as I am productive—but not beyond." That seemed agreeable to him and I continued, "I may not know when I'm not productive, but you will. I don't want to hang on beyond that time."

That was the guideline he used each year when the staff was evaluated. He added one requirement to it in later years—that I give him several months notice when I saw a need to retire.

Brother Dale didn't give me assignments, apparently expecting me to make my own. Knowing my boldness concerning outreach, I was afraid his gentle nature would hesitate to call me to task, so I tried to walk in my self-given assignments gingerly and prayerfully—that was a good lesson for me to learn.

We soon learned he could be firm in the midst of his gentleness, and when he contended for the faith (*Beloved . . . ye should earnestly contend for the faith . . .* Jude 3) there was no mercy offered.

His first years as our pastor prepared the church body for later steps of moving forward with the Lord. They gave me grace to face Jay's approaching death, a hurdle I knew would exceed any previous one.

I remembered Mama's death a few years earlier. It was during the Christmas season, and I had put out my first decoration—a floor mat at our front door imprinted *Ho-Ho-Ho*— when the call came that she had died. Mama always made Christmas a fun-loving time, and I continued experiencing it on a higher plane after I met Jesus; I never thought it sacrilegious to combine the two.

When I came home from her funeral, walked up to our front door, and saw *Ho-Ho-Ho* I threw a *hissy fit*—Daddy would have call it that. I picked up that floor mat, and slammed it at the side of the house saying, "It's not Ho-Ho-Ho. It's Woe-Woe-Woe." I burst out sobbing for my fun-loving Mama.

I remembered Daddy's death and burial ten years before Mama's. He died after a long illness. Just before his death while he was in intensive care, a young preacher boy who didn't know any better went to see him each day pressing his need of a Savior. Finally, Daddy admitted he wasn't good enough to go to heaven, asked the Lord for forgiveness, and was born again— right on his deathbed. The peace and joy that flooded my soul at his conversion stayed with me during his funeral and after I came home.

Death was a bottomless pit to me before I knew Jesus, but when I met Him death changed to a doorway to heaven. Even so, I knew that for me to keep rejoicing as Jay left this earth on his ultimate trip without me beside him, it would require all the grace and mercy that God can bestow on one of His children.

Jay stayed on his feet, continued going to church with me, enjoyed his daughters and grandchildren, and loved me and Peti right up to the end. As his death approached, all his family gathered around him, and we celebrated his homegoing together.

It came at 8:28 a.m. on Sunday morning, May 23, 1993. At eleven o'clock Len Alfano, Debbie's husband, rounded up the family members saying, "Let's go to church—that's what Jay would say." Our young preacher grandson, David, stayed with me to watch the service on television. A young nurse's aide was still here, and David led her to the Lord while we worshiped via television. She was another soul on her way to heaven with Jay. There were scores of others with whom he had been a part of sharing the Way who were already there.

Soon after Brother Dale came as our pastor, we discovered that he is anointed in a special way when he preaches a funeral message. I went to most of the church funerals, and there were times in the midst of some when it seemed I caught a fleeting glimpse of heaven. That was true of Jay's funeral as Brother Dale preached and our grandson David assisted him.

After the funeral service in First Baptist Church, Fort Smith, we buried Jay in the family plot out of Little Rock alongside Mom and Daddy and my baby brother. Brenda's husband, John O'Neal, brought the graveside message. A young man strummed a guitar softly alongside the open grave before the burial. When he played "In the Garden," it seemed the birds hushed their singing in the quietness of the beautiful cemetery. It was my church site as a child where I vowed when I was ten years old, "I won't stay in that ground if they ever bury me." And sure enough, I won't.

There is a double monument marking Jay's grave:

Albert J. Curtis	Ann M. Curtis
1916–1993	1922–

Carved under Jay's name are the words: *Well done, my Good and Faithful Servant.* A daughter asked, "Mother, why didn't you have it say 'servants' to include you?"

I replied, "That can't be said until the end of the journey." She seemed to think that was a done deal. *Lord, may it be,* was my silent request.

I came home from Jay's burial grieving, but still rejoicing. When the family left, *loneliness* descended. This was an enemy I'd never faced before, a formidable foe to the soul, one that Satan must count his choice ally in stealing one's joy. If my church family hadn't reached out in ministering to me, my joy would have escaped me. I accepted them as ministering angels, and I truly believe the Lord sent them one by one.

After I had written all my thank you notes and tended to seemingly myriad business matters, I started rearranging my household. I was embarrassed when I saw what a terrible shape it was in. The years I had taken care of Jay kept me just skimming the surface of housekeeping, and the result glared at me. The last two years Mama lived she rotated staying with her three children. When she was with me, it was almost impossible to keep my household presentable. She was incontinent, Jay was, and even Peti—but the Lord's grace was sufficient. A painting of the outstretched hands of Jesus hung at the foot of the stairway, and as I came down each morning I seemed to hear His words: *Come unto me, all ye that labor and are heavy laden, and I will give you rest* (Matt. 11:28). But *loneliness* was worse than labor had ever been.

Peti finally bonded with me, but not as he did with Jay; he wanted me to take care of him, and I continued to be a caregiver. We grieved together our first year without Jay. I even wrote love notes to heaven:

LOVE NOTES TO HEAVEN

Jay, do you remember:
How you loved me in my teens,
Through the turbulent years of my twenties,
With agape love in my thirties,
Adoring and abiding love in my fifties—
Then *Alzheimer's* invaded your brain cells,
And you never knew I grew any older.

I remember how you loved me:
    Foolishly, romantically, seriously, devotedly,
    All that a woman could ever dream to experience.

I remember waking up that first year we were married
    With you sitting quietly on the bed beside me waiting
    For me to open my eyes. You said my eyes were the most
    Beautiful eyes in the world. When I looked in the mirror,
    I didn't see what you saw. I just saw two eyes.
    But you said they danced with joy, sparkled with anger,
    Winked with excitement, dreamed with love;
    And you loved the expectancy you said they revealed
    When I first woke up in the morning.

Do you remember telling me on our honeymoon,
    "I know you don't love me as much as I love you—
    But that's okay; I'll love you enough to make up for both
    Of us."
    I didn't know what you meant as I thought I loved you, too.
    Later, I realized mine was a selfish love compared to yours.
    Even Mama said, "Ann, you're not as good to Jay as He is
    To you."
    But you did love me enough to make up for both of us, and
    Slowly my love for you lost some of its selfishness.

How did I love you? In so many ways—
    I loved your hair—the feel of its crispness at the back of
    Your neck after a hair cut. Your feet and ankles—
    I often told you that you had the dressiest feet
    Of any man I'd seen.
    I loved to buy you shoes and socks to accentuate them.

It pleased you, but do you remember asking me not to tell
Anyone but you? I didn't, until our daughters were teenagers,
And we all laughed together about it.

I loved your full lips.
Last week I said to a young friend, "That is my husband
In his twenties,"
Pointing to a large picture of you on my dressing table.
She traced your mouth with her index finger and said,
"Um-m-m, he must have had kissable lips."

I loved your slim waist and firm stomach that never bulged.
I loved your deep voice, especially when you were speaking
Or singing in my ear alone.
I loved your one-line wit,
Your Love and devotion to our two daughters,
And to our five Grandchildren.

I marveled at your reverence for the sacredness of life,
Especially for the small creatures.
Deer were all little Bambies to you;
A dead sparrow had to be carefully disposed of,
Not just thrown into the trash.
Then your love for little Peti,
The Yorkie dog that God created for you,
As surely as He prepared a gourd for Jonah.
(Peti still lets me know that he is your dog.)
And little girls,
You truly thought they were made of sugar and spice
And everything nice, didn't you?
You could walk in a room a total stranger to them,

And they came scampering to you,
Drawn by a magnet of love.

Your mother said you transferred your heart of love
For her to me the first day you saw me.
She wasn't jealous, and neither was I,
When you put another before me
When you turned forty years old.
It was to our Lord, and that enhanced your love for me
To its highest level—*Agape.*

I remember the highest compliment you bestowed on me,
But in retrospect, I see that it reflected your love
More than my lovability. Marriage seminars were first
Becoming prevalent and a revival team held one in our
Church. "Men, come and learn to love your wives."
Afterward, you stopped abruptly on our way to the car
And said in amazement,"Why would a man have to
'Learn' to love his wife?"

The Bible says love covers a multitude of *sin,*
And you certainly had your share,
But your love for our daughters and me covered everyone
Of them,
Until Brenda, Debbie, and I thought you
Were almost perfect.

Jay, if you can look over the portals of heaven today
And see me, what do you feel?
I hope that same total love and undeserved admiration
That you showered on me in our earthly life together.

18

Final Assignment

I poured out my aching heart to the Lord and in my journal—
one I had kept off and on all my life, but mostly off until I was
alone. My daughters urged me to write my life story, and I began
to think that writing might be a solace to my lonely heart.
Westark Community College offered a non-credit course for
senior citizens in how to begin an autobiography, and I enrolled.

My first class assignment was to write in fifteen minutes a
subject describing a deep emotion. I wrote on death.

A WALK THAT CHANGED MY LIFE

It was Sunday morning May 23, 1993, and rain was falling softly, trickling down the window panes like tear
drops on a child's face. At 8:28 a.m. Jay, my husband
for 52 years, left our house at 1408 No. C Street and
went to his heavenly home.

I stood at the foot of his bed cradling his feet in my
hands while his earthly life came to an end. His eyes
had no side vision, and I liked to stand where he could

look up and see me each time he opened his eyes. I caught the last glimmer of love his eyes reflected as Brenda leaned over his bed and said, "Daddy," but before she could finish the sentence, he was gone.

As Jay left that bed, something left me. I cannot name or define it, but it was not just an emotional feeling. As real as my hands and feet are a part of my physical body today, and I would know the instant one was severed, I knew at that moment a definite part of me broke loose and departed with Jay. Believe me when I say it was tangible—not just a feeling— although I still feel the vacuum created when it left. The Bible says in speaking of marriage that the two shall become one. Now, I walk alone—half of what once was a whole.

After several months and writing a few chapters of my story, I felt an urge to write a book of my whole lifespan that would reveal what God can do in lives that are led by Him. I put it on hold for a future project when I could no longer "Go" for the Lord, and in my mind I set age 85 as my goal. In the meantime I claimed His promise that His children are never alone, and though loneliness continued to hover, it failed to erase my joy.

Grieving was a process that I moved through one step at a time. Finally, a challenge began forming in my mind to take a more active involvement in Pastor's Class outreach. Over the years we had done mail-outs, telephone surveys, newspaper ads, billboards, television and radio spots, as well as door-to-door visiting to invite people to come; however, there were still literally thousands of Fort Smith residents who had never heard of the Bible teaching offered in the Pastor's Class.

I remembered asking the Lord at the beginning of the class in 1976 to let us get an invitation to every household in the city. A door opened, and I gave myself an assignment under Pastor Dale's leadership to walk through it.

We ordered labels according to postal guidelines and prearranged by courier-route. Class volunteers did the work, and when the invitations were taken to the Post Office, each postman had his assignment ready to deliver—not just by zip code, but box by box. This lowered the postal rate to a nominal fee compared to zip by zip mail-outs. Volunteers followed simple, but meticulous instructions; they prayed over the invitations as they stuck on the labels and then rejoiced at seeing the results when the people came on the opening Sunday of each new series which Brother Dale began.

It took four weeks to complete the procedures from planning stage to delivering the 65,000 invitation cards to the Post Office. Harley Bilyeu made the deliveries in every Pastor's Class mail-out. Donna Prough served faithfully as captain over the volunteers in the new mailing procedure. They counted, completed cutting assignments, and checked that each phase was followed in exact detail. Under her eagle eye not a single postal assignment was rejected—as it would have been if one card had been out of sequence.

Planning and overseeing this strategy involving scores of class members became my main outreach. We executed this plan two and three times a year until I retired. I had served thirty years as the Pastor's Class Assistant from the beginning in 1976 until January 1, 2006.

PETI LEAVES

Little Peti died on Wednesday, January 19, 2000, at 6:08 a.m.—six years after Jay. I wrote in my journal that day, *Peti took his last breath. Was breathing at six o'clock and soon after his mouth opened and there was no more. It seemed he waited until I woke up. I came in and he left.*

At the end of the day, I wrote:

> To dust you will return
> Even as I one day.
> Thereafter I know what is for me,
> But there is silence on
> What is for you.
> But if there is more,
> I know for sure
> Your reward will be:
> "Well done, my good and faithful Peti;
> You fulfilled the task
> I created you to do."

I wondered, *Did a ministering angel embody little Peti to take care of Jay?* Only heaven will tell.

We buried him outside the front side window. Anita Schafer took me to purchase a burial box, but when she saw it was no more than a cardboard box, she said, "We can't bury Peti in a plain box—let's go get some material, and I will make him a casket."

We did. She covered it with burgundy velvet, and lined it with gold silk. A sofa pillow, made from Jay's ties soon after his death, fit snugly inside the covered casket which cradled little Peti's body.

Jack Garner, a dear Pastor's Class friend and a public accountant, stopped right in the middle of the tax season to come dig the grave. When he saw Peti's casket he told Anita, "I want you to make mine if there's not one available when I die." Jewel Page came and cried with me. Cindy Grebe made a video of the doggie funeral. The sermon was one sentence as we all echoed together, "Thank you, Lord, for little Peti."

LONELINESS

My daughters, grandchildren, and families lived too far away to fill the vacuum of my loneliness after Peti died. When they went home from visiting, my house as well as my heart felt empty.

Some women tend to rearrange their furniture when under stress, but I needed more than that. I began a whole makeover project to eliminate the stains Peti left and to beautify my household. I began with having the upstairs floor covering removed and replaced with cranberry wine carpet. Next came new drapes throughout the house.

In the midst of my decorating urge our Music Minister, Brother Kendall Lucas, called asking, "Ms. Ann, can I do something to help you around your place?"

I answered, "I don't think you can, but maybe someone in your choir can. I bought new drapes, and it will take real expertise to hang them in the upstairs windows because of the dome ceiling."

Before I could finish he said, "I can do that." He came and did what no one else could, or would do. He installed the drapes standing on the loft rail over a fourteen foot precipice.

Later someone remarked, "The best way to get a man to do something is to imply that he can't." That was not my intent, but he started a whole line of people offering to help in my beautifying project.

Jane Owen, Crawford County Art Director, had the vision and inspired helpers to completely remodel the bathrooms. The young man responsible for the unique architectural lines in the house seemed to have had no vision for the bathrooms beyond their being utility rooms. Except for the conveniences plumbing and running water made, I often thought, *They are just a cut above the outside toilet with its cracked mirror of my childhood day.*

Jane was the decorator, made the window and shower curtains, and selected the trimmings and colors. Don and Anita Schafer laid the floor covering, installed the cabinets, and did the painting, plumbing, electrical, and all that was needed to make the bathrooms beautiful—the upstairs in pink and ivory, the downstairs in beige and gold. They put in hours and hours—a labor of love done after their regular workdays. Debbie replaced the kitchen oven; Jerry and Shelby Ezell provided a new Whirlpool refrigerator. (Ten years later, they replaced it with another new one.)

Walt and Mary Ann Willard came by during the planning stage of the project, and when Walt heard the amount I allotted for the material required he said, "Well, that won't pay for much more than the floor covering in those bathrooms."

The next day Mary Ann handed me a check for $2500. Jane stayed within my first quoted allotment, and I thought, *I can go on the Evangelism Explosion Cruise that Dr. James Kennedy is sponsoring.*

I fully expected Mary Ann to agree to be my partner, and I began shopping for a whole new wardrobe. Alas, she refused when she discovered no one was going from this area whom we knew and who could oversee our traveling itinerary. I was stuck with a small fortune to use any way I wanted. I set it aside to use for personal luxuries that a woman growing up during the Great Depression would hesitate to put in her annual budgets—a cleaning lady, nails, and so many things Jay prayed for me while he was here on earth.

At Christmas time Jane Owen with all her art expertise sponsored a decorating party each year. Our joy bells rang in the midst of holiday beauty throughout my house. Nick and Beverly Graham came at Thanksgiving season and put the tree up and came back at New Years to store it away with all the other decorations in an upstairs closet.

After finishing the remodeling project I wondered, *What do I do now?* My daughters suggested I start attending some singles activities saying, "Mother, there are men who would love to take you to dinner—just go to be seen where they can meet you." I had guarded against that happening, and Jewel Page walked me to my car to prevent anyone from even walking out of church with me.

Finally, I came to grips with my loneliness problem. Paul said, *I have learned, in whatsoever state I am, therewith to be content* (Phil. 4:11). Contentment was a learning process, and I set about it. I looked for a role model to emulate, and Eula Mae King instantly came to my mind. She was the godliest woman I met soon after coming to Fort Smith, and when her beloved husband died in the prime of life she never remarried. She continued serving the Lord in the children's ministry both in her church and as a consultant throughout the Southern Baptist

Convention. She remained attractive, joyful, and seemingly content. Her family rose up and truly called her blessed. Erasing loneliness is still a learning process with me, but thank the Lord, it isn't stagnant.

My daughters and my church family continued to rally around to meet my every need. Debbie dressed me in the finest clothing available; Brenda showered me with Mary Kay cosmetics, and I felt like the richest lady in town. Carol Martin led the church family group by being whatever I needed at the moment—even my hairdresser when Sophelia was battling cancer and I needed a comb-out. Jimmie Garner replaced Betty Walpole as my faithful prayer partner after the Lord sent Betty a preacher husband who moved her to Texas. Jimmie seeks to have clean hands and a pure heart before God, and I asked her to censor every word of this book before its final typing that I might not cause some young reader to stumble.

LONGING FOR EVANGELISM

It seemed as my physical strength lessened the Lord surrounded me with beauty, ease, and ministering angels to compensate, but I longed for a fresh wave of evangelism, and I chafed at its slowness in arriving. I knew it was coming though, as I caught a glimpse of an apparent schedule Brother Dale had jotted down on a card once when he shared his vision with the staff. Evangelism was on the agenda, but it was several lines below other steps listed in preparing for it. I thought, but I didn't voice it, *Put evangelism first and the other will fall in line.* Not so in a conventional, 150-year-old church body—preparation was necessary. I continued to learn that the Lord's way is not my way. In the meantime the Thursday morning evangelism teams going out and sharing the Good News with new mothers gave me an outlet for my pent up zeal.

In the fullness of God's timing evangelism edged up toward the top of the church agenda. It began with Brother Dale surrounding himself with a chosen staff. Brother Kevin Kilbreth came on staff as Associate Minister of Discipleship. He had a heart for evangelism and was equipped to fill any slot in the Kingdom's work—preaching, teaching, singing. When the need arose, he was anointed to fill it. His daddy, Bro. Leon Kilbreth, was a motivational speaker to our Evangelism School and the entire church body in March, 1971. He challenged us with the test of a Soul Winner by using Luke 9:57–62. After passing this test he said, "Jesus will anoint, appoint, and commission you."

Then Greg Ford came as Minister of Missions and Evangelism. Finally, *Evangelism* had a leader. First Baptist was already strong in Missions, ranking second in the entire Southern Baptist Convention for giving to the Lottie Moon offering that goes directly to foreign missionaries, but evangelism here lagged.

Greg was young, unmarried, and his zeal for evangelism made me want to be a soul winner. When I saw how it affected other single women I jokingly remarked, "If I were younger, I would run them a race." But seriously, I told him, "I began praying twenty years ago for the Lord to send an Evangelism and Outreach man—and it must have taken Him that long to prepare you."

CANCER

But as the church agenda began changing, so did mine. *Cancer* altered my life schedule, and believe me, it takes priority when it invades one's body. I opted for surgery, but with no radiation or chemo treatment.

Soon after recovering from surgery I was back on schedule, but again tests showed cancer was still on my agenda. I earnestly sought wisdom from the Lord in putting everything in order for my allotted time on earth.

First, since none of my family lives here, I entrusted Paul Gean, the godliest attorney I know and a member of First Baptist, along with my bosom friend Jewel Page to oversee the details of my last days on earth should I not be capable. This will free Brenda and Debbie and their families to surround me with their love without making heartbreaking decisions.

I already had a caring doctor of faith, Dr. Chris Hardin, who knows my medical history. I am confident of having the best available care, and there is comforting power in that assurance.

I shared with Brother Dale my need to retire at the end of the year—2005. I asked him to wait to announce it until near the time so I wouldn't be a lame duck leader in the Pastor's Class for the coming months. He made me feel productive my last year on his staff, and he did it from a pastor's heart.

At the end of the year he announced my retirement after thirty-five years on First Baptist staff, five as Evangelism Assistant and thirty as Pastor's Class Assistant, and he led the church in planning a reception fit for a queen honoring my retirement.

A monetary love gift from the church family made me feel like the richest lady in town again. In addition I could continue living in my Mansion in the Sky rent-free for as long as I desired. My prayer is to move from it to the real one prepared for me in heaven.

Another chapter in my life began with retirement. It was already outlined on my life agenda except it came at age eighty-four instead of eighty-five as I had planned. I would now finish writing my life story, and I began immediately setting myself a writing schedule.

Brother Dale encouraged me by transferring all my office furnishings including my desk and computer to my house. Jane Owen again sponsored transforming the upstairs sitting room into a writer's room.

In January, 2005, I began writing *the rest of my story*. The Lord provided Jan Cutsinger to do my typing. I visited her family when they moved to Fort Smith and discovered she was writing a book. I had just begun classes to write my life story at that time, and now ten years later I needed a typist. I asked her who she had type her manuscript, and she said she did her own. She had retired from working several years for Arkansas Best Freight as a writer and editor, and she was available. She has worked patiently with me as I have given her handwritten copies week by week to type.

Claude Eubanks, a published author, encouraged me immensely when I heard him tell another after he read the first section of this manuscript, "I write, but Mrs. Curtis is a writer."

I know his comparison is not valid, but when others asked me what I do since my retirement, I reply, "I am a writer." The power of encouraging words is often underestimated.

At 9 p.m. Friday, July 28, 2006, I pushed my chair back from my desk saying, "Thank you, Lord. It is finished."

GOING ON

Revival winds are blowing in First Baptist Church—people are being saved and baptized. A future plan for a Sanctuary/Gatheria (worship complex) is being formulated that reminds one of the grandeur of the New Jerusalem that John caught a glimpse of in Revelation 21:2—*And I, John, saw the Holy City, the new Jerusalem, coming down from God out of heaven. It was a glorious sight, beautiful as a bride at her wedding* (The Living Bible).

Looking back over my eighty-four years on planet earth, I see the sovereign hand of God loving me, guiding me, calling me, saving me, molding me, and one day in the fullness of his timing, ready to welcome me *HOME*. It may be days, weeks, months, or even years; but may I live them joyfully serving Him in my limited physical capacity.

My next assignment made by the Lord Himself:

DEATH

It is appointed unto men once to die,
But after this the judgment.
Hebrews 9:27

Then face-to-face with my Lord and Savior
I shall behold Him . . .

AMAZED BY GRACE

Hallelujah!

Mrs. Ann Curtis went to heaven on February 21, 2007.

Afterword

You may wonder if I ever found out why Randall failed to show for our date when I was a teenager and why he sent Jay in his place. You decide.

In later years Randall was diagnosed with a terminal illness and his friends asked Jay and me to come and share the way to heaven with him.

We did. As we left, I stopped on his doorstep. With his wife standing behind him and listening carefully to our conversation, I couldn't resist asking, "Tell me, all those years ago when you didn't show up—why did you send Jay instead?"

He and Jay exchanged knowing expressions, but all Randall said was, "Jay was the best man."

Jay remained silent.

HAVE YOU FOUND THE WAY TO HEAVEN?

The passion of Ann Curtis' life was to tell everyone how to get to heaven by knowing Jesus Christ personally. Her passion was driven by the fact that she had lived thirty-four years before anyone told her. She and Jay learned the way to heaven at a funeral and on the way home prayed a simple prayer that changed their lives completely.

Ann responded to her new relationship with Jesus with a lifelong commitment to evangelism. She recognized that Christians hold the keys to heaven, yet often fail to share them—thus denying friends and family critical knowledge for eternal life.

The calling to evangelism was evident from the time of Ann's spiritual birth, but it became the driving force of her life. She personally shared the way to heaven with a large number of individuals and motivated many believers to do the same.

If Ann were with you today it is highly probable she would ask you to consider two vital questions:

1. Do you know for sure that you are going to be with God in heaven?

2. If God were to ask you, "Why should I let you into My heaven?" what would you say?

These two questions which came through Ann's Evangelism Explosion training provide entry into the critical issues of eternity. If you find yourself struggling to know for sure your eternal destiny and the basis for entry into heaven, consider the words of Jesus and his early followers.

- *I am the way, the truth, and the life: no man cometh unto the Father, but by me.* (John 14:6)

- *That if thou shalt confess with thy mouth the Lord Jesus, and shalt believe in thine heart that God hath raised him from the dead, thou shalt be saved.* (Rom. 10:9)

- *These things have I written unto you that believe on the name of the Son of God; that you may know that that ye have eternal life, . . .* (1 John 5:13)

Don't delay. Today, right now, complete the personal transaction with Jesus Christ through a simple prayer of commitment like Jay and Ann did traveling over Mt. Gaylor in the Ozark Mountains. Confess your sins, express your faith in Jesus, and invite Him to take control of your life. Your decision will make an eternal difference.

If you already know Jesus and the way to heaven, commit yourself to sharing that knowledge freely and often.

For more information see Evangelism Explosion website
www.eeinternational.org

Appendix A

Recollections upon Hearing of Frank Laubach's Death

October 7, 1970

> If you give me a fish, you have fed me one meal.
> If you teach me to fish, you have fed me for a lifetime.

A presence filled the sanctuary as His spokesman, Frank C. Laubach, quietly spoke these words. Just as a radio must be plugged in, turned on, and tuned in to the station, so must the worshipper in the pew be plugged in to God, turned on, and tuned in to His spokesman before his message is received.

My heart warmed to a visit recalled by Dr. Laubach. Instead of fish, their need was fruit, vegetables, and clothing. Small children grabbed the apples and crunched loudly, chewing with their mouths wide open. A teenaged sister pulled an avocado green sweater from the clothing box, stroking it delightedly as she held it to her face. The aging mother fondled a Bible as she lifted it and began turning the pages in awe. "Mama can't read," chirped one small son between apple bites. "Sister can't either. She done quit school," piped another.

The warmness cooled, but then I said to myself, "Such as you had, you took to them in the name of Jesus."

"Teach them to read," came the soft words with the force of the Almighty God from the heart of the speaker, Frank Laubach, and I startled from my reverie.

I'm not a school teacher. I am a Bible teacher. If they could read, I would gladly teach them the Word of God, my mind retorted.

"Teach them to read," relentlessly the speaker forged. "It is the Jesus way to save our age." He stopped speaking and looked directly at me and made his electrifying contact. The 81-year-old educator proclaimed, "The one who can save the world is wearing your clothes. You hold the key." In that instant he recruited another prayerfully concerned volunteer in his mighty army against illiteracy.

Teach me to teach, was my unvoiced reply, and he immediately outlined his schedule for training teachers in the city. Can a speaker have this rapport with one listener seated in an audience of 800 people? Frank Laubach did. This world-renowned and heaven-bound educator spent his next two weeks painstakingly training a small group of people in his miraculous method of teaching adults to read.

Each day I sat directly in front of his desk, and two times I looked into his eyes searching for an answer. He stopped teaching the lesson and began talking aloud to God as naturally as a child speaks to his father. I completed the course trained more in his concept, than in his method of teaching. His textbook and Teacher's Guidebook supplied the method, and I launched out to save the world—the world of illiterates—and to win them to Christ.

TEACH THEM TO FISH AND TO KNOW THE MASTER FISHERMAN AND THEY WILL NOT HAVE ONE MEAL, BUT AN ETERNAL BANQUET was my goal. Four years later the Compassionate Army is marching on reaching and teaching the silent billion, the illiterates, the little people.

Laubach's startling rapport from the pulpit to the pew was transcended by messages intermittently flashed from New York to Arkansas. I was unprepared for the learning difficulties which I encountered in teaching. Yet, skills I did not possess and words I had not formed projected themselves unobtrusively. I was aware of miraculous power, but I pondered in my heart these engrafted experiences that were couched in the words and the tone of Frank Laubach.

"Frank C. Laubach died last month," an editorial in the July issue of "Christianity Today" read. *But he could not have, he talked to me in class last week,* was my response. *He that heareth my word, and believeth on him that sent me, hath everlasting life, and shall not come into condemnation; but is passed from death unto life* (John 5:24). Prayer, the mightiest force in the world . . . does it continue in heaven?

Ann Curtis

APPENDIX B

THE POSITIVE INFLUENCE OF GODLY GRANDPARENTS

My grandfather, Jay Curtis—a gentle, kind, and loving man—showed all of the fruit of the Spirit in his everyday life. He was a godly man. You could look into his eyes and see that he knew Jesus well. Even when he became ill there was a sense of peace about him. It was evident to me as a young child that he loved God and God's Word. My most fond memories of him are of the numerous times I would sit in his lap and he would read Scripture to me from a little Precious Moments book. When my first child was born I bought a similar book and I read it to each of my children. What a legacy! Thanks, Grand Dad!

My grandmother, Ann Curtis, is a strong, prayerful woman with a zeal for witnessing. She tells just about everyone about Jesus. (I would like to be so bold.) She is a lover of God and His word. She told me once that she chooses a different translation each year to read the Bible through. She gave me the *Amazing Grace Devotional* and God has really ministered to my spirit through it. Thank you, Jesus, for the spiritual heritage You have given me!

. . . But showing love to a thousand generations of those who love me and keep my commandments.
(Deut. 5:10 NIV)

Written by Shannon Terry 12/25/05

Appendix C

Feeding The Five Thousand
What Did I See?

A *VISION*—first illuminated in the face of Bro. Bob Lever as he shared his plan of feeding 5000. There was no hesitancy or wavering in his manner, but instead a confident exuberance as he visualized the unfolding of his vision to the staff.

I caught a glimpse then of the glory to be revealed and progressively the excitement continued to mount. Thousands of cans of sweet potatoes miraculously became available, as well as cookies for the children, to add to the hundreds of roasting chickens in the well-stocked baskets of food.

A spirit not unlike the mystery of Christmas pervaded the fellowship of members as they met praying in small groups. Feeding the 5000 became a by-word throughout the city. Strangers at the mall asked, "Are you from that church that is feeding the 5000?"

Then came the *DAY*—Tuesday, November 20, 1990.

Counselors were instructed to arrive at 9 a.m. As I approached the church area, multitudes of people were scurrying toward every visible entrance. The streets were filled, and as I moved slowly through throngs of eager people, my heart leaped with joy and expectancy.

The halls were full when I made my way inside. Bread of life ministers created a convention-like atmosphere as they joyfully registered the people and directed them toward the sanctuary entrance.

I continued my way through the masses—white, black, yellow, red, skinny, fat, clean, dirty, elderly, middle aged, young adults, youth, children, and babies—all with one common denominator, a hushed and expectant expression. There was no bedlam, no pushing or shoving, none of the irritation of a crowded mob of people.

I approached the sanctuary entrance and caught a glimpse inside. There was a *SHEKINAH* glory unmistakably visible as hundreds of people crowded every pew. Not a single seat was available on the lower floor at 9 a.m. and the time to begin was 10 a.m.

I literally floated down the carpeted aisle looking right and left. First Baptist members never filled that beautiful sanctuary with the pomp and glory that showed from myriads of faces as they sat in holy wonder in being in such a magnificent place of worship.

Chairs were brought in to fill the aisles; people were escorted to the choir loft and soon filled it. The balcony overflowed with people. Chairs set up in the foyer soon filled, and outer doors were opened revealing people sitting on the entrance steps. They crowded in the hallways and everywhere they could find a place to look inside and behold the wonder.

Food for Thanksgiving dinner had prompted the multitudes to come, but the *BREAD OF LIFE* welcomed them when they arrived.

Music began one hour later, and the opportunity for the crowds to voice the worship that was mirrored on many faces was joyfully released.

Pastor, DR. RON HERROD, greeted the congregation and won the hearts of the multitudes as he voiced the joy and blessing we at First Baptist Church were receiving from having all of them present. Then he said, "It is more blessed to give than to receive." He asked, "Is that right?

Their audible voices answered, and "Yes-s-s-s" filled the sanctuary.

Then he said, "Many of you will receive Jesus Christ as your Savior before you leave today, and it may be that Jesus will bless you with a job during this coming year, and you can come back next Thanksgiving and be one to give instead of to receive."

HOPE and challenge appeared on faces around me from hearing his words. I remembered seeing that same expression on faces of illiterates when years ago Dr. Frank Laubach said, "You will learn to read and then one day you too can use this method and be a teacher of others."

Bro. William Blackburn stepped forward, and a wave of love exuded from the crowd. He was no stranger to many, as he is the Bread of Life minister at First Baptist Church. He is involved each Friday in the giving of food to the needy on a smaller, but just as meaningful scale. As he gave his testimony and opened the Word exalting the Name of Jesus, a cascade of worship like a waterfall flowing upward enveloped the sanctuary. We invited the people to come to Jesus and more than 200 people rushed to the altar—at least 100 of them came to be saved. Fourteen were baptized on the spot. Many had other church preferences, and some wanted to wait.

Later, the crowds unhurriedly left the church carrying supplies for a bountiful Thanksgiving dinner. Some had tears in their eyes, but all left with their heads up looking like the VIPs they truly were.

IF YOU GIVE THEM A FISH, YOU HAVE FED THEM ONE MEAL. IF YOU TEACH THEM TO FISH AND TO KNOW THE MASTER FISHERMAN THEY WILL NOT HAVE ONE MEAL, BUT AN ETERNAL BANQUET.

Ann Curtis

Additional copies of
A Farmer's Daughter . . . Amazed by Grace
may be ordered from the following address:

Open Ear Publishers
P.O. Box 2212
Batesville, Arkansas 72501

Please include in the order:
1. Payment

$19.95 per copy
<u>$ 4.00</u> handling and shipping per copy
$23.95 total per copy

Number of copies _____ x $23.95 = $_____Total Order

2. The shipping address:

Name_____

Street_____

City/State/Zip_____

Copies may be ordered online from the following website using an approved credit card:

www.openearpublishers.com

Allow up to two weeks for delivery.